TRAVELLERS' TALES

TRAVELLERS' TALES

Stories from the ABC's Foreign Correspondents

Compiled by

Trevor Bormann

ABC
Books

Published by ABC Books for the
AUSTRALIAN BROADCASTING CORPORATION
GPO Box 9994 Sydney NSW 2001

First published March 2004

National Library of Australia
Cataloguing-in-Publication data
      Travellers' tales: stories from the
      ABC's foreign correspondents

      ISBN 0 7333 1364 7.

      1. Voyages and travels. 2. Foreign correspondents –
      Journeys. I. Australian Broadcasting Corporation.

910.4

Cover image courtesy of Gary Yeowell/The Image Bank/Getty Images
Cover and internal design by Nada Backovic
Typeset in 11.5/14pt Goudy by Kirby Jones
Colour reproduction by Colorwize
Printed and bound in Australia by Griffin Press

5 4 3 2 1

CONTENTS

Introduction

BY MAX UECHTRITZ

If, as the American photographer Larry Burrows said, the role of the correspondent in war is 'to show the interested people and to shock the uninterested', the ABC has an unequalled history of commitment to showing, and sometimes shocking, Australian audiences with what is going on in the world. Some of the truly memorable scenes sent back to Australia have moved us out of our complacency – we've covered every conflict the World War II. We've covered famine, disasters and terrorism campaigns. For the many reporters we've had posted overseas for the ABC, most of them are awed and feel privileged that they have had a ringside seat at history – and have taken audiences along with them for the ride.

But as the stories in this book illustrate, we've done much more than just report on the dark side of humanity. Our correspondents get under the skin of the culture they're temporarily engaged with. Our splendid isolation means Australians have always been fascinated by what our neighbours, near and far, are up to. And for so long 'culture' was something we went elsewhere to get. That is clearly not the case now; we've lost that cringe we were once famous for. Our willingness to embrace people from other countries goes far deeper than eating at the local Thai takeaway. It emerges in an enrichment of our culture, taking the best aspects of all the people from all the countries who make Australia home. And that leads us to take a great interest in where those people came from, what their country is like, their political systems, their beliefs, their art, their industry.

Our audiences have grown up with our correspondents, they have confidence in their ability to tell the stories of other people – but looking through Australian eyes and interpreting what they see in the most appropriate way for Australian audiences. I think our audiences also appreciate that our correspondents are often operating in the most extreme and difficult environments to bring back the story. What could drive this home more dramatically than the death in northern Iraq in 2003 of Paul Moran, the victim of a terrorist attack as he went back to get that one last, great image? It was one of the saddest tasks of my life to bring Paul's body back to his family in Australia in the company of his wife, Ivana.

But these *Travellers Tales* are not gloomy. They're a celebration of people, their lives and the places they live; they're about the triumph of the human spirit. They tell the stories behind the stories you've seen or heard on ABC Radio and Television. You'll be surprised by these tales: what was Craig McMurtrie doing in a lift with 'that woman', Monica Lewinsky? You'll be stirred by the derring-do of Mark Corcoran and the mercenary who flies him at

270 kilometres an hour over the jungle in Sierra Leone, just metres above the treetops because 'it makes it harder for them to hit us with a missile'. You might weep at the unbearable scenes of genocide Sally Sara witnessed in Rwanda, and the man she met there, Emmanuel, whose only reminder of his wife and six children murdered that day in 1994 is a deep indentation in his head, the result of a bullet that his family's murderers assumed had killed him.

These reporters are continuing a fine legacy that began in 1932 with the appointment of our first London representative, Arthur Mason. In the late 1930s and early 1940s, correspondents were engaged in Berlin, Moscow, Shanghai, Tokyo, Manila, Singapore and New York. We mobilised for the second world war, with correspondents in London and New York, in the Middle East, and the Mediterranean, and then in New Guinea and throughout the South-West Pacific when, as an ABC note advises, the Commonwealth Government charged the public broadcaster with providing war coverage for all Australian radio stations, including the commercials. Our reporters served with distinction in covering the Korean War, the first 'television war' in Vietnam, and the various Gulf Wars. We opened more bureaux – in Singapore, Jakarta, Kuala Lumpur, Washington, New Delhi, Tokyo, Port Moresby, Hong Kong, Bangkok, Wellington, Beijing, Brussels, Moscow, the Middle East, Berlin, South America, Johannesburg, Nairobi, Hanoi and Auckland.

We don't have as many bureaux as we once did: as global power shifts around, as budget cuts bite, a bureau might be closed here, but another might be opened there. Yet despite budget cuts and reductions in some of our international bureaux and operations, the ABC remains fiercely resolved to maintain our commitment to bring the world to Australian audiences. And even after the cuts we've had to make, the ABC still stands head and shoulders above the rest of the media in Australia with the number of overseas reporters and bureaux and, dare I say it, the quality and depth of international reporting spread across our programs on radio, television and online. This is particularly so of our specialist program *Foreign Correspondent* where so many great travellers' tales come so vividly to life.

As long as Australians maintain their great interest in what's happening in the world, the ABC will see it with Australian eyes and bring it to Australian audiences.

Max Uechtritz is a former foreign correspondent and is the ABC's Director of News and Current Affairs.

JENNIFER BYRNE started in journalism early, as a cadet journalist with the *Age* newspaper in Melbourne in 1972. She covered all major rounds as part of her training, and went on to become a specialist in environment and planning, a feature and editorial writer, and co-editor of the *Monthly Review*. At the age of twenty-three, she was posted to San Francisco as the *Age's* West Coast correspondent.

During her time at the *Age*, Jennifer took three years leave during which she worked on Fleet Street in London, writing for a range of publications from the *Sunday Times* to the mass-circulation *Weekend Magazine*.

In 1981, Jennifer moved to Sydney as founding reporter with Channel Nine's *Sunday* program, and five years later moved across to *60 Minutes*. In 1993, she became the morning presenter of ABC's Radio 2BL, and then in 1995 she was appointed publishing director of Reed Books.

In 1999, having spent a couple of years as stand-in presenter for both ABC-TV's *7.30 Report* and *Lateline*, Jennifer took up the anchor's job at *Foreign Correspondent*, and has spent the last five years as host and reporter travelling with the program.

She has continued to write both features and book reviews and is a regular host with Radio National's *Breakfast* program.

In 2004, Jennifer took leave from ABC-TV to write a weekly feature interview in the *Bulletin*.

Foreign Correspondent

The best jobs are often hatched in the shabbiest offices, and from the beginning I knew *Foreign Correspondent* was one of them.

When I joined the program at the start of 1999 it lived in a run-down outhouse on the edge of the ABC car-park – a sort of corporate Siberia, from which we came and went unobserved except by people who dropped in for a cigarette or a chat on their way to the canteen.

We had real air instead of air-conditioning, stained carpets, over-stuffed bookshelves and too few desks. In short, it was absolutely perfect, since what more does a travelling journalist need? A telephone, a passport, top colleagues and a shared sense of inquiry and adventure. Sounds like *Foreign Correspondent* to me.

The ABC's pride is its network of foreign bureaux – one of the finest and, despite cutbacks, still one of the most extensive in the world. The Australia-based reporters have a different challenge. The world, literally, is our beat, and while I wouldn't swear that no-one's ever tried the old pin-in-the-atlas trick, I do know we spend a lot of time and energy arguing over which story to cover, where and when.

Although sometimes events break upon our heads and upend all the bookings and the plans in an instant. For example, the attack on the Twin Towers, on 11 September 2001.

ABC correspondents scrambled to reach Ground Zero – some were already in New York and Washington; others came from as far as South America and Europe. I was heading towards the opposite side of the Atlantic, to London, on the first leg of a long-planned trip taking in Ireland and Turkey. London-based producer Bronwen Reid was already waiting for me at Shannon Airport in Ireland's green south.

I checked in at Heathrow's Aer Lingus counter, the bags were loaded and I was heading on board when I got an urgent message in the departure lounge. Cancel the flight, retrieve the bags, and beg, borrow, or steal a ticket to New York. Pronto.

The airports, of course, were in pandemonium, full of jittery and confused passengers. All flights to America had been suspended. Bronwen managed to scramble back from Ireland and we holed up overnight in a London hotel, ringing on the hour, until, miraculously, we found ourselves sitting in the pointy end of the first flight cleared from London to New York. An unfamiliar setting for an ABC correspondent, but the only seats going.

Does it sound callow to talk of excitement? Of a tingling sense of anticipation? This was both a human tragedy and, of course, a vicious act of terror – with political repercussions no-one could yet guess at, but everyone knew must follow.

It is one of the core truths of foreign journalism: that we rush to the scenes most people run from, whether it be bombs or battles or natural or man-made disasters. It's not a matter of courage, nor of adventure lust: it is both what we love to do and it is our job to do. This sounds obvious but I'm often amazed at the number of people who ask, 'But why do you want to go? I couldn't think of anything worse!' There's no proper answer, but I do know that once someone has lost that intense hunger – to be there and see it and record the story – it is a clear sign that their time is up, and they should be thinking of a different job.

The al-Qaeda planes had struck a few days before, but the whole of lower Manhattan was still barricaded off, black smoke hanging heavy over the city. There was no transport or power to the zone, clearly everything was going to have to be done on foot. So we booked into the closest hotel (ironically, also one of the city's smartest, the Soho Grand – though they had suddenly dropped their rates dramatically) and joined the hundreds of international journalists jostling for access to the site. We went in the next morning.

You've seen the images, they are burned in all our brains: the buckled steel base of the towers, the mountains of rubble, the ash-white faces of the emergency workers as they hosed water onto the underground fires which still raged. What the pictures couldn't show was the thickness of the air and the smell of the smut and cinders which fell constantly from the sky.

Where had these people gone? So few bodies found, so many thousands killed. As New York's pre-eminent columnist Jimmy Breslin said to us later, the vast majority had simply vaporised, and it was more than dust that was in the air, it was fragments of real people, falling onto your head and clothes and getting into your lungs. It was ghastly, it was extraordinary and – let's be honest – it was one of those rare moments when one is conscious of being there, at the very centre of a world-changing event.

Over the days that followed, we spoke with a gentle man from the Bronx, about to celebrate his daughter's first birthday, who still went out searching each day for news of his wife and her girlfriend, both workers in the Towers.

We spoke with exhausted firefighters, who shared their sandwiches on street corners. With priests. With dazed New Yorkers, hypnotised – as were we all – by the yawning gap in the shining Manhattan skyline. I introduced the program against that backdrop, as the city lights came on for the first time since the attack.

As often happens, the encounter that moved me most was never seen, because it was never recorded. He was a businessman in late middle-age whom we found standing slightly apart from the crowd at one of the impromptu search centres, plastered with photographs of the missing, which sprang up around the edge of the barricades.

He was holding a large yellow envelope, staring at nothing, his tie just slightly askew but otherwise dressed in a good suit, his thin hair neatly brushed – a bit like one of those blank-faced men in a Jeffrey Smart painting.

He explained that his wife was still missing. He said the search organisers had tried to warn him hope was fading, but he remained full of optimism and talked at length about how they had met, relatively late in life, and what that had meant to him. How she had changed everything . He spoke of her in the present tense, with deep love, and refused even to consider the possibility of her not being found. They had no children.

He had agreed to an interview when I thought to ask him what he was carrying in the envelope. Her toothbrush and hair comb, he said distractedly. The officials wanted these intimate objects for DNA analysis, and he'd brought them along to help with the search.

I felt like crying out, but this is for matching with body parts, this is for dead people – but realised he was a man in deep shock. What he was saying was in direct contradiction to what he was doing. And the truth, he knew, was in that envelope.

It struck me as unutterably sad. We rang that afternoon to cancel the interview and wish him well as he tramped the pavements. The next day, Ground Zero officially went from being a disaster site – that is, where they were still hoping for survivors – to a retrieval site. No-one would be found alive.

The day after that, we left New York. And arrived, belatedly, in Ireland.

This is the joy of *Foreign Correspondent* – of life on the road, full-stop. You don't forget where you've been, or what you've seen, but the scenery shifts and you collide into other lives and sometimes, it seems, other universes. In this case, Bronwen and I found ourselves the only women in a monastery full of Benedictine monks.

The story was that the monks of Glenstal Abbey had produced a modern-day prayer book combining the old texts with the 'people's prayers' of southern Ireland, all overlaid by Celtic mythology. And it was selling like hot cakes. Our story was intended as a postcard but ended up three times the expected length because what we found was so marvellous, so irresistible, we simply couldn't put down the camera.

Yes, the Abbey was beautiful, and the choir did a splendid Gregorian chant of an evening, but it was the monks themselves who captured our imaginations. We felt we'd found ourselves in a golden, springtime version of *The Name of the Rose*: there was the elegantly handsome one, the crabby one with the gentle soul, the mysteriously distant Abbot (fuelling schemes over his successor) and the fey gardening monk who was creating a garden from all the plants named in the Old Testament.

One shy, bent monk is his eighties had been delivered to the monastery as a very young child, discovered his lack of vocation in his teens, yet stayed, enduring a life of silent disappointment, because he had nowhere else to go. We met a scholar with a flowing Oscar Wilde hair-do, in high demand on the international lecture circuit, and strode through an emerald forest with a fierce environmentalist and anti-globalisation campaigner who'd spent many nights in jail for his devotion to the cause.

To come from the smoking ruin of the World Trade Center to this peaceful place of the spirit was a balm and, it seemed to us, an inadvertent act of grace.

We talked with the monks about terror, and God's will, and the blackness that lurks in the human heart, astonished that men in retreat could be so well-informed and so wise. We ate honey from their bees and drank milk from their dairy and, at night, shouted each other drinks at the local pubs.

In the best Colleen McCullough tradition, I fell a little in love (but chastely) with the handsome author of the prayer book. The crusty one took a huge shine to Bronwen and used to sneak out of church to gossip, enjoy a furtive smoke and show us his carving shed full of wooden pots and bowls, which he sold on the internet. And though I say we were were the only females, we were closely watched and eventually befriended by a woman from the local village, a vision in spandex and glitter, who desperately wanted to become a monk and regularly badgered the Abbot to change the rules. She had to resign herself to singing lustily with her good brothers and fathers each morning in the pews.

It was a wonderful week. And for that brief period, as we commuted each morning from our simple B and B, it seemed like a wonderful world. But again, it was time to go.

We were scarcely halfway through our trip at this stage. Still to come was Turkey, and a complex political story of a nation on the cusp of Islam and the West. We would be staying in the magical city of Istanbul overlooking the Bosporus, meeting generals and imams and the man who was then a renegade, banned from political life for reciting a verse from the Koran, but who is now the country's prime minister. We would hear from women whose careers had been shattered over the right to wear a veil, and the man who did the shattering.

We had another postcard to shoot in the spectacular lunar landscape of Cappadocia, where hermits took refuge from the world's follies in giant caves. Later, during the religious wars of the 7th and 8th centuries, Christians fled here clutching their precious icons, to save them from destruction. I would always remember the sight, when I rose early one morning to explore, of a dazzling sun striking the white rock of their cells.

After that, the UK. And after that?

This was one trip in one year. There have been dozens more, and each time it is different, and astonishing, and difficult, and rewarding. From the over-stuffed prisons of Rwanda to Wall Street in the grip of dot-com hysteria, to the shadowy menace of Haiti. You try in your stories to transmit a sense of the taste and the smell of these places, above and beyond the facts and figures and personalities.

Of course it is a job, but it is also a life, which you share at the time with your colleagues on camera and sound, and later, in a dark room, with your editor. You'd be surprised how little most of us talk about it when we get home, to our friends and loved ones. We know it can be alienating, it can even be boring, hearing about other people's adventures and disasters – particularly for those who've had to shoulder the domestic burden while their partners are away.

Is it an addiction, the accusation that's been thrown at me more than once? In all honesty, it probably is. But it's also true that Australia never seems dearer, nor more beautiful, then when flying home to it after a long absence.

One of the many reasons I feel overwhelmingly grateful to have worked for this program.

CRAIG McMURTRIE has been a foreign correspondent for seven of his twenty-two years in broadcasting, first with TVNZ in the early 1990s and then for ABC Television. He was posted as Washington Correspondent from 1997 to 2001 where he covered the Lewinsky scandal, the Clinton impeachment trial, the cliff-hanger Bush–Gore presidential election and the events of September 11.

Craig began his career in radio in New Zealand, moving to television news and current affairs with TVNZ in the mid 1980s. He moved to Sydney to join the ABC as a news and current affairs reporter in 1992, and was Diplomatic Correspondent based in Canberra before his Washington sojourn.

He is currently the ABC's Political Editor based in Canberra.

Craig is married and has three children.

September 11 ...

So there I was in a lift standing next to Monica Lewinsky.

She was a vision in pure white – one of hundreds clothed head to toe in the same colour for a Jewish peace conference at the hotel I was staying in, on Times Square.

She pretended not to notice my slack-jawed gape as I took in her porcelain skin, long eyelashes and big hair. On any other day I might have summoned up a witty aside, some sort of self-deprecating remark that could have endeared me to her, but she'd appeared so unexpectedly I was temporarily tongue-tied.

The gathering of these white wraiths was occurring on Rosh Hashana, a religious occasion I knew nothing about at the time, except that it had something to do with the Jewish New Year and there seemed to be a prohibition against anything resembling work, which prevented the white-clad figures around me from pushing buttons to select the floor they wanted on the lifts. I had already been implored to rescue several of them, punching out the required floor numbers. Now fate had delivered me to the most famous former intern in the world. It was hard to equate this smiling vision in virginal white with the vixen that was, according to the Clinton cronies, a sex-crazed stalker of the President. Then again, she had kept the semen-stained dress.

It's a terrible thing to stand next to someone you've read about, someone the whole world has obsessed over, and not be able to think of a thing to say, especially if you're a reporter. There was an excuse, though. I was covered in dust and was not exactly at my aromatic best, which might explain why she didn't attempt conversation. As for me, my brain was mush after a long and sweaty day picking my way around all that was left of New York's twin towers.

Only a few days before, the world had seemed to be orbiting on its usual axis. The eastern seaboard of the United States was ablaze in the fiery hues of autumn and New York was its usual frenetic self. A twenty-year-old kid from Adelaide had won at Flushing Meadows, and not just one match but the whole US Tennis Open. He was skinny, brash and yelled at himself a lot, but Lleyton Hewitt made Pete Sampras look like a lead-footed old man that day. He was ferocious.

After the post-match press conference I caught a plane back to Washington to help my daughter blow out her birthday cake candles. It was 10 September 2001.

Next morning I was sipping coffee, staring out the window at our backyard, wondering how much our landlord would mind if the place were overtaken by ivy – when the phone rang.

Perhaps it's possible to measure the import of a story by the amount of time it takes a reporter to pack. I ran up the stairs, opened the suitcase I'd only just emptied and threw my clothes back in.

Minutes later, in our beat-up black Dodge van, my wife and I were in the clogged streets of downtown Washington. It wasn't hard to see why there was virtual gridlock. A great plume of smoke snaked skywards on the other side of the Potomac River. As if the horror unfolding in New York wasn't enough – an American Airlines jet had just ploughed into the Pentagon.

The ABC bureau is two blocks from the White House and after abandoning the van I was legging it across the Washington Mall. A glorious outdoor promenade, it stretches over several kilometres from the marble solemnity of the Lincoln Memorial to the massive dome of the US Congress. Piercing the sky at its centre is a giant obelisk, an oddly impersonal tribute to George Washington, all angles and edges.

Beneath it I could see a group of tourists with their maps and guidebooks, confronting a policeman. Amazingly, even though the US Military Headquarters was burning, the sky was darkening and the city was emptying around them, they were demanding to know why they were being denied entry to the monument.

Over the years of my posting, the Washington Mall had always thrown up surprises, a frequent theatre of the absurd. In October

1997 a group called the 'Promise Keepers' held a rally of biblical proportions to atone for their sins. There were nearly a million of them and for a repressed male from down-under, it was somewhat confronting. In a classic case of collective hysteria, they swung wildly from exuberance to chest-heaving tears while very publicly casting off their sins. We tiptoed among them filming it all, and were largely escaping notice too, until they decided en masse to prostrate themselves before God.

I don't know that I've ever felt more exposed than when those souls, hundreds of thousands of them, lay down all around us, planting their faces in the dirt. We slunk off, trying not to step on anyone.

But I digress.

In the ABC office the editor was on the phone and he was unequivocal. Everyone else might be trying to get the hell out of New York, planes and trains might be stopped, bridges and tunnels might be closed, but I had to find a way in.

It is still amazing to me that in the midst of all the chaos of that day, with breathless news reports comparing it to the attack on Pearl Harbor, I was able to walk into a rental car agency and hire a car. ABC Radio's Michael Carey came with me and we didn't even tell half-truths. The bright-eyed staff behind the counter seemed perfectly comfortable with the fact that we were reporters from Australia's national broadcaster and that we wanted to take their nice shiny sedan somewhere near the smoking heap which was all that was left of the World Trade Centre. The sales assistant didn't even linger over the insurance option in the rental contract.

Three and a half hours later we were on the wrong side of the Hudson River, staring at a smouldering, gaping hole in the New York skyline, trying to figure out a way of getting across. We had no choice but to keep driving north, hoping for a miracle. Just when it was beginning to look like we'd wind up in Canada we came across the Tappanzee Bridge. It was well north of the city but at least it was still open. Thirty minutes later we were over the river and driving south to the Bronx.

New York is a truly wondrous place. I love the edgy exuberance of it. The narrow breakfast diners that serve everything except privacy, where the waiters greet you with a friendly bellow and then shout your order over the heads of everyone else. I love the delicatessens with jars of pickles you've never heard of and blackboard specials that require a doctorate to follow. I love the minimalist chic of the 'in' bars with their uncomfortable furniture and thin, twitchy people in black. I love the overdressed doormen, the underdressed dog walkers and the hurtling yellow cabs.

But there were no cabs weaving crazily through traffic on this day. In fact there was hardly any traffic at all. The great city had been struck dumb and we were still over a hundred blocks from the World Trade Center.

We spotted a subway station and discovered a train about to leave for midtown. There wasn't time to park the rental car properly, so we dumped it in a seedy lot across the road and shoved a handful of greenbacks at the bemused attendant. Explain that one to the ABC bean counters, I thought as we scampered onto a deserted platform and into an empty train, half expecting never to see the shiny sedan again.

For the final dozen or so blocks there was no option but to walk. Despite the massive size of Ground Zero it wasn't easy to approach, let alone see, from street level. We only knew we were getting close when we started coming across smashed and burnt-out cars. Then there were shreds of paper, pads and pens, the detritus of countless offices strewn everywhere in a fine, choking dust. The towers' ash remains coated cars, steps and ledges and though it seemed to burn to the touch, people had traced out peace signs and devotions to New York in wobbly heart shapes. As we drew closer facemasks and bottled water were being handed out. We took our share.

Closer in, the grim reality of it all was inescapable. From the other side of the river it had looked as if there was nothing left, but here, the edge of the smoking, mangled mass towered several storeys above us. It was already being called 'the pile' and it was almost impossible to find a familiar shape in the jagged, beaten, twisted metal. Alien and formless, it was like a misshapen growth, malevolent and hissing. Columns of eager firefighters were swallowed up by it, only to stagger out, much later, covered in concrete dust and grime, completely spent. They were barely coherent as reporters and cameras swarmed around.

Armed soldiers stood behind barricades preventing access to the site, and on some level I was relieved. One look at the worn faces and dull eyes of those who'd been scouring the wreckage told me all I needed to know about what they were finding in there. Handlers were afraid for their dogs who were being sent into the dark, still unstable crevices. Firefighters would describe how the frenzied activity on the pile would be broken by long, aching silences when everyone would freeze because someone thought they'd heard something – a scratching sound or tapping.

We interviewed one crew from New Jersey who worked a night on a human chain passing buckets and were going home, not to rest, but for their regular shift at the station house. Like many others, they weren't supposed to be at Ground Zero but who would dare refuse them? For these men it was deeply personal; hundreds of their own had been swallowed up in the calamity.

They told us of a scene of wild cheering and celebration as several fellow firefighters were pulled alive from the ruins. Their description was vivid and beautiful, but a few minutes later, after they left, we learned that it had all been a mistake. The men pulled out had been second-wave rescuers, caught very briefly in collapsing rubble.

In the midst of the hubbub we came across a male nurse from Tasmania, jogging along the footpath with a daypack on his back. He was looking for directions after interrupting a long-planned American holiday to volunteer his services. Others might be wandering around in a daze but he was all business. He had some experience, he assured us, having been involved in the aftermath of the Port Arthur shootings, and since a large ship was about to arrive to be used as a gigantic morgue, he thought he might be of use.

Like a slowly unfolding nightmare, the scale of the disaster became more apparent as photographs of the victims began appearing on walls and fences all over the city. At first there were only a few faces, then dozens and finally hundreds stared out. It was inexpressibly moving. Makeshift shrines of candles and flowers grew up around them, children left toys and drawings. It was the same story outside fire stations but these were images of sturdy-looking men, striking a tough pose. They were hypnotic, the last markers of so many broken lives.

The shock of it was producing behaviour that was plainly out of character. New Yorkers do not normally queue well. Now, though, long lines of next of kin were forming up outside hospitals and city offices, or any other place offering information on the missing. They were waiting their turn, anguish etched on their faces.

A city usually obsessed by individualism was sharing its pain. Grief-stricken relatives wandering the streets with pictures of missing loved ones were being approached and comforted by complete strangers. Students came out with placards and flags to cheer weary police and firefighters. Billionaires and millionaires were offering unheard-of donations. A volunteer at one charity showed me a broom closet full of plastic rubbish bags stuffed with cheques they hadn't had time to count yet.

This outbreak of open civility even extended to a drugstore owner at three in the morning. The sky opened up while I was making my way to a satellite truck for a live cross and he gave me the only umbrella in the shop, his own. The downpour ripped it to pieces within a few minutes.

Perhaps it was an omen, because that was the only deadline I didn't make that week. For some inexplicable reason, previously porous police roadblocks were now locked tight and my coveted NYPD press pass made no difference. The fact that I had an accent also seemed to have lost its novelty value. By the time I found a way through I was running, darting down narrower and narrower streets until I was completely alone, with a broken brolly and no torch, in an unlit alley in an unfamiliar part of New York's financial district. A can or bottle rattled somewhere off in the darkness, and as the sound reverberated around me I realised that this was, perhaps, less than wise. Lost and more than a little unnerved, I did the only thing I could think of. I began swearing out loud at all those bastards at the ABC who'd put me in this predicament, as I marched straight on.

Which might explain the startled reaction of the police patrol I stumbled into.

Recognising that I was both foreign and mad, they directed me to a brusque senior officer standing near the entryway to the closed Brooklyn Bridge. I needed to get across; the bridge was due to reopen shortly, but not soon enough. He told me to get out of his face and walk the hell over the bridge if I wanted to – so I did.

The rain was thumping down again, it was pitch black, I was wearing a sodden dark suit and time was running out. About halfway over I thought I was delivered when a patrol car skidded to a stop and two cops yelled at me to get in. As we continued across the bridge they wanted to know if I had a death wish, and then they had an argument about whether there were any satellite trucks on the Brooklyn side. I handed them a soggy bit of paper with the address and they agreed I was definitely going the wrong way. Noting my look of barely restrained panic, they dropped me at a subway to catch a train back. The seconds were ticking away when I emerged where I'd started, in lower Manhattan, shivering and exhausted. The mobile phone rang; it was the cheery truck operator ringing to see where I was. He had a great shot, he assured me, looking back at Ground Zero from Brooklyn.

Slowly, New York stirred and came back to life. Times Square lit up, crowds returned, and in no time street hustlers added twin towers memorabilia to the other trinkets of dubious taste on offer. Previously commonplace World Trade Center mugs and calendars were now billed as 'commemorative' editions, already there were Osama T-shirts showing the bearded terrorist caught in crosshairs.

Wall Street reopened for business, and there was the bizarre spectacle of traders in business suits being herded by armed soldiers out of subway stations to checkpoints where they had to present their bags and photo identification in order to get anywhere near the Stock Exchange. Getting the markets going again had been intended to reassure everyone, but it didn't look promising: more than a few were clearly petrified.

They weren't the only ones.

I hailed a cab and no sooner had I got in than the driver informed me he was from Pakistan. 'That would be Pakistan, not Afghanistan, right?' he told me at least half a dozen times. He had the Star-Spangled Banner flying or taped to every nook and cranny on the vehicle and he was still very worried. Perhaps he had cause to be, since in his enthusiasm he'd also covered the back seat. How would most of his customers feel, I wondered, about sitting on their flag?

In the immediate aftermath of September 11 there was a spate of hotel bombscares; they were happening so often it was almost easier to sleep fully clothed. A city-wide security clampdown quickly followed, and that led to a mercy dash back to the Bronx to rescue the shiny sedan. It was either that or a jumpy police force was likely to have it towed away or blown up.

Weeks later I was back at the Pentagon where frenzied rebuilding was already under way. As construction workers set about undoing the murderous work of the terrorists brick by brick outside, America's military top brass was plotting its retribution inside. My guide was the supervisor of the reconstruction project, Lee Evey. A compact man who looked every inch an engineer, he took me to an inner ring of the massive building where a white circle marked the spot where the doomed Boeing jet had finally come to a stop. In a matter-of-fact way Lee described how it had roared in so low it had snapped aerials off parked cars and forced joggers to dive for cover. He promised the repairs would be finished by the first anniversary of the attack. He was better than his word. It was ready ahead of schedule.

The psychological blow landed by the hijackers wouldn't be erased nearly so easily.

Before the twin towers fell, American society and newsrooms across the world had been preoccupied with the sex life of the libidinous Bill Clinton, and mysterious things called butterfly ballots and pregnant chads, and whether George W. Bush was a legitimate president.

On the night I stood next to Monica Lewinsky in a hotel lift the world was changing profoundly – and I didn't realise the extent of it yet. On top of their grieving, Americans would soon be confronted by deadly anthrax sent in the mail, while others elsewhere would face suicide bombers, and in Afghanistan and Iraq there would be war.

I didn't know, and at that moment didn't care. I was frozen to the spot, remembering how we'd all pursued her – the baby-faced Ken Starr, hound-dog Republicans and a battalion of reporters. I remembered I'd said 'oral sex' on live television and wondered if my mother would ever forgive me. I remembered it all – the thong, the beret and the cigar.

Of the six billion souls on the planet, she was now one of the very few known by just her first name, a fully-fledged celebrity culture diva.

Even though I was covered in World Trade Center dust and muck, the white-gowned Monica smiled as I stepped out and the doors closed behind me.

It was after all Rosh Hashana – the beginning of the Days of Repentance.

ERIC CAMPBELL has been an ABC foreign correspondent since 1996, having previously worked for Channel Nine's *A Current Affair* and the *Sydney Morning Herald*. He has been based mainly in Moscow and Beijing, but has reported from more than thirty countries.

His assignments have included covering conflicts in Afghanistan, Chechnya, Kosovo and northern Iraq, where he was wounded in a suicide bombing that killed ABC cameraman, Paul Moran.

A three-time Walkely Awards finalist, Campbell won the 2003 Logie Award for outstanding news coverage for a world exclusive report on an al-Qaeda training camp outside Kabul. In 1999 he was awarded a World Medal from the New York Festival for a story on the plight of the Siberian tiger.

His hobbies include spending every holiday in a weird country.

Pul-i-Khumri, Northern Afghanistan: September 1996

An Afghan warlord is plying me with vodka and he wants to know what I think of heavy metal.

'So you guys are from Australia?' he asked again. 'You like AC/DC?'

I start forming the words 'well, umm' as he summons a servant to bring in a giant sound system and CDs. Another fills my glass with more Russian vodka. I notice the brand is 'Black Death'.

I am starting to feel woozy but the warlord is just getting started.

'The Taliban are all fucking Pakistanis. They are all fucking homosexuals. Tomorrow I'll show you some prisoners. All Pakistanis.'

Within minutes the sound system is set up. The strains of 'Highway to Hell' start blasting at full volume across the room and out to the Hindu Kush Mountains.

The warlord is singing along: 'Highway to hell, uh, uh, uh! Highway to hell, uh, uh, uh!'

It is turning into a very strange night.

Eleven days earlier I'd been sitting in the ABC Bureau in Moscow when news flashed that an obscure group called the Taliban had seized the Afghan capital, Kabul.

Back in 1996 very little was known about the Islamic purists who would later help spark a world war. *Foreign Correspondent* had shot a story in their base in Kandahar, southern Afghanistan, showing them hanging TV sets in the streets like executed criminals (they believed television was un-Islamic). A few newspaper articles had talked about their bizarrely repressive policies towards women. But most of the world had lost interest in Afghanistan after it descended into civil war in the early 1990s. It was widely seen as a pointless conflict between equally vile warlords in a failed state that no longer mattered.

The Taliban's seizure of the capital changed that in an instant. Suddenly a horde of apparent lunatics was on the verge of conquering the whole country. What's more, they were vowing to spread their brand of fundamentalism throughout Central Asia.

The Executive Producer of *Foreign Correspondent*, Dugald Maudsley, rang to say they wanted a story 'as soon as possible'. But 'soon' and 'possible' were not words that sat easily with Afghanistan.

After seventeen years of continuous war, first against the Soviets, then against each other, landlocked Afghanistan was one of the hardest countries in the world to get to. All air links between Moscow and Kabul had long been severed.

My cameraman, Tim Bates, and I would have to go in through one of the increasingly dysfunctional countries surrounding it: Uzbekistan, Turkmenistan, Tajikistan, Pakistan or Iran. All were grotesquely bureaucratic in their visa requirements and none except Pakistan was even remotely welcoming to journalists. And no matter which country we got into, the next step of crossing into Afghanistan was going to be even harder. Unless we could hitch a ride on a UN or Red Cross aid flight, we would have to drive in through roads that had been bombed into obstacle courses, risking bandits and tin-pot warlords along the way.

It was going to take at least three weeks to get in, get a story, get out, get the tapes to Australia and get the story to air.

We'd debated about whether I should head to Kabul, the target of most foreign news journalists. But I felt the story would have moved on by the time my feature was broadcast. So we decided to focus on the man who might just determine the Taliban's success – a kingmaker and rogue named Abdul Rashid Dostum.

General Dostum was the kind of warlord who made other warlords blush. He was not just brutal and corrupt, he was breathtakingly treacherous. He controlled six provinces of northern Afghanistan like a private fiefdom and his allegiance was for sale.

Known as Pasha, an ancient term for king, he was a hard-drinking ex-communist who had long been changing sides in Afghanistan's long-running war – backing the central government of President Rabbani when it suited him and shelling Kabul when he judged it to be in his interest.

With the central government now on the run, he could be crucial to the country's future. If he swung his support behind the Taliban, there would be little to stop them taking over the rest of Afghanistan. But if he sided with the ousted government forces, they might just have a chance.

Dostum's territory bordered the former Soviet republic of Uzbekistan. It was a separate country now, but hadn't yet cut every link with Moscow. We discovered we could enter Uzbekistan with a Russian visa and stay for three days. That would give us time to get to the Afghan border. We could transit through there on a Russian visa. But we still needed an Afghan visa to cross. That was going to be a bigger problem.

The central government, which had fled to the remote Panjshir Valley north of Kabul, had an embassy in Moscow. But there was no guarantee Dostum's people would accept one of the ousted government's visas. Like any self-respecting major league warlord, he issued his own visas. He just didn't have any embassies.

We went to the ousted government's embassy in Moscow, just in case. A plaque on the wall announced it as the representative office of the Islamic State of Afghanistan – a state that was now effectively confined to a valley. Smooth diplomats in expensive suits were still carrying on business as usual. We had to write a letter listing the places we wished to visit – all of them outside their territory – before we were issued with expensive but probably worthless visas.

Waiting in the queue we ran into Tom Szypulski, the ABC's former Moscow producer who now worked for the television news agency APTN. He decided to chance the journey through

Uzbekistan with us. We flew out of Moscow at midnight on a battered Aeroflot plane, crammed into tiny, malodorous seats surrounded by hundreds of Russian traders and Uzbek families. As always, the other passengers had brought on half their baggage as hand luggage – cramming some of it into the overhead lockers and laying the rest along the aisles. Surly flight attendants wandered between the bags, ignoring every request for food and drink and lighting up cigarettes next to the No Smoking signs. It was impossible to sleep. We landed in the Uzbek capital, Tashkent, just before dawn and queued for an hour to clear customs. After a further four-hour wait in the crumbling, Soviet-era airport, we boarded a domestic flight to Termez on the border of Afghanistan.

Sure enough, we found our Afghan visas were worthless. The local United Nations' office in Termez explained we would have to send our passports to Dostum's capital, Mazar-i-Sharif, to get 'Dostum visas'. The UN Director, a Bulgarian named Petar Bojilot, offered to take them with the next UN vehicle heading to Mazar. We'd just have to wait three days.

Termez is possibly the most boring place in Central Asia to wait for anything. The town is over a thousand years old, perched on the ancient Oxus River. But the Soviet Union managed to remove almost every trace of history and charm. Where oases and ancient mosques once rose up from the desert, the first sight to greet travellers now is squat, ugly apartment blocks.

By chance, we had also struck an impromptu daytime curfew. The Uzbek president, Islam Karimov, was due to be passing through town any day. So the authorities ordered everybody to stay off the roads. Karimov was the former communist leader who re-labelled himself a democrat after the Soviet Union collapsed. Not much else had changed. He rigged the first elections in his favour and maintained power through brute forced and a secret police force inherited from the Soviet KGB. A couple of times we ventured outside to grab a kebab, but mostly we stayed inside the UN compound.

It was a relief when our passports finally arrived with Dostum's elusive visas. But Petar Bojilot was nervous about us going. The news the UN was getting from across the border was consistently bad. The Taliban were advancing rapidly towards Dostum's territory. Dostum was trying to negotiate but there were fears the Taliban would just sweep in.

'In three days they could be at the border,' Petar warned us. 'If you are on the other side, the Uzbeks will not let you back in. You will be trapped.'

We debated our options. Tom, a Polish-American with unfaltering self-confidence, was determined we should go in. He was the only agency journalist in the area and dozens of TV networks were waiting for any pictures he could send. Tim, a quietly spoken Tasmanian, was more cautious about war zones after an earlier shoot in Chechnya where he'd inadvertently walked into a minefield. But he was willing to give it a go. The Taliban weren't targeting foreigners and there was every reason to believe we'd get through the worst-case scenario of being overrun. Being stuck in Afghanistan couldn't be much worse than hanging around Termez. At least we'd have a story.

The border was a heavily fortified bridge over the river. It had been built by Moscow and named the Soviet Friendship Bridge. The Soviets then used it to invade Afghanistan.

Now it was in the hands of corrupt Uzbek border guards. They gave us the usual shakedown for money, seizing our Uzbek currency and inventing various fines. Eventually they agreed to let us cross.

A small Uzbek man in a dark suit with dark glasses watched them take our money. He was clearly KGB. Just as we were about to leave he asked to see our documents.

After a few seconds he handed back my passport and Tim's. Then he turned to Tom.

'You cannot cross,' he said. 'Your Russian visa has expired.'

Tom checked and saw that his multiple-entry visa for Russia had expired the day before. He'd been meaning to renew it when he was scrambled to Uzbekistan. Then he remembered he wasn't in Russia.

'This is Uzbekistan,' he said. 'And I'm going to Afghanistan. Why do I need a visa for Russia?'

'You must come with me,' the spook said.

'Look,' Tom said, 'I haven't got a visa for France either. What does it matter?'

But logic had nothing to do with it. The Uzbek KGB man just couldn't move on from the fact that Russia and Uzbekistan were no longer the same country. He led Tom away.

'Don't worry, I'll be fine,' he shouted to us. 'I'll see you in Mazar.'

We waved and turned towards Afghanistan.

As we crossed the river, Soviet suburbia gave way to Arabian Nights. A small village of mud-brick huts straddled the bank, full of bearded men wearing the traditional *shalwar kamiz* (pantaloons and long cotton shirts with camel-wool waistcoats). The market in the centre was a cluster of stalls selling spices, lamps and offal. Apart from the odd Russian car, it could have been a scene from the 19th century. Afghanistan was so improbably exotic it felt like a filmset for a Rudyard Kipling epic.

A UN translator had crossed with us to help organise transport into Mazar-e Sharif. It was late afternoon and there was no such thing as taxis here. Eventually we found a car that was driving to Mazar. The only problem was it had four large Afghan men inside it. Tim and I would have to share the front passenger seat.

We put as much gear as we could into the boot but still had to stack boxes on the floor of the front seat. Then we both squeezed in on top of them. None of the Afghans spoke a word of English. The translator wished us luck and we headed off across the desert.

We bounced across potholes and bomb craters as Tim tried desperately to keep his bum off the gear stick. I struggled to stop my head banging on the roof. It was a painful three-hour drive but the landscape was extraordinary. The road wound over sand dunes beside a line of low mountains glowing in the evening sun.

We arrived just after dark, bruised and cramped. Mazar by night was almost as exotic as the border village, with pools of light from the few public lamps illuminating market stalls and ghostly passers-by.

It was the last place on Earth we'd expect to meet a gay Scottish flight attendant. But as we walked into the UN guesthouse a man with epaulettes named Derek looked up and smiled wickedly. 'What are you boys doing here? he asked.

It turned out that Dostum had his own airline, Balkh Air, leased from a British aviation company complete with a British flight crew. They lived in the guesthouse and spent every night drinking German beer and moaning about how Dostum wasn't paying his bills. None of them seemed particularly worried abut the prospect of the Taliban army arriving any day. 'We can always fly out', Derek said.

The next morning Tim and I sought out Dostum's Foreign Ministry to register our visas and find a translator. The official translators had already been assigned to the handful of journalists who'd arrived before us. But some students were hanging around outside looking for work. We hired a young man named Wahid who spoke passable English and was intensely eager to please.

'You are a guest in my country and it is my duty to serve you', he said. 'Whatever you need, I can do for you.'

The first thing we needed was some local currency. Wahid took us to a market to change our US dollars for afghanis. It was an open area creamed with dozens of traders waving wads of notes and shouting the latest changing exchange rates. Dostum printed his won afghanis, which were slightly different from those of the central government. And he'd been printing a few too many of them of late, fuelling massive inflation. The value of Dostum's afghanis was also plummeting as the Taliban army approached. As a result, money was no longer measured in face value, but in bulk.

We gave Wahid fifty US dollars. The moneychanger calculated the size of the pile of afghanis and carefully measured them out. It was a wad of notes about a metre thick.

'How are we supposed to carry that?' I asked.

'No problem,' Wahid said. 'They will give us a bag.'

So, clutching a dirty black plastic bag of near-useless currency, we started shooting our story.

Dostum Pasha was not an easy man to meet. After traipsing around a series of government offices we found his senior general, who promised to pass on our request for an interview. He would surely have an answer any day, he promised. The general was impressed that we had come from Moscow, where he had studied to be an officer. 'Moscow is the most beautiful city in the world,' he said in fluent Russian.

I wondered which part he'd been to. Moscow had a historic centre, but its surrounding suburbs were among the planet's ugliest. Mazar-i-Sharif, on the other hand, was one of the most beautiful, wonderful places I had ever seen.

We wandered around the town gawking like kids in a sweetshop. Everywhere Tim turned the camera there were magic images: camel trains, donkey-drawn carts, wizened old men in turbans, women in *burqas*, nomads in shawls, tiny street stalls and frenetic markets full of ethnic Uzbeks, Tajiks and Hazaras.

At the centre of town was the Blue Mosque, the tomb of the Prophet Mohammed's son-in-law, and one of the holiest shrines in Islam. It is an extraordinarily beautiful building, decorated with magnificent inlaid mosaics and turquoise minarets. Tourists and pilgrims used to flock to it before Afghanistan descended into endless war. Now the only people pouring in were soldiers.

Mazar was filling with fighters from Dostum's tribal allies. Some were uniformed, some wore traditional clothes, but all had weaponry left behind by the Soviets. Swaggering teenage boys carried machine-guns, Kalashnikovs and grenade launchers.

This had been a secure base for the Soviet Army during the occupation, when Dostum commanded an ethnic Uzbek militia that sided with the Russians against the mujahideen. He rose to the rank of defence minister in the Soviet puppet government of

President Najibullah. But his commitment was always based on self-interest rather than ideology. He betrayed Najibullah to the mujahideen after the Soviets left and routinely switched sides during the ensuing civil war.

He now enjoyed absolute power in his provinces, along with a cult of personality. Giant portraits of Dostum hung on every square and street corner, his thickset head and bushy moustache smiling or glowering at every subject. For all his brutality, he was popular with most of his subjects. Mazar had escaped any serious fighting during the long years of war and was prosperous by Afghan standards. The shops were full of imported goods and the streets were clogged with expensive four-wheel drives weaving past rickshaws and camels.

But having thrived in the deadly game of Afghan politics for more than a decade, Dostum now faced his most difficult choice – to accommodate or to fight the Taliban. His life could depend on the decision. A few days earlier, the Taliban in Kabul had castrated and murdered his former boss, Najibullah, hanging his mutilated body from a roadside pole.

It wasn't a good time to be chasing Dostum for an interview.

The next day, to our amazement, our friend Tom Szypulski arrived. He had managed to persuade the Russian consul in Termez to renew his visa in a day, an astonishing victory over Russian bureaucracy. Satisfied he was now properly documented to travel to Russia, the border spook let him cross into Afghanistan. Tom added his name to the request for an interview.

Walking around Mazar it was not hard to see why people were nervous about the Taliban. Mazar was as close as you could find in Afghanistan to a secular city. Most of the men smoked, some even drank and everyone enjoyed loud music, just some of the evils the Taliban had banned.

There was a thriving university open to everyone, another sin against God according to the ultra-fundamentalists. Many female students wore the suffocating veil, the *burqa*, on the streets, but changed into casual clothes when they reached the campus.

Wahid pointed out his girlfriend, a pretty young student he said he was saving up to marry.

'Aren't you too young?' I asked.

'No, it is time!' he said. 'I am twenty.'

We went to a restaurant for dinner. More than a hundred men in traditional clothing were watching a tape of *Baywatch*. I could tell the Taliban weren't going to take this place without a fight.

By day three, there was still no reply from Dostum. But his general invited us to film a tank drill. We expected to see just a couple of soldiers raising and lowering a turret, but it seemed like half the army had assembled for us. About fifty Soviet-era tanks fired up and began driving aimlessly in circles around the desert. Tim wedged himself in the manhole of one as I clung to the back. They were great pictures for about a minute – until the cloud of sand shaken up by the tanks covered us and the lens in a thick blanket of dust. Tim resembled a plaster statue that had mysteriously come to life and learned to shout expletives.

Back at the guesthouse, a messenger told us Dostum had finally agreed to an interview … or rather, an audience. We could meet the pasha but we were forbidden to ask him questions.

His aides took us outside town to Dostum's fortress, a huge palace surrounded by an adobe wall that could have been fashioned by Hollywood for a remake of *Beau Geste*. Heavily armed guards stood on the crenellated turrets as farm boys marched around the courtyard below, learning to be soldiers for battles that could start within days.

We were led into a grand meeting room where Dostum was poring over maps, ringed by tribal commanders and his senior officers. He rose as we entered, a giant of a man in a bulging military uniform, with a crushing handshake and a deceptively friendly smile.

'I think we have met before?' Dostum said to me through his translator.

'I don't know if we've met before, no,' I answered. 'But I've seen your face many times.' On every street corner, in fact.

Unable to ask questions, I tried to appeal to his vanity.

'We saw your army today,' I said. 'We were very impressed with their preparedness.'

Dostum smiled. 'You have seen one or two brigades. If you go to other places and see all of them, they are very much more prepared than this. By the help of God I am not weak militarily.'

He then launched into 'The Dostum Story', describing his peace-loving history as a warlord. Laying siege to Kabul and shelling it, for example, was something that had been forced upon him.

'This war was forced on us,' he lied. 'We were against the war and were forced to participate.'

As always, Dostum was hedging his bets. He confirmed he had just sent a delegation to the Taliban in Kabul.

'We'll try to stop the war and come to a political conclusion to end the conflict peacefully,' he said. 'My proposal to the Taliban is that there is now no need for war and political problems in this country.'

Then he sat down and returned to planning for war.

'We are here,' he said to his generals, pointing to the map. 'Here are our tanks.'

The aides hustled us out.

Finally, I had a centrepiece for an exclusive story. Now it was time to find the Taliban.

While Tom waited in Mazar for an aid flight that could take out his tapes, we drove south toward the Salang Pass. The Taliban had temporarily halted their advance on the other side of the pass, at the mouth of a long highway tunnel. To reach Mazar by force, they would have to fight their way through the tunnel or make a quick dash over the mountains. Neither was an easy option, so the Taliban were waiting to hear if Dostum would invite them in.

Our plan was to drive across what was still a relatively cordial frontline and continue to Kabul. But as we arrived in the town of Pul-i-Khumri, just north of the pass, it was clear something extraordinary was going on. Hundreds of soldiers from different militias were milling around the highway. Wahid went to investigate and came back breathless with excitement.

'Rabbani is here,' he said. 'You can talk to him.'

Burhanaddin Rabbani, president of the ousted central government, had not been seen since fleeing Kabul eleven days earlier. But he had come to Pul-i-Khumri to negotiate an alliance against the Taliban.

Wahid led us up to a large tent where dozens of warlords had assembled. Dostum's representatives sat alongside the independent mujahideen commanders. It was an extraordinary spectacle. As we watched, they formed the united front that would become known as the Northern Alliance. It was a moment in history – and by complete chance Tim and I were the only foreigners to witness it.

Then they invited me to ask some questions of Rabbani. The problem was I had no idea which one he was.

I began by thanking the president for the opportunity to speak to him, waving my head around and focusing on each old man with a beard in the hope of making eye contact with the right one.

After my remark was translated, one of the beards answered back, thanking me for coming. I stopped waving my head around and looked at him as intently as I could.

'We intend to stop this invasion, throw out the invaders and end the war,' he said. 'That is why we have had talks with Dostum by phone and in person.'

Dostum, as usual was playing off both sides.

President Rabbani continued to insist they were ready to launch a counterattack any day. He sounded remarkably confident for an unpopular president who had high-tailed it out of his capital just days earlier. While he spoke in a measured voice, the translations became increasingly strident. There was something distinctly odd about his interpreter, a young Afghan dressed in a general's uniform.

He not only had an American accent, he appeared to be embellishing the answers, peppering every statement with derogatory remarks about Pakistanis.

After the audience was over, I thanked Rabbani and withdrew.

Minutes later, the interpreter came out.

'So you guys want a beer, or what?' he shouted.

It turned out he was the local warlord, Sayed Jafar Naderii. His father was a powerful commander who had sent him to be educated in New Jersey, hence the accent. He was rumoured to have ridden with the Hell's Angels. But he had come home to take over his father's private army.

Naderii arranged for us to tour the front line to see how they were going to stop 'the fucking Pakistanis'. Pakistan was known to be backing the Taliban, and some extremist mullahs had stirred up Pakistani villagers to fight alongside them. But Naderii seemed oblivious to the fact that many of the Taliban's supporters were simply rebelling against corrupt feudal warlords, like himself.

His main general took us to a ridge overlooking the Taliban forces. Light snow was falling on the pass. He boasted they would have no trouble holding them back.

'Except for this tunnel there is no way through for the Taliban. All the passageways over there are filled with snow.'

In the distance, we could hear the faint sound of artillery shelling. The counterattack had just begun.

We went back to Pul-i-Khumri to spend the night with Naderii.

As we were led into his mansion, we could hear him shouting animatedly into his satellite telephone, directing the fighting. He switched to English when he saw us, shouting, 'Sit down, I'll get you guys a beer. Cold, I suppose?' then continued to bark orders over the phone.

The servants led us downstairs to a room where a banquet had been laid out on a low table. Three extremely evil-looking men were already eating, one of whom introduced himself as a former ambassador to Syria.

Naderii's family belonged to a branch of Islam known as the Ismaelis, led by a long line of playboys bearing the hereditary title, Aga Khan. It was clear they had a more relaxed interpretation of religious strictures than the Taliban. The room was well stocked with alcohol. A mat on the wall was inscribed with the words 'Sex, Drugs and Rock and Roll'.

Eventually Naderii joined us and the alcohol began flowing. He held court in English, talking about motorcycles (he had a Harley), Pakistanis (with whom he had serious issues) and AC/DC (of whom he was a huge fan). His cronies continually and nervously laughed at what they took to be his jokes, even though they clearly had no idea what he was saying.

My glass kept filling with Black Death vodka and – in what should have been a warning – it was starting to taste good. AC/DC was even sounding good.

The more we drank the more he expanded on his hatred of Pakistanis. He talked about how he was going to 'kick their fucking asses' back to where they came from. His cronies laughed even louder, presuming he had made another joke. Naderii waved his finger at me and shouted: 'Don't you put this on your fucking camera!'

The room began to spin as 'Jailbreak' thumped out of the sound system. I could feel something unpleasant stirring in my stomach. The warlord was getting blurry. I pleaded tiredness as he poured me yet another glass of Black Death. Finally, he agreed to let us leave. Tim and I stumbled to our room and collapsed.

I woke with the worst hangover I have ever had. The Black Death vodka had been aptly named. It was as though horsemen were galloping across my skull while pygmies in muddy boots danced on my tongue. It appeared I had also eaten something rich in bacteria. I staggered to the toilet, a foul-smelling pit in the next room. As I retched into the black hole, gagging on the fumes, a servant arrived at the door. 'Gentlemen', he said. 'Breakfast is served.'

Tim was not much better than me, and we walked uncertainly into the dining room. I sat down in the designated chair. A sheep's head was looking up at me from the plate.

The evil men from the previous night joined us, Wahid translating. They explained Naderii had had to leave early to go to the front and would not be able to see us again. But he wished us to enjoy the sheep before returning to Mazar.

The fighting meant the road to Kabul was closed and our shoot was effectively over. All that remained was the long journey home.

But for now, I was wondering if I'd live through the morning. My stomach rumbled. A fresh wave of nausea washed over me. Naderii's cronies stared at me expectantly, gesturing towards the sheep. Its dead eyes met mine. I picked up the knife and began slicing into its face.

MARK SIMKIN went to Tokyo in January 2001 as the winner of a prestigious Asialink fellowship. He worked at NHK, Japan's national broadcaster, and with the *International Herald Tribune/ Asahi Evening News*, a major newspaper.

Several months later, he was appointed the ABC's North Asia Correspondent. Reporting for radio and television, Mark is responsible for covering Japan, North Korea and South Korea. He has reported from all three countries, and has covered stories such as the soccer World Cup, the rise of the charismatic Japanese Prime Minister, and the North Korean nuclear crisis.

Before becoming North Asia Correspondent, Mark was Economics Correspondent and Co-Bureau Chief for ABC Radio Current Affairs in Canberra. He has also been a senior reporter with *Lateline*, a political reporter in Canberra, and was ABC TV's Finance Correspondent during the Asian currency crisis.

North Korea

It was like something out of a spy movie. The Tokyo hotel room was tiny, and filled with cigarette smoke. The two men sitting opposite me were North Korean government officials. They had introduced themselves as 'tour guides' but the trips they specialised in were likely to be of the one-way kind. They wore dark suits. They exchanged furtive glances. They took notes in little black books. And they knew an awful lot about me.

'You may be allowed to visit our peerless country to view a mass gymnastic performance held in honour of the Great Leader,' the senior spook said. 'But you will have to abide by certain rules.'

The list that followed made it clear that this was to be a package tour like no other. 'You will not file "political stories". You will only film what is permitted. You will not talk to people on the street unless permitted. You will not leave your hotel without a guide. You will not use the local currency. We will determine where you go and what you do.'

I was overjoyed. Sure, the rules were tough – almost as tough as covering an Ashes tour – but the prospect of getting access to the world's most inaccessible country made it worthwhile. In an increasingly globalised, homogenised world, the 'hermit kingdom' lives up to its nickname. It is hermetically sealed and truly unique. The Berlin Wall has come down, the USSR has broken up, China and Cuba are experimenting with 'market socialism', but North Korea remains committed to its communist philosophy of *juche*, or self-reliance. It's the world's last outpost of Stalinism, the cold war's final frontier, the globe's most controlled state. I couldn't wait to get there.

Two weeks later, accompanied by my Japanese cameraman, Jun Matsuzono, I was sitting on board North Korea's national airline en route to the eastern end of the 'axis of evil'. A ride on Air Koryo is an adventure in itself. It's the only airline I've ever flown where the stewardess wanders around as the aircraft lifts off, and doesn't bother with a safety demonstration. Then again, the plane didn't need one – the sum total of its emergency equipment was a sign on the bulkhead saying 'Escape Rope'. No wonder the country's Dear Leader, Kim Jong Il, only travels by train.

We were met at Pyongyang Airport by Mrs Park and Mr Goh. They were from the government and they were there to help. 'Welcome,' Mrs Park said with a disarming smile. 'We are your guides. We will accompany you everywhere you go. May I have your passports? I'll look after them for the duration of your stay in our peerless country.'

The road from the airport into Pyongyang was a masterpiece of engineering: straight, flat and wide enough to land a jet fighter on. Actually, you could have landed an entire squadron without disrupting the traffic. Apart from our little van, the vast ribbon of concrete was utterly, eerily deserted.

It was a road for the elite – North Korea is desperately poor, and most people can't afford to buy food, let alone a car. Aid agencies talk of people eating grass and bark from trees to survive. After the Korean War, the North was actually richer than the South. Now, each year, South Koreans throw away more food than the North produces.

The evidence was all around us. On either side of the expensive, modern freeway were scenes from another time, testaments to the priorities of a 'workers' paradise'. Crumbling concrete apartment blocks towered over desolate fields tilled by fifty-year-old Soviet tractors. Oxen pulled rudimentary ploughs through the dust. I asked Mrs Park what they were trying to grow in one particularly barren patch of dirt. 'Rice,' she replied, straight-faced. It was as if we'd entered a bizarre parallel universe – a place where things were familiar, yet radically different. It was disorienting, fascinating, and occasionally frightening.

The capital was unexpectedly pretty, albeit in a sterile kind of way. Like North Korea itself, Pyongyang is very centrally planned. It's one of the greenest cities on the planet – there are fifty-eight square metres of garden for every citizen (by contrast, Paris has twelve square metres and Seoul manages just three square metres). Ancient, rusting trolley buses trundle around the streets or, more often than not, sit idle during the electricity stoppages. It's very clean and quiet, perhaps unnaturally so. There are no animals or birds. There's no pollution (because there are few cars) and no advertising, apart from giant billboards featuring the Dear Leader and his father, the Great Leader, Kim Il Sung. Their faces adorn posters, the sides of buildings, and the lapel badges worn by everyone you see.

The city has a huge edifice complex – it's full of massive monuments glorifying the fathers of the nation. There are monuments 'to glorify the victory and heroic struggles in the Fatherland Liberation War, in which the Great Leader defeated the armies led by the American imperialists'. There are monuments that 'reflect the unanimous desire of the people to praise the exploits of comrade Kim Il Sung and immortalise his revolutionary achievements'. And there are monuments that 'symbolise the victorious advance of the Communist Party grown up from the root of down-with-imperialism-union'. It's like a giant socialist theme park.

The biggest building of all is truly spectacular – a 105-storey pyramid, complete with five revolving restaurants. The Ryugyong was to be the biggest hotel in the world, but in 1991 the government ran out of money and construction was suspended. It now stands in the city centre, like a giant inverted ice-cream cone, a monument to grand plans and inadequate resources. It's a touchy subject; our guides tried to pretend the building didn't exist, even though it was visible from almost everywhere we went. So while they were able to give us the most minute details about all the other monuments – 'the 170-metre high Tower of Juche Idea has 25,550 stone slabs, one for each day of the Great Leader's life' – they were uncharacteristically quiet when it came to the Ryugyong Hotel. 'Why did they stop construction?' I asked. Silence. 'Did they really need five revolving restaurants?' Utter silence. 'Why would you want to build the world's biggest hotel in a country virtually no one is allowed to visit?' Utter silence accompanied by death stare.

Our hotel was conveniently located on an island – convenient for our guides, that is, because it made it impossible to leave without being seen. It was, we were told, a typical North Korean establishment: there was a revolving restaurant on the top floor, a bowling alley in the basement, and an anti-American display in the foyer. 'The US aggressors committed bloodcurdling atrocities of mass slaughter everywhere they went during the war,' the text said. 'However, the Korean People's Army – whose soldiers are capable of beating any enemy with a single blow – won a brilliant victory in the war.'

Hatred of America drips from the very walls of Pyongyang. There are posters that feature North Korean missiles smashing the Capitol. The local newspaper, *The Pyongyang Times*, even featured a poem celebrating the pretzel that caught in George W Bush's throat:

Oh cake, my dear and laudable cake,
You're strong enough to knock Bush down.
You devote yourself,
You set yourself afire,
To avenge the grievances of the world's people.
Oh Bush, you fighting cock, who is the supporter of the cake
*   terrorist attack?*
The cake manufacturing country will soon come to an end.

On a river in central Pyongyang, the hatred takes tangible form. The USS *Pueblo* is the country's proudest possession – an American spy ship intercepted off the North Korean coast in 1968. Eighty-three US crew members were captured. They were released eleven months later, after Washington provided a grovelling apology. You can still see the bullet holes in the *Pueblo*'s hull.

The man who showed us around the vessel was involved in its capture. 'The US imperialists are our sworn enemies,' Kim Jung Rok told me, his chest bristling with military medals. 'Their plan has not changed. We are not part of any "axis of evil". The fact that Bush said so proves he is trying to find any excuse to wage war against us. Our People's Army and our people will destroy whatever plot the US imperialists hatch.'

After the little history lesson we returned to our hotel. 'Sleep well,' Mrs Park told us. 'Tomorrow a great honour awaits you.'

It turned out the 'great honour' was a major dilemma. I was escorted to a florist, and instructed to hand over ten US dollars for a tatty bunch of near-dead flowers. Then we walked to Mansu Hill, the grandest monument of them all. It features a twenty-metre-high bronze statue of Kim Il Sung, his right hand outstretched, 'showing us the way forward,' Mr Goh explained. My cameraman was given strict instructions only to film the whole statue – images of the Great Leader with his feet or head cut off are not permitted.

A group of school children stood there, as their teacher related the glorious exploits of Kim the elder in a trembling voice. 'Our Great Leader was so gracious he helped us serve him honourably even after his death by building this statue,' the teacher declared, as several children wiped tears from their eyes.

The kids moved on, and then it was my turn. 'You now have the great honour of bowing to the Great Leader and presenting your flowers,' Mrs Park said. From nowhere, a government official appeared to record the moment with an ancient movie camera. It was a very awkward situation. I didn't want to show deference to a dictator who apparently sent vast numbers of people to their deaths, but nor did I want to insult my hosts. In the end I compromised, tossing the flowers at the giant bronze feet but not bowing.

As we left, the florist began picking up the flowers, presumably for recycling.

The whole incident demonstrated what sets Pyongyang apart. The people are utterly brainwashed. They think the country is a paradise ruled by a virtual god, and there's no outside media or internet access to spoil the illusion. Our hotel featured one television channel, and one subject – the glorious life and times of the Dear Leader. The evening 'news' provided a rundown of everything he'd done during the day: 'Today, the Dear Leader provided on-the-spot guidance at a catfish farm and chicken farm,' one lead story began. (Curiously, everywhere he goes, the Dear Leader appears to be accompanied by a bevy of ladies wearing army uniforms with very short camouflage skirts – his so-called 'pleasure brigade'.)

North Korean children are fed unhealthy doses of propaganda from birth. Each week, schools spend six hours teaching the 'revolutionary history of the Great Leader', six hours on the 'exploits of the Anti-Japanese Woman Revolutionary' (Kim Il Sung's wife) and six hours on the revolutionary activities of Kim Jong Il. The children's books – many of them supposedly written by the Great Leader himself – are full of communist allegories where brave peasants rise up against their malevolent landlords. The colouring-in books feature pictures of the North Korean military destroying the vicious American invaders. I was told – but didn't see – that even arithmetic is taught from an ideological perspective ('because he loves his people, the Dear Leader kindly gives a grateful farmer ten cows, but the US Imperialists kill three cows in a cowardly surprise attack. How many cows are left?') 'I love my country,' one schoolgirl told me. 'I love North Korea very much, because this is the country established by the Great Leader, and the country that comrade Kim Jong Il will lead to victory.'

Halfway through our stay, we were taken to a concrete example (actually it was marble) of this astonishing cult of personality. The International Friendship Exhibition is a massive shrine to the glory of the Great Leader. It's a sacred place. You're not allowed to film or take photographs, and you have to wear covers over your shoes. There are vast polished floors, imposing staircases and one hundred and fifty cavernous rooms. Unfortunately, the effect is somewhat undermined by the lack of electricity, which kept the lights flickering on and off – the one kind of power struggle North Korea seems comfortable with.

The Exhibition is living proof that you can't take it with you when you're gone. It houses 210,00 presents given to the Great Leader by other, lesser leaders – a testament, we were told, to 'the esteem with which Kim Il Sung is held by the entire world'.

That's not exactly true. It seemed the only people who had sent presents to Kim senior were fellow dictators. Nicaragua's Daniel Ortega sent a stuffed crocodile holding a plate (what else do you give a guy who's got it all?). Joseph Stalin sent a full-scale luxury train. Not wanting to be outdone by a comrade, Mao Zedong presented an even grander one. An assortment of African hard-men sent animals – some stuffed, some live (but now dead). Former East German leader Eric Honecker gave a rifle… so did ex Romanian leader, Nicolae Ceausescu, and he generously threw in a bear he'd used the gun on.

After wandering for several hours, we were ushered into one final, very special chamber. The door was opened, the lights flickered on, and some rickety marching music started playing. There, in front of us, was a life-like statue of the Great Leader himself, standing among some plastic palms and fake fronds of *Kimilsungia* (the national flower). Our guide immediately bowed her head and burst into tears.

Outside, she behaved as if she had just had a life-altering experience – which she probably had. 'There are only two wax statues in the entire world,' she told us breathlessly. 'And that is one of them – the Great Leader.' Obviously, Madame Tussaud's is yet to visit Pyongyang.

The foreign media often predicts the imminent collapse of North Korea, but I can't see it happening any time soon. Kim Jong Il's cult of personality is holding the place together. Aid groups believe millions of people have starved to death over the last decade, but there is no apparent dissent. There are no protests, there's no graffiti, and there's no criticism. Just veneration of a man whose annual cognac bill tops a million dollars, whose video collection contains 20,000 titles (including all the James Bond films) and who, according to the CIA, is so concerned about his height he wears ten-centimetre lifts in his shoes.

Then again, this is not the sort of place where dissent is tolerated. North Korea is a totalitarian state, dominated by its million strong army. The secret police is still active. If you're considered 'ideologically suspect', three generations of your family are wiped out. Defectors tell harrowing stories of midnight knocks on the door and relatives being dragged away to concentration camps, never to be seen again.

Early in our stay, we were invited to watch a military parade. It was a scary but hugely impressive spectacle. Imagine a vast square adorned with massive pictures of the Dear Leader and Great Leader. On the left are seated the army's top officers, their medals shining in the sun. On the right stand the foreign diplomats and tourists (most of whom are from Eastern Europe – presumably in town to revisit the good old days). In the background, thousands of civilians wave fronds of *Kimilsungia*. In the foreground, hundreds of thousands of men and women goosestep in perfect formation, bayoneted guns in their hands.

The sea of soldiers took several hours to pass. When it did, something amazing happened. The normally reclusive Kim Jong Il appeared on a balcony several metres from where I was standing. He waved to the crowd, and the masses went absolutely crazy. They erupted into deafening chants of praise, and several people around me burst into tears. One woman grabbed me by the arms, looked me in the eyes and said, 'Do you realise how great this honour is? You have been in the presence of the Dear Leader!'

A few days later we travelled to the demilitarised zone, or DMZ, the strip of land that divides the peninsula. It's the most heavily fortified border in the world. Bill Clinton once called it 'the scariest place on earth' and it's easy to see why. On either side are rolls of razor wire, electric fences, guard towers, minefields, tank traps and hundreds of thousands of soldiers. Above it all flutters an absolutely enormous North Korean flag attached to a flagpole one hundred and sixty metres high. Perhaps the most alarming thing we saw was a humble road sign. 'Seoul: 70 km', it read, emphasising just how vulnerable the South Korean capital is to attack.

A North Korean major guided us through the eerie no-man's-land. He told me that his country longed for peace, but in the very next breath made it clear what that peace would involve. 'For Korea to be reunified,' he declared, 'the first thing that must happen is that the US Imperialists must withdraw from the South. Then the South Korean army must turn its rifles on the US Imperialists. That is our precondition.'

The major went on to give us Pyongyang's version of the Korean War. Apparently the American Imperialists invaded from the South, but the People's Army won a series of stunning victories and forced the enemy back. The US aggressors then got down on their knees to beg for mercy, which was granted. The truth, of course, is somewhat different. In 1950, North Korean troops stormed across the 38th parallel. The war that followed lasted three years and cost more than one million lives.

No matter how it started, the conflict ended with an armistice rather than a peace treaty. The North and South are still technically at war. Our guide took us to a small museum, where we were shown the agreement that put an end to the fighting. Unfortunately, we did not get to see the museum's most prized exhibit: the axe that nearly started a second Korean war.

In 1976, a group of South Korean and American soldiers ventured into the DMZ to prune a poplar tree that was obscuring their view. The work party was intercepted by troops from the People's Army, who demanded a stop to the pruning. When one of the US officers refused, the North Koreans grabbed the axe and used it to beat two Americans to death. In the United States, there were calls for an immediate retaliatory strike, but President Gerald Ford chose a very different response. A week later, a second work party was sent into the DMZ – this time backed by twenty-seven helicopter gunships, three B-52 bombers and an armed platoon – to finish the job of chopping down the tree.

I didn't have a run-in with an axe, but I did get to see my hosts' less hospitable side. The whole purpose of our visit was to film the Arirang Festival – a mass gymnastics performance held to celebrate Kim Il Sung's birthday. Before the show began, Mr Goh announced that we would need to cough up four hundred US dollars cash if we wanted to move around inside the stadium. If we stayed in the designated media area, though, there would be no charge. Reluctant to hand over any of the ABC's meagre resources, I chose the latter option.

It was a big mistake.

Our guides showed us to the special media section, and helped set up our camera gear. We'd been filming for about ten minutes when all hell broke loose. North Korean soldiers declared that we had not paid the four hundred US dollars, and ordered us to stop filming. No matter that we'd been given repeated assurances that we *would* be allowed to record pictures – no bribe, no access. We tried to argue, but North Korea is not used to dissent. Several soldiers manhandled Jun and tried to wrench the camera from his shoulder. When I started to film the scuffle with a smaller camera, I was grabbed, thrown down a flight of stairs and wrestled to the ground.

Things were getting ugly.

Then I caught a glimpse of a cameraman from Japanese television filming the fight. 'Look!' I screamed to the soldiers. 'Now the world will see what your country is really like!' It was as if someone had hit a pause button. The wrestling stopped. For a few moments nothing happened, then we were seized, whisked out of the stadium, and taken back to our hotel.

That night, senior government people came to apologise, admitting that the security forces had got carried away. I shouldn't have been surprised, though. It might be a communist country, but North Korea has a thorough understanding of the power of the greenback. Hardly a day would pass without our being ordered to hand over US dollars for 'special filming fees' or 'special access rights'. On my last evening in Pyongyang, two government goons paid a late-night visit to my hotel room to demand nine hundred bucks for 'satellite costs'.

The ugly incident overshadowed the festival itself. Which was a pity, because the show was simply spectacular. A cavernous 150,000-seat stadium. Rousing military music. Tens of thousands of performers on the field, contorting and coordinating their bodies on cue to form massive scenes – a divided Korean peninsula, a hydro-electric power plant, radiant farmers tilling bountiful fields and so on. Tens of thousands more in the stands behind, raising and rotating cards above their heads to produce massive images – even animation. The programme gives you an idea of the messages that were conveyed: 'Towards a New Fatherland', 'Defending the Republic with Blood' (this featured North Korean soldiers bayo-neting their enemies), 'My Socialist Country is Best' and so on.

The overall intention was to demonstrate how North Korea, 'a country with a bitter past, has entered the arena of world history as the most dignified nation in the twenty-first century'. It made the opening ceremony of the Olympics look second rate. I was told that many of the participants were ordinary people, and that they'd spent many months practising their routines in sub-zero temperatures before and after work. They weren't given any money for the privilege. In many ways, the Arirang Festival was the ultimate allegory for the entire country: everyone moving in unison with military precision. And not getting paid.

The next day it was time to return to the real world. Our guides saw us off at the airport. 'I hope you can now correct all the American lies and propaganda in the Western media,' Mrs Park said. 'Please remember this: everything in our country is held together by the teaching and guidance of the Great Leader and the Dear Leader. We are happy because we are under their guidance. We are happy. We are very happy. Please take this truth with you.'

I was able to take a lot of things away from the trip: a genuine North Korean CD (which included great tracks like 'Peace is on the End of Our Bayonets'), several bruises from the brawl at the festival, and a sense of despair for the Korean people. But, despite my guide's exhortations, I wasn't able to bring back many North Korean truths. There simply aren't enough to go around.

EVAN WILLIAMS
• EVAN WILLIAMS •

EVAN WILLIAMS was the ABC's South-East Asia Correspondent based in Bangkok for five years between the end of 1992 and mid 1998.

In that time the stories changed from the UN-run election in Cambodia, the lifting of the US embargo on Vietnam, the release of pro-democracy leader Aung San Suu Kyi from six years of house arrest, the Cambodian coup, the fall of Suharto in Indonesia and the installation of that country's first democratically elected leader.

One of the things journalism allows is access to some of the remarkable people who lead remarkable events – the good and bad, mighty and humble. And sometimes we get extraordinary access.

These are just a few of *Foreign Correspondent*'s encounters with them.

Gus Dur: The Man Who Would

Breakfast with a nation's leader is a rare opportunity for a reporter – one you fight hard for – but one I was starting to regret.

Indonesia's former President, Abdurrahmin Wahid, is of course blind. And as I sat there with him, camera-rolling, he started chasing a slippery sausage around the presidential plate with his fork.

The faster he poked at it the quicker it rolled away. It's happened to us all – but this was the president, elected leader of 220 million people – and his sausage could not be stilled.

From their polite distance palace staff eyed the contest with increasing concern, frozen by doubts over correct protocol.

Sitting right next to him I was overwhelmed by the urge to stretch out a hand and arrest the rebellious sausage so it could be speared with due presidential dignity.

He's blind, and I figured he wouldn't notice – but just as I was about to, Wahid downed the fork, grabbed the sausage with his hand and took a huge victorious bite – consuming it with gusto as he continued telling me how he was going to defeat a parliamentary putsch to oust him from office.

It was typically, endearingly Wahid. When frustrated, he simply took matters into his own hands – regardless of how it looked.

It was a trait hated by Jakarta's etiquette-obsessed elite – but one that spoke most clearly to the tens of millions of Indonesians whose nation's wealth has been plundered by decades of dictatorship and corruption.

As President, Gus Dur was very much a man who saw what he believed had to be done – and did it. He was stubborn, perhaps a bit vain, but had a genuine belief in trying to reform a corrupt, out-of-control military, in talking with secessionists instead of killing them, and in getting parliamentarians to do something more than look after themselves.

He was, of course, like us all, a man not without faults.

Some say his life as the hereditary leader of Indonesia's largest Islamic group – where he is unquestioned as a mystic saint – left him ill-equipped for the deal-making and consensus needed to forge a unified parliamentary coalition. It's true he did not show much interest in building the political consensus he probably needed to get his reforms off the ground.

Just as in the sausage incident, he would see what had to be done and would just do it, regardless of appearances. He was at times mercurial – to keep his political adversaries off guard – but this confused many at a time when the nation seemed to be screaming out for clear leadership, direction and a new dream.

Fundamentally, Gus Dur was a reformer, on the side of greater transparency, less self-interest, curbed military powers and account-able public office.

It made me think of other leaders and what they really stood for. It probably changed the way I assess them, made me look more carefully at their motivations.

Soon after the breakfast Gus Dur was in trouble. The politicians formerly in power, and those he'd made enemies of, had formed a coalition of convenience to get him out of office. The military, under pressure from Gus Dur to get out of business, couldn't wait to join them.

He thought he was playing some of the politicians, but instead they were playing him. It was classic Machiavellian betrayal.

Events moved quickly. There were claims Gus Dur had corruptly misappropriated some public funds – claims a parliamentary inquiry found to be false. But by then it didn't matter. It was just an excuse to have a parliamentary vote to oust him – a vote Gus Dur's political mishandling meant he no longer had the numbers to win.

As the final days approached, Gus Dur granted me unique access to the Presidential Palace more than once. He outlined elements of his strategy – to play one party off against the other – and revealed he saw it as a battle between Parliament and the elected President's right to stay the full term.

He believed Parliament could not constitutionally oust the President – especially with no legal cause. It was that belief, I think, that was the basis of his decision to seek military backing for a type of emergency, or martial law, to hold on to power however the vote went.

It was a mistake, at least in terms of perceptions. His enemies, especially the military, pounced on it immediately. The man who'd presented himself as the beacon of parliamentary reform had discussed a type of martial law! What more proof did people need that he was simply seeking to stay in power? So the argument went.

And anyhow, there was no way the military was going to help out the guy who'd tried to curb their money-making activities.

Instead, tanks were lined up in a park across the road from the palace, turrets menacingly pointed towards the palace. The generals insisted they were there to protect the President from any popular uprising. But the message was clear.

In the palace grounds the tension escalated. Middlemen came and went in a flurry of black cars and cameras. The pressure on Gus Dur was enormous.

To get to him, you had to go through layers of protocol and protection.

First there were the military police at the palace gates. I had no official Palace Media Pass, but because the President himself had allowed us in we had been through the gates repeatedly before and sort of got away with it.

That got you as far as the presidential media gang who were corralled in a room near the side entrance of the palace. Like newshounds the world over, they dashed outside en masse whenever a car came or went – trying to get something, anything of substance on the latest twist or turn of the crisis. Deals were being made. Just no-one knew what they were.

Once you got to that point, it was up to the President himself and his closest minders to decide whether you got any closer to the inner sanctum.

Usually, it was better to encounter the President during his very early morning walk around the palace grounds. These were wonderful moments for a journalist – and hell for the cameraman who'd usually have to walk backwards while filming for extended periods, as Gus Dur regaled me jokes, inside strategy and insights on the next move.

These walks usually happened at about 4.30 am. Doctors and military adjutants would flank him, but as the blind cleric-President walked and talked he was sometimes at his most lucid – before the rigours of the day sapped too much of his diabetic body's reserves.

For us, it was unprecedented access to a national leader – especially at a time of crisis – and access that was also highly personal, unvarnished. He would walk in his shorts and an old T-shirt (no style counselling here) and I believe that was one of the reasons the story – and the President – somehow struck a chord not only with Indonesians, but also with Australians.

I am forever grateful to filmmaker Curtis Levy (who produced a documentary on Gus Dur) and to Gus Dur's biographer, Greg Barton, for the tip that these walks were accessible. Not something your average hack like myself would have even thought of – especially if it means a 4 am start!

But the drama was so great we had to be at the palace as much as we could. Instead of chasing news all over town during the day it was a matter of trying to stay focused on the personal story of a President struggling to stay in power.

Gradually we were piecing the story together. It meant long waits and a big gamble: that we would get enough access to the President at such a critical time to make twenty minutes of television that was different from everything else that was being broadcast – something personal, the inside story, or – as I joked to cameraman Geoffrey Lye – it felt like putting everything on '21' in a game of roulette.

The day before the parliamentary vote we were again allowed to join the early morning walk. By now the military police on the gate were sort of used to two weird Australian journalists turning up in the dark at 4.30 am to enter the palace, and begrudgingly they would let us pass.

We joined the walk. And Gus Dur started speaking about politics. We were rolling. He had, he said, secured a deal with the (former ruling) Golkar Party to vote with him and against the ousting. The others, he said, would 'rush to push me off the cliff and instead fall over themselves as I step sideways'. Ending with a huge toothy laugh.

The plot had thickened, and we were getting the inside story of how it was unfolding.

But then the day of the vote arrived, and everyone's true colours were revealed.

Gus Dur had been outflanked. Golkar had voted with the block to oust the President.

Straight after the vote we left the media pack on the steps of Parliament and went to the Golkar Party offices. Golkar chief Akbar Tanjung (who was himself to face massive corruption charges) and senior party people were sitting around on plush leather chairs.

When I asked Tanjung what had happened to the deal with Gus Dur, he just said with a curl of the lip that they had never, ever had any intention of backing Gus Dur. It was all a ploy – all politics – and Gus Dur, desperate for the numbers, had fallen for it. Then they all laughed.

This was Tuesday afternoon. Our story was planned for *Foreign Correspondent* the following Wednesday – eight days away.

Then my boss called. We all agreed that would make the story too old. We had to get it to air this Wednesday – now less than twenty-four hours away – and we still didn't have Gus Dur's reaction to the vote that had taken him from power. But we thought we could manage it.

I started writing the story, guided tremendously by producer

Nick Greenaway, and cameraman Geoffrey Lye, who'd shot it all despite a bad flu, started editing it.

As I wrote a page Geoff would cut it. We worked right through the night till the next morning, knowing that our best chance of getting Gus Dur was in his normal morning walk at about 4.30 am.

I grabbed half an hour's sleep; I don't think Geoff got any. By 4.30 am we were in the car heading to the palace. It was dark and the few cars on the road glided past in dreamy silence.

When we got to the palace something had changed. The military police on the gate were not only different, they were aggressively anti-foreigner. This was of course after East Timor, and these guys were not going to do any favours for Australians.

I pleaded. They ignored me. We had no palace passes, it was five in the morning, we were Australians *and* journalists and insisting we get in to speak to a President who'd just been ousted by Parliament? You must be joking.

No, I was very, very serious. And we were due on air in several hours.

I managed to peer around the palace gate. Dawn was filtering through the giant trees in the grounds and to my horror I saw Gus Dur and his tiny entourage already doing their laps.

I phoned his main personal advisor and actually watched him answer his mobile; he would do everything he could. I phoned his biographer; *he* would do everything he could. They were now getting close to their last lap. I thought, if he goes inside, that will be it. The events of the day will overtake us and we'll never get to him.

I phoned again. The guys on the gate were getting increasingly icy.

Greg Barton outlined the situation. The President was no longer in charge of the palace, the guards were from a new unit, the military adjutant was now taking his orders from elsewhere and was actually running security, no-one was getting in. The noose was tightening around Gus Dur. There was speculation he would refuse to leave the palace. It was an extremely tricky moment, and not one the Jakarta establishment would like to have scrutinised by any outsiders – least of all an Australian TV crew.

My heart sank as I saw Gus Dur and the entourage enter the presidential quarters. But soon after – a break. The advisor came and escorted us to the waiting room. He would ask the President if he would see us.

By about 8 am – as the world's media was filling the airwaves with speculation that Gus Dur would virtually have to be blown out of the palace – we were allowed into the private reception area where Gus Dur was meeting a select gathering of Islamic leaders and supporters who appeared to be trying to comfort him.

As we approached, his personal doctor stopped me. 'You can interview him,' he said, 'but no questions on politics.' It would upset him and could further damage his precarious health. They were concerned he might have another stroke – his third.

No politics! You must be joking – this was all *about* politics. But I also didn't want to spark a stroke. We eased into the conversation and were soon led to a light breakfast.

Gus Dur was clearly in shock and depressed. Yet it was here – over the same table where he'd done battle with the sausage months ago – that he gave me his personal reaction to the vote.

Why did it happen? Because he had underestimated the danger of making deals with the self-seeking parliamentary blocks; the establishment had fought back; the new president would be their puppet; the dirty deals would continue. Yes, he would accept the vote, and leave. How would he be remembered? Management chaos, unique personal charm; a man who tried to make a difference, tried to reform an unaccountable, corrupt military/ political elite; a man who tried to give the President's office back to the people and who tried to use his considerable standing as an insightful, moderate Moslem leader to span religions and reject extremism.

The full import of that aspect of Gus Dur's leadership would not be felt until the Bali bombing.

General Wiranto

Before he left, one of Gus Dur's major successes was against the military chief, General Wiranto, the man many believe did know or should have known about the military's control of militia in the East Timor carnage.

Wiranto has never been named or charged in relation to those tragic events – and is now a potential presidential hopeful himself.

Soon after the killings that followed the independence ballot in East Timor, Gus Dur was in a showdown with Wiranto that finally ended in the President sacking the General as Armed Forces Chief.

At the time it was a major victory for the elected democratic government over an unaccountable military led by a man who was not only nearly impossible to access but also known for his temper.

It was May – several months before East Timor's historic and bloody independence ballot – when I had my chance to meet General Wiranto.

We were doing a story on the future of the Indonesian armed forces after the downfall of Suharto. Just as we finished, the very first reports were starting to emerge of an attack on a village in East Timor. It looked like standard Indonesian army tactics, but in the days that followed it emerged this was something quite new – the first attack by pro-Indonesian militia – organised, trained, supplied and paid for by the Indonesian armed forces in a bid to intimidate the Timorese into voting to stay with the Republic.

None of this was yet clear. The story would still be: the military back away from politics and give democracy room to breathe in Indonesia. But the East Timor ballot was looming, and during the shoot it became more and more obvious that a vote to break away didn't gel with anything the Indonesian army stood for – even if they were to withdraw from national politics.

No-one got to General Wiranto – not foreign journalists anyway – yet he was the man everyone wanted to hear from. In my application, and crawling to various rungs of his officials, I focused on the positive (the military's desire to transform) and after a few weeks of to-ing and fro-ing with minor officials he took the bait. I would have an on-camera meeting.

Disturbingly, they kept calling it an *audience* – never a good word when what you want to hear is the word 'interview'.

In situations like this it's always a matter of negotiation, slowly edging the skittish prey into an on-camera session if that's as far as you can get at the outset, then warming them to the idea of a few words, and then hopefully at least a few key questions with some wonderfully revealing exclusive comments. Easy – right?

But as I was quickly to discover, my idea of an on-camera interview and General Wiranto's idea of an on-camera audience were two very different things.

First, his underlings kept stressing, with a rather unfortunate choice of words, 'Pleeease – don't interrogate the General.' To this I happily agreed, not to my knowledge having interrogated anyone before.

'Right, no interrogation, got it. I will not interrogate General Wiranto – no problems. But I can ask him a few questions, can't I?'

'A few questions, yes. Just, pleeease – *no interrogation*.' I kept getting the feeling they thought the questions should be nice and polite, like: 'How's the weather? Oh, I do love what you've done with the trophy case.'

As cameraman Tim Deagle set up, I was led to a formal setting of two seats side-by-side, a doily-covered table between them. This was not looking good: horribly close to the kind of picture-opportunity settings you often see for lowly officials meeting high-powered presidents before the cameras are told to leave.

General Wiranto entered, friendly enough. He had a commanding, almost charismatic presence – but the air of someone who could turn very quickly.

We sat down, and he started reading in English from a prepared statement: 'Thank you for taking interest in the Indonesian armed forces' attempts to transform ...' and so on. Then he started to get up to leave – eeek!

I quickly thanked him for the chance to meet – and knew I would only get a couple of questions in at best – so to get him to say something I started: 'Is the military willing, as part of transformation, to withdraw from politics?' This seemed fair enough and on the topic.

He answered. I followed up, and he answered again. But he was clearly starting to get edgy. The smile was dropping, a hardness flared in his eyes and he started inching his way off the seat. This was it, then – my last shot.

'Do the Indonesian armed forces support the independence ballot in East Timor?' That was it. He went red and glared at me with such fury I thought he was going to hit me. Then he just jumped up and stormed off – screaming in Indonesian as soon as he got to the door of his office.

The room we were in was absolutely silent, but through the wood panelling we could hear the General ranting uncontrollably at full lung. I've rarely heard a man so angry. It was reverberating around the walls as his ashen-faced officers in our room stared either at me or the ground. Every one of them looked like they'd shat their pants. It was extraordinary.

Tim and I looked at each other amazed. I think I said something like: 'What – was it something I said?' That's certainly what I was thinking. Even though he'd said nothing on the subject, his furious reaction – on camera – said it all in spectacular fashion.

But we were the only ones thinking that. The General had gone silent now, and as we tried to quickly pack up and get out of there the General's personal adjutant came over. 'We will have that tape.'

'Ohhhh no, sorry, I simply can't do that.'

'No, we *will* have the tape.'

'Nope, sorry, I can't.'

'We will have the tape.'

There was a sort of steel in the comment that Tim and I both agreed later was not negotiable – steel that says: 'Give us the tape or you're not leaving the room …'

I still refused, but then he offered: 'The General is sorry about what happened and will do it again for you. But we must have *that tape*.'

That sort of got me. The General would do it again, which to me meant I could ask the East Timor question and this time get an answer. Whatever he said would be hot, and – given his initial reaction – it could be dynamite.

I agreed. I was led to General Wiranto's office where, calm now and back in control of himself, he explained in not-very-good English that he didn't want to answer the question because his English was not good enough. I said it didn't matter, this was Indonesia, he should speak Indonesian and we'd translate it. No, he said, it's very complicated and should be answered in English because we are a foreign TV crew … However, when the time was right, he said he would tell me everything.

That was great. But right now I really just wanted one answer. He agreed to do the 'audience/interview' again. I handed over the tape, which I soon regretted.

I returned to my chair, cameras rolling, we filmed the hand-shake, sat down – and General Wiranto read the same opening statement in English. Then, before I could even open my mouth, he got up and quickly marched off.

Disaster! Now I had nothing except a patsy handshake, a prepared statement, and me sitting there looking like some meekly deferential goose.

This was not good. I protested, but was told to leave – now. Pack up and GO! The room emptied of officials, the panelled doors closed. 'Audience' over!

I had learnt my lesson – never, ever give up the tape.

It was with some keen interest I later watched Gus Dur move against Wiranto. But I still hope to take the ex-General up on his offer – to tell me everything, when the time is right.

Hun Sen

Of course, General Wiranto is really just one in a long line of still-powerful Asian strongmen.

Being shouted at by one of these dictators can be unsettling – but being threatened by one is, to be frank, a little scary.

Cambodia's Prime Minister, Hun Sen, a former Khmer Rouge guerrilla, is a man with a false eye and a short temper. It's said he was once so angered by a local TV news story he shot the television screen with a pistol.

To be fair, that may or may not be true. But I *do* know Hun Sen up close and angry is not a pretty sight: his lips curl, his glass eye veers sideways … grown men go pale, reporters meek.

In 1996 the United Nations spent US$18 million restoring democracy to Cambodia – or so it thought. An election left Hun Sen sharing power with the Royalist Party, his civil war opponents. It was a marriage made in hell … and soon fell apart.

In June 1996 Hun Sen ousted his partner and took complete power in a coup.

While we were in Phnom Penh covering news we were also shooting a *Foreign Correspondent* story, the main focus of which became the flight of many ousted Royalist Party members before they were hunted down and killed by Hun Sen's henchmen. About a hundred were murdered.

The coup had given Hun Sen complete control of Cambodia, but the international reaction was not positive. Australia wasn't happy, the United States was indicating it might not accept the coup's results, and even Cambodia's ASEAN neighbours, some of which still had aspects of dictatorship in one form or another – were not exactly overwhelming Hun Sen with support.

It looked as if Cambodia could be heading for international isolation unless Hun Sen allowed his Royalist rivals back into some form of power-sharing. Things were not going well for Hun Sen.

But he was not giving interviews and no-one had yet obtained his reaction.

We discovered he was heading for a rural function, a typical Cambodian Communist Party style event where hundreds of poor peasants were trucked in to spontaneously wave flags and hear their leader speak. And it would be our chance to get him to talk.

Hun Sen had flown in to the function by helicopter, and to get back to it he had to walk from the secured stage across an open field. Perfect for the 'ambush' or doorstop interview – where you basically stand in front of the subject with a camera, throw as many questions as possible, and hope to get more than a bullet.

On his way back to the chopper, Hun Sen had stopped at a small knot of local journalists. This was my chance.

'Samdech Hun Sen,' I blurted. 'Do you now regret the use of force …'

As I said this I could feel the fear run through the Cambodians around me. No-one had directly challenged Hun Sen on the use of force yet. His government was even vigorously disallowing the use of the word 'coup' to describe what had happened. Of course it *was* a coup, it's just no-one was meant to say so.

As the question was translated Hun Sen adjusted his oversized glasses and turn his face to me – a curl started lifting one corner of his mouth and I swear the glass eye started moving sideways.

Then he pointed at me – and yelled: 'IT WAS NOT ME WHO FIRST DECIDED TO USE FORCE!' jabbing his finger at me to emphasise each word. 'It was [Royalist Prime Minister] Ranariddh who was preparing to use force to oust me.' (Hun Sen accused Ranariddh of importing weapons to overthrow him. It could have been true but was likely a set-up.)

'What did YOU want me to do?' Froth started appearing. I was no longer sure which was the glass eye – both were glaring with such rage.

'Just wait there for them to attack? No! I attacked them first – to defend myself from their attempts to push me from power …' He was furious. His official aide almost whispered the words, eyes bowed to the ground. The Khmer journalists were wide-eyed in fear. But he wasn't finished yet …

For weeks Ranariddh had been announcing that he had secured the surrender of Khmer Rouge leader Pol Pot, still at that stage holed up in a Thai–Cambodia border crossing called Anlong Veng.

Hun Sen now pointed at me: 'You go to Anlong Veng and stop a bullet with YOUR head.' The crowd audibly gasped. Then he said in English: 'You go Anlong Veng … eeeehhhhhhhh … shoooo-TING by Pol Pot!' And stormed off towards the chopper.

I thought it was a pretty good grab. It revealed motivation for the coup, or at least was his first official statement of why he'd launched it, and it revealed something of the man – both his anger and the pressure he was feeling.

But my Khmer journalist friends quickly pulled me aside and in hushed tones explained something to me. In Khmer 'stop a bullet with your head' is a direct threat – translated roughly as 'I will shoot you / would you like to be shot / you will be shot / you're really pissing me off / you're going to die.' Or possibly all of the above.

OK, then, clearly we'd hit a nerve. I looked across the dry rice paddy to the prime ministerial chopper, to see Hun Sen just glaring at me through the glass … A slight chill ran down my spine. Maybe, just maybe, this was serious. It was Cambodia, after all, and people had been shot for less.

That night I was followed by two reasonably ugly Hun Sen style heavies.

One had a large scar across his face, the other had no neck. Both kept turning up wherever I was and just staring at me. First in a bar, then at a restaurant, then in the bar again, and at one point I swear one of them just looked at me and nodded slowly. No smile, just a nod and a steely gaze as if to say, 'Yep smart-arse, you really *have* pissed off the boss this time. We know where you are. Don't do it again.' It might have been my imagination – but I don't think so.

I left, and didn't see them again. But then, I was a visitor. Cambodian journalists, and the many who work under similar pressure in some other countries, don't have that luxury.

The Skipper

Some of the most memorable people I've met have not been at the top of the political heap at all.

There were the brave young teenagers who helped us through a hellish two-day walk in the Cambodian jungle. Their boots were falling apart and some were later to be abandoned to a Khmer Rouge attack by their officers – but they had a spirit of can-do toughness and generosity that I've never forgotten.

Then there was the canoe skipper.

We were doing a story on Malaysian logging in Papua New Guinea and had been dropped into the remote south-western jungle – a vast expanse of huge rivers and thick forest canopy that was rapidly being destroyed.

The lines of the clearing had crept gradually from the coast deep into the interior, and we had to get to the village where a group of traditional landowners were deciding whether to allow the loggers to proceed further. Some wanted the money. Others saw what devastation had been wrought on their neighbours' traditional lands and were rejecting the offers.

To get there we had to travel upriver to the Wavi-Gwava Falls. After travelling for days collecting material for the story, we finally arrived at the river. Days of torrential rain had swollen it into a series of thick, fast-moving swirls.

Our transport lay on a muddy bank: a four-metre dugout canoe made from a single log and not much wider than a human bum. This was going to be interesting.

It was already 4 pm and we were told it was a four-hour journey upriver. That meant that even if we left immediately, two hours of the journey would be in darkness. But in this remote area we had little choice, and the skipper said he reckoned he could do it.

We loaded about fifteen boxes of TV equipment, the large cameraman Geoffrey Lye, producer Mark Worth and me. We all sat in a line getting our bodies used to the terribly tippy flat-bottomed dugout – I felt for sure we were going to go in at any moment.

The skipper's offsider – a young fella with a fixed grin – took up position at the canoe's bow, and the skipper pulled the rip-start in the motor, a pathetic nine-horsepower Evinrude which whined in what seemed an ineffectual way. I looked at the motor, then at the whirlpools swiftly moving down the thick brown river, then back at the motor ... This wasn't going to be good.

Suddenly the rope tying us to a tree branch was let go, the skipper pushed the motor and we nosed out into the torrent – immediately rolling towards the downriver side as the gushing water caught under the canoe.

Some quick rebalancing, and we managed to survive and get back on level, our tiny outboard screaming in the effort to push us out into the current.

We were off.

The river was so high we were actually passing the branches of trees, and couldn't even see the river bank. But once we'd calmed down, the late afternoon light cast a mesmerising tranquillity on the surrounding jungle as we edged upstream.

It's true we did see a giant black crocodile – only moments after Geoffrey had been standing on a similar bank to get a shot of us.

Shortly after that, an empty fibre-glass dinghy, water-logged and floating just a few centimetres above the surface, silently passed us. A bad sign indeed – where were its occupants?

The river snaked towards the interior, and with amazing skill the skipper would ease us into the rapidly moving waters of each bend, shoot across the worst part and nudge our tippy boat along one bank or the other until the next hair-raising bend. This went on for hours, each bend a new unsettling adventure, and each handled with incredible skill by the old bloke on the Evinrude.

At one point we pushed through a gorge, with walls of sheer rock on both sides forcing the water through a narrow channel.

Oh – and I forgot to mention the logs, branches and entire trees racing down the river at us all the time – most of which the skipper avoided with the aid of yells and much arm waving from his offsider at the bow. Had we hit one side on, we would have been history. God knows if any of us would have survived a dunking like this – or where we'd have ended up.

Finally, inevitably, it started getting dark. Gradually the calming effects of green trees began to disappear into an unknown landscape of dark shadows and strange sounds.

It was the logs coming downstream I was most concerned about – a concern which did not diminish when I saw the bow hand take out a small, old, cheap-looking torch – you know, the kind whose connections always fail just when you need it.

Well, it was our only hope. He pointed its sickly glow into the on-coming maelstrom of water and logs, barely buying himself a few feet of vision, shaking and banging the torch as it flickered and spasmodically went out.

I asked Geoff if he was OK, and he dryly replied he was wondering if he should take his boots off ready for the swim.

Undaunted, our skipper stayed steady at the helm, dodging and weaving among the logs, reading the whirls and torrid waters of each bend. Then the moon came out, and for a while everything seemed magical, unreal, a sight you would never normally see because you would not normally be there.

Finally the river seemed to ease and broaden. We nudged up to a steep red mudbank and tied up. We'd made it – we were at the Wavi-Gwava Falls village, a collection of timeless community houses, dim fire lights and whispered chatter.

When we and our gear were all in our raised hut, the skipper came to see us. A gathering of local men crammed in around him. In true Papuan style he started speaking – an oration worthy of the great fire-lit speeches of man through the ages.

One of the young boys translated for us.

'I am the first of our villagers to come up this river with a motor,' said the skipper, metaphorically beating his chest.

'Ooooh,' the crowd responded in hushed approval.

'I am the first man to come up this river with a motor while it was in full and dangerous flood,' the orator continued.

'OOOOooooh,' said the crowd slightly more approvingly.

'I am the first to ever successfully come up this river with a motor, while it was in full and dangerous flood – and at NIGHT!' he declared, puffing out his broad chest.

'OOOOooooooh,' said the crowd of young men in enthusiastic awe.

'When did you do all this?' I asked, thinking it was in the seventies or something.

'TONIGHT – with you!'

The things you do for a story.

Aung San Suu Kyi

She was the leader of a party that had been overwhelmingly elected as Burma's government. The military refused to hand over power, instead putting her under house arrest and savagely repressing any pro-democratic protests.

Many times on trips to Rangoon for news stories had I passed her house, hoping to get some shots or even catch a glimpse of her at the window. But I never did.

During my first few years as the ABC's South-East Asia Correspondent, based in Bangkok, there were constant rumours of Suu Kyi's imminent release that never amounted to anything.

The ruling military junta was trying to lure foreign investors into the country while keeping itself in power. Yet something had to give, it was thought, for Myanmar (as they had renamed it) to escape the constant pressure over its human rights record. The release of Suu Kyi, it was thought, was inevitable. But there were constant false alarms.

Then one Saturday morning, while in a Bangkok shopping centre, I received a call from a well-placed contact in Rangoon. It might be worth my while being in Rangoon as soon as I could, he said, and certainly before Tuesday morning.

That was good enough for me, and I got myself quickly to Rangoon, using the journalist visa I always tried to keep updated.

Rumours were flying thick and fast. Then we were called to a media conference at her house – the same place I had viewed furtively from outside the gate. I was the only foreigner among ten Burmese journalists working for various agencies.

We were sitting on the floor of a tiny front room. I was sweating profusely in the humidity. Then a door opened and there was Aung San Suu Kyi – the first time anybody outside the military had seen her in six years.

I think she wore a dark blue traditional Burmese skirt and top, smiled gracefully, and with wonderful double meaning said something like: 'I'm so sorry to have kept you all waiting.'

I could barely believe it. I was there at her first media conference after six years, and her message was defiant. Yes, she would still fight for the recognition of the elections and restoration of democracy. No, she had not agreed to any special deal with the military for her release. No, the people should not fear the military because all they had was guns.

Some in the military truly believe they have to stay in power to prevent the nation from falling apart, but many are in it to protect their massive business interests – and to stay out of court on human rights charges.

Rarely is there a story with a really clear-cut division between right and wrong – this has always seemed to be one of them.

Suu Kyi's first media conference was quite a performance, conducted with her now signature poise, charm – and iron will.

The next few days were a blur. Thousands of supporters came to her house, sitting in the heat outside on the street to hear her speak from behind her gate.

The people's support was clear.

Then, over the next few months, the military's real reason for releasing her emerged.

All of those most active around Aung San Suu Kyi in the pursuit of democracy were slowly rounded up, her key supporters arrested and given heavy jail sentences – some up to fourteen years. By releasing her, the military junta had flushed out the underground support network. Maybe they had thought that by releasing her they could gain some international breathing space, perhaps they intended to talk but saw the movement was getting way out of hand. But I think it was a deliberate, cynical ploy.

Suu Kyi remains steadfast. At times criticised for not being more flexible about a power-sharing deal with the military, she remains firm on the installation of the elected government because she feels an obligation to the vast majority of Burmese people who voted for that.

Today, after an attack by army-backed thugs which some think was an assassination attempt, Suu Kyi remains incommunicado, back under house arrest.

GEOFF THOMPSON joined the ABC in 1996 as a television cadet. After his cadetship year he was posted to Darwin as the *7.30 Report's* Northern Territory Correspondent. At the end of 1998 he took over the bi-media job (reporting for radio and television) of North Australia Correspondent, a job he did for just three months before the call came to go to East Timor.

He stayed in East Timor for much of the next nine months before winning the job of South-East Asia Correspondent, based in Bangkok. From there he covered stories across the region and beyond, including the Fiji coup of 2000 and the American-led attack on Afghanistan in 2001. Geoff was the first Australian broadcast journalist to enter Kabul as the Taliban were defeated.

In 2002, Geoff took over the job of South Asia Correspondent, based in New Delhi, where he remains today. He was part of the team covering the war in Iraq, spending a month embedded with the US Marines as they invaded Iraq from Kuwait to Baghdad.

Geoff won a Logie Award for Most Outstanding News Reporter in 2002 for his work in Afghanistan. He is also the recipient of two Walkley Awards: one for an investigative radio report with Stephen McDonell in 1996, and the other for a TV current affairs exposé of a fake aboriginal artist in 1998. In 1999 he was named Northern Territory Journalist of the Year.

First Day Out: East Timor

I was nervous and sweating and my stomach was churning. I couldn't help babbling out stupid questions. 'So what exactly is meant to be happening today? It's like a protest, right?' The ABC's experienced Indonesia Correspondent, Mark Bowling, listened patiently. He had a relaxed cowboy-like cool that I had always envied. 'Let's just see when we get there,' he said. 'It will probably be nothing.'

It was Saturday 17 April 1999, and in less than an hour we would be touching down in East Timor. Less than an hour before my foot would touch the tarmac in another country, transforming me suddenly, somehow, into a foreign correspondent. Well, technically, at least. Just days before I had been making weekend plans to go bushwalking in Kakadu National Park, and now, instead, I was on a plane to a place of spasmodic, inscrutable violence, where I would end up living for much of the next nine months. We were flying from Bali on the Indonesian airline Merpati. A joke popular with the Jakarta press corps went like this: 'It's Merpati and I'll die if I want to, die if I want too, die if I want toooo. You would die too if it happened to you.' I'm glad I heard that joke a bit later, because I certainly wouldn't have found it funny that Saturday morning.

Rewind. Why the hell was *I* on that plane? The answer is: completely by accident. Or perhaps more accurately: by default. Just two days before I had been meandering around Aboriginal communities near Darwin making radio features about indigenous music. East Timor was only four hundred kilometres away, but when the call came to go, it was the furthest thing from my mind.

Now, on the day the pro-Indonesia militia had threatened to invade East Timor's capital, I was on a plane to Dili. I really knew very little about East Timor, while many of my worthy friends carried East Timor's indignation as if it was their own – a fact that always made me feel guilty, especially as I was now the ABC's

North Australia Correspondent and East Timor's terrible troubles were so close. Sure, I knew about Indonesia invading in 1975, and about Australia's blind-eyed complicity, and of course the killing of five journalists at Balibo – but that was kind of it. Oh yeah, and I also knew who Xanana Gusmao was, but not much more. It was the sort of thing Tim Palmer (later a correspondent in the Middle East and Indonesia) did know. He also *spoke* Indonesian. So of course he was asked to go, but he couldn't at that time.

So it was that one Wednesday night I returned to Darwin from an Aboriginal community and discovered my mobile phone full of messages. 'Geoff, would you like to go to East Timor? … You've got to be there by Saturday,' the first one said. I gulped when I heard it. I'd wanted to be a foreign correspondent since my teens, but I'd expected such an opportunity would be years away, if it ever came at all. Then, in the end, it all happened within forty-eight hours. Well, I thought. Careful what you wish for.

Strange pictures from East Timor had turned up in the Darwin newsroom a few weeks before, sent out by a news agency. One image struck me deeply. A young boy lay on his side on a hard tile floor, breathing heavily. With his back to the camera he looked almost completely normal except for a long, gaping hole along the side of his torso. It wasn't really bleeding, but it was dark and wide and all the more horrible because it was unexplained. It scared me shitless. The questions that hole asked had not been answered and that mystery sickened me. Apparently the cameraman who took the pictures didn't know precisely what he was shooting at the time. I learned later that it was the aftermath of the Liquica massacre, one of the first of many militia attacks which would bloody the road towards East Timor's independence referendum a few months later. It's thought that more than forty people died in the Liquica attack. I was thinking about the hole in that boy – its horrors and its questions – as our plane touched down in East Timor.

So much happened over the next nine months that my memory of landing in Dili is sketchy. I remember palm trees.

I remember how small, unremarkable and vulnerable Dili looked – like a country town hung out to die on a rocky bit of coast. I remember Indonesian police uncomfortably gladwrapped in uniforms of brown nylon. But what I remember most was my own confusion and fear – of violence and of failure.

We were waiting for our bags as Mark made a call on his mobile. His face scrunched with concern. 'Really,' he said. 'Now?' Hanging up, he looked at me. 'Manuel Carrascalao's house is on fire.'

In a panic to fudge my ignorance of East Timor I had squeezed some cramming into the past forty-eight hours, and had managed to learn who this man was. From an established pro-independence family, he had recently opened his home to villagers who had fled to Dili to escape the military-backed militia terror campaign in the countryside. Manuel's daughter Christina had lived in Darwin and was well known there among the East Timor independence lobby.

Unlike me, Mark knew what to do. 'Let's quickly drop the gear at the Turismo [Hotel], and head straight there.' We piled into a couple of taxis and drove towards Dili. On the way into town the streets seemed quiet, but the air was thick with the anxiety I couldn't help projecting onto it. We entered Dili's main waterfront road and the atmosphere changed. A large gathering of men came into view. They were standing in rough rows, like a parading army of hobos, draped in rags of red and white, the colours of Indonesia's flag. As we passed they were starting to disband, breaking off and getting into trucks. 'That's the militia,' said Mark, 'and that's the Governor's office they're standing in front of.' It was at that gathering that the Indoneisan-army-backed militia leader, Eurico Guterres, gave the order to hunt down and kill supporters of East Timor's independence. But I didn't know that then, and just gawked naively out the window as we drove by.

The Turismo had seen it all. It was the one Dili landmark with which everybody was familiar, and through years of terror, struggle and strife, the Turismo somehow managed to generate optimism within all who arrived at its gates. It was an open place, a place where Timor's clandestine movement met with outsiders, a place where secrets were whispered and plots were hatched. And all the time the bizarrely bright blue-on-white lettering of the sign 'Turismo Hotel' branded the proceedings, making it look like a scene from a 1960s holiday postcard.

It was here that I met Joao on that first day, the first of many I would spend living at the Turismo. He was a spritely old man, always grinning and gentle. He had been working at the Turismo when the Indonesians invaded in 1975, and he was there when they departed late in 1999. When I returned to Dili after the carnage in September, there he was, at the Turismo. We embraced and he sobbed. 'First they come and now they leave,' he said. His trembling and his tears said everything else.

We dumped our gear in our rooms and drove towards the house of Manuel Carrascalao. The street was blocked by Indonesian police who were donning riot helmets and goofily padded protective suits. I remember they reminded me of Teenage Mutant Ninja Turtles. Mark pointed out a house which was black with ash but no longer burning. There were still a few people hovering around the front. It was there on the bonnet of our taxi that I wrote my first ever foreign story. I could hardly read my own scrawl, my hands were shaking so much. I borrowed Mark's phone and tried to ring it in but I couldn't get through. As I hung up, the phone rang and I handed it back to Mark. A fellow journalist told him that the offices of *Suara Tim Tim* were being attacked.

Suara Tim Tim was East Timor's daily newspaper, staffed by young journalists, all smiling and mild and ludicrously brave. We made our way to the Mahkota Hotel, which sat on the main waterfront road just in front of the newspaper office. Much later the Mahkota would become the last bastion of courage for most of the world's media in East Timor – where we were corralled and shamed all the way to the airport, stupidly scared witless by soldiers and secret service agents performing mock attacks on the hotel. But we were running for our lives from … bad melodrama. On the evacuation plane to Bali we saw an enlarged photo in an Indonesian newspaper and realised that the long-haired man who had been threatening to throw a grenade into the Mahkota Hotel was wearing a wig – no doubt an Indonesian intelligence agent dressed as militia and ordered to scare foreigners out of Timor. For the most part, it worked.

But on this day, day one as a correspondent, all I knew was that a lot of loopy-looking men dressed like Manchester United supporters were waving around a gangland arsenal of pipe guns and swords. A few truckloads of them edged to the front of the hotel as we ran into the lobby. I remember panting and my heart pounding as we ran upstairs to the roof to get a look at the newspaper office from above. We could hear gunfire all around. I was recording all the time, and the stupid young reporter in me was thinking 'Wow, I've recorded gunfire, wow, isn't that cool, gunfire, yeah, cool, yeah …'

On the roof Mark Bowling was ducking and moving to the edge which overlooked the *Suara Tim Tim* building. As there was only sky above us, I couldn't see the point in ducking, but neither did I go very close to the edge … just a quick peek, that was all. The attack on the newspaper office seemed to be winding down. Just a few of the militia men were shooting at it, breaking glass and lighting fires. ABC cameraman Terry Macdonald was determined to film them, and stuck his camera over the roof edge. Mark was anxious for him. 'Terry, be careful,' he said. 'Be fucking careful.' Terry angled his camera and popped off a few shots.

We had to figure out what to do next. We were guessing that now the hotel was pretty well surrounded by those fancy-dressed loons. I was learning a lesson: in Dili, being inside a building, a proper formal building like a hotel, did not afford any protection. In Australia I kind of carried with me this naive belief that if I ever got into trouble in the street I could run into a pub, or a shop, or a hotel, and thus avoid the dark, private world in which homicidal maniacs tend to thrive. In that uncomfortable moment, I understood that in East Timor security only existed where Indonesia *wanted* it to exist, which most of the time was nowhere.

We gathered at the top of the hotel's stairwell with a few other reporters and photographers. A snapper for Associated Press, Charlie Darapak, was there. He was this too-cool Thai–American with a relaxed 'how's it going, man?' manner. He was much, much more experienced than me, which of course wasn't hard because I had no experience at all. I was wide-eyed and sweating, suddenly aware that we couldn't stay on the hotel roof because it was entirely possible that the militia would come up and find us there. And that's why I just about wet myself when too-cool Charlie turned to me and said in an American accent: 'Hmmmm … not a good situation, huh?'

I said 'yeah' as quickly and calmly as I could manage, anxious to shut my mouth before my heart leapt through my teeth and bounced off Charlie's forehead and onto the floor where – I had no doubt – it would run around in panicked circles all by itself.

'We've got to get out of here,' said Mark, just as I was beginning to fantasise that the hotel was really quite cosy after all. We all knew that getting out of there meant running the gauntlet, past the trucks of thugs out the front. 'Let's go,' said Mark. And I followed, too confused to question.

We got downstairs and saw that, yes, there were now two or three big pick-up trucks full of militiamen. Some were looking wired-up and angry, others were laughing wildly, the way that little boys do when they taunt small animals. I was of course to learn later that nearly all the militia conscripts in East Timor were village men and boys who had been rounded up and trucked into town under threat of terrible things happening to them or their families if they did not obey. Of course, there were some *real* nasties among them, but many would have been more frightened and confused than I was that day. I didn't know that then, though, and amidst their fear and frenzied desire to please their tormentors, they weren't exactly men you wanted to try and reason with either.

Anyway, we bolted. Out the front door of the Mahkota as the militia men shouted and, I think, began to give chase (but I don't know for sure, because I was too busy running).

Then something *wonderful* happened. A beautifully beaten-up little blue Timor taxi sped in front us and kept moving. 'Alfonso!' shouted Mark. I'd met Alfonso at the airport. He was a small and smiling man (but that doesn't tell you much because just about all East Timorese are small and smiling) with a plume of grey hair sticking straight up (but there *is* a story in that). Alfonso didn't speak a word of English, but driving from the airport to the Turismo Hotel, Mark had told me that he was once a Falintil fighter and had been captured and interrogated by the Indonesians. They burnt off all his hair.

So you can understand why, on that day, Alfonso might have been a little anxious, and why his little taxi kept driving away from us as we chased after it. 'Alfonso!' yelled Mark again, and the taxi slowed down just enough (thank God) for us to open the doors on the run and jump in. 'Get us out of here,' is what I assume Mark then yelled in Indonesian. But Dili is very small, and there weren't many places to go.

My thinking at that moment was: 'Yes, let's go, let's find safety, yes safety, yes, yes.' But then the reality returned that ... *oh fuck* ... we are journalists – correspondents, no less! – and our job is not to run away but to get as close as possible. As that sank in, I felt like the butterflies in my stomach had just flown through a cloud of amphetamine dust.

Mark suggested we drive to Telkom – Dili's telecommunications centre – where I could make a call to the news desk in Sydney. On the way we saw truckloads of militia men circling the small city like sharks. Mark and Terry dropped me off and went elsewhere to shoot some pictures.

The scene around the Telkom building was tense. I learned later that when trouble was cooking, Dili's locals would shut up shop and stay at home. It was one of those days. There was a heavy atmosphere in the empty streets, the ordinariness broken only by a shout or a flash of movement – a glimpse of someone being chased, or a passing figure languidly wandering in the distance, weapon in hand.

I spoke to a Telkom worker who led me into a small booth of cracking brown lino and I looked down at a decaying old phone. Scribbling on my pad, I attempted to tidy up the radio news story I'd written earlier on, adding bits and pieces I had picked up along the way, and dialled the news desk. When someone answered I realised how scared I was. I was shaking and my breathing was shallow. I so wanted to sound professional and brave, but I wasn't. It took at least five attempts before I could deliver the story in anything like usable quality. I knew they would have quite a time editing out my stumbles and curses. A guy named Barney was staffing the desk that day. Months later he was kind enough to tell me I did well in East Timor. 'I wasn't sure about you at first,' he said. No wonder. Neither was I.

I can't remember how I got back to the Turismo, but I did, just as it was getting dark. Mark and Terry were there and I wondered aloud about what to do next. 'I've heard that twelve people were killed today at the Carrascalao house,' Mark said, 'including Manuel's fourteen-year-old son. Why don't we go down to the church hospital and have a look? There must be some wounded there.' That was another lesson: the morbid checklist, which becomes familar to all reporters covering conflicts. After violence, go to the hospital. There will always be a story there.

Our taxi pulled up outside the clinic behind Dili's Motael Church. There was a breeze blowing off the sea, carrying with it the scent of death. Of course, at that very moment, for me it was an odour without a name. It was an ignorance short-lived.

Very dark outside, there was a dim light in the doorway of the clinic. A nun stood under it, dressed in white, talking to some people. As I approached, I heard wails of pain. I stepped through the door and walked into a wall of humidity pungent with the pong of antiseptic and blood. Another nun dragged a mop backwards and forwards across the floor, turning a thick liquid from bright red to dull brown. Someone released a long, lingering whimper. On my right I saw a man lying motionless. Completely still. I leant over him and realised that, for the first time in my life, I was looking at the body of a man drained of his.

I turned on my mini-disc recorder and walked through the clinic, weaving between the bodies of wounded and dead. I spoke haltingly into my microphone. *There are people with machete and gunshot wounds in their chests, their arms, their legs, their heads ... a lot of pain.* Some of the victims' faces were screwed up in agony, while others stared blankly, shocked and frozen in confusion. I tried to interview some of them. When I finally stepped back out into the night, I was shivering. But it wasn't cold at all.

Back at the Turismo I found Mark and Terry sitting in the dining area, eating something. Mark told us that in the morning there would be a funeral at Bishop Belo's house for Manuelita, the fourteen-year-old boy killed in the Carrascalao house. The word on the street was that the Indonesian military had removed the bodies of the twelve others killed – refugees slaughtered in the only refuge they could find.

Mark walked with me to my room on the ground floor. He checked the door and then went to the windows which faced onto the street. There were flimsy bars on them which he held and shook as he looked through, left and right, exhibiting a protective instinct that only agitated my anxiety. 'Tomorrow we might try and get you a room upstairs,' he said, and left.

Alone, the events of the day began to sink in. I still had to write a few radio stories for the morning, but first I needed to take a few moments to try and process how my daily realities had shifted so radically in just three days. I became aware that my clothes were caked in sweat and grime. I went into the bathroom – where washing meant a bucket and cold water – and taking off my shirt, looked into the mirror and realised that for probably the first time in my life I had forgotten to eat for an entire day. A dull bare light bulb hovered above my head. It was one of those rare existential moments that never leave your memory. Looking at myself, I wondered who I was, where I was, and why. It was an indulgence thankfully short-fused by pouring a bucketful of cold water over my noisy skull.

I slept feverishly, waking constantly to the emptiness of a strange room dappled with street lights from the new and frightening world outside. At dawn I got up and wandered down the street to the early mass at Bishop Belo's house, which was just on the next corner. Dili is that small – few places in the city are more than half an hour's walk away. Soon I could hear the singing, the exquisite voices of East Timor's Sunday faithful. Brutal days, followed by mornings of serene worship. Death, then dignity. That was Timor's weird circle of survival, turning round again and again for almost a quarter of a century. Winding through the crowd I spotted a huddle of bodies embracing. Getting closer, someone told me it was the Carrascalao family receiving friends and relatives who had come to pay their respects to young Manuelita. His sister Christina was there, red-eyed and exhausted, and hugging a sobbing woman. I edged next to them and guiltily recorded their wails of grief, adding it to the catalogue of suffering I would put on the radio the following Monday morning.

It was perhaps eight months later that the missing bodies of the others killed at the Carrascalao house were finally found. They were discovered by the UN in a seaside grave only about one hour's drive east of Dili. Just next to the road, the graves were clearly marked with names and the date, 17 April 1999. Hundreds of journalists had driven past them hundreds of times, but no-one had ever bothered to look. We had moved on to other stories, those right in front of us which were easier to tell. The thing is, those graves were right in front of us too, but we hadn't seen them. Much as the world, for twenty-four very long years, had chosen not to see East Timor.

SALLY SARA is the ABC's Africa Correspondent based in Johannesburg. She has reported from more than twenty countries on four continents, including assignments to Iraq, Zimbabwe, Congo, Sudan, Israel and Indonesia.

Sally grew up in the small town of Port Broughton in rural South Australia. She began her radio career at a community radio station at Bourke in outback New South Wales, before joining the ABC as a rural reporter in 1993.

Her ABC career includes two years covering the rough and tumble of Australian federal parliamentary politics in Canberra.

Sally has been a finalist in the prestigious Walkley Awards for excellence in journalism. She is the winner of an Australian national radio award – the Dalgety Award for Rural Journalism – and was South Australian Young Journalist of the Year in 1996. In 1999 she won the British Prize for Journalism.

Johannesburg: March 2003

'Nothing personal, mate,' he said. 'But I just don't think they should be sending a sheila to Africa'. Clunk. The phone call ended.

I was twenty-nine years old and two weeks away from starting my posting at the ABC's bureau in Africa.

My mobile phone had become an instrument of warning. Producers, colleagues, friends, friends of friends of people who knew someone in South Africa were calling with messages of caution.

'Do you understand what you're getting into?'

'My brother's boss knows a South African and they said it's not safe over there.'

'I knew a woman who was dragged from her car at gunpoint, right in Johannesburg. Dreadful place.'

'Are you sure you can live there?'

The answer to *that* was easy. No.

I spent some of my last nights in Australia on the internet – which is about the worst thing you can do before you move to South Africa. The world wide web is full of statistics so that you can work out, right down to the last decimal point, how likely it is that you will be raped, robbed, hijacked or murdered in Johannesburg … I knew the numbers like a model knows her measurements.

Johannesburg is one of the most violent cities in the world. It frightened me, from my ten-minute daydreams to the solitary half-dreams of the darkness between sleep and dawn.

I grew up in a small country town in South Australia, a peaceful place where locks and keys rarely chinked together. A one-policeman outpost. A place where a stolen bike was news in the district newspaper.

I was preparing to leave for Johannesburg, wondering whether I would be back home before the jetlag had even worn off.

I imagined making a stuttering phone call to my boss. 'Errr, yeah, I'm really sorry. But, look, I just can't live here. I've got to come home. I'm scared.'

Clunk. Phone call ends, shortly followed by my career.

I was caught between excitement and fear. I was on the way to Africa for the first time in my life.

My parents farewelled me at the airport, as if I might be on my way to a distant execution. It was a teary goodbye. Most of what was being thought wasn't said. It was communication by gestures. Squeezed hands, looks, hugs and pats. Little words conveyed larger messages.

'You make sure you're …' Sentence stopped.

'Dad and I, we'll be …'

'I know, Mum.'

It's uncomfortable to be the centre of a difficult send-off. I felt responsible.

But this was also the start of a longed-for adventure. Below the guilt was wild excitement, pounding anticipation and fear.

My first sight of Africa wasn't a shape or a place or a person. It was a colour. Gold. The cloud and the smoke of a winter afternoon were mixed together in a broth of golden light. It was the kind of scene that seems to deserve orchestral accompaniment, like the start of a B-grade biblical epic. The plane descended through the haze as if it was about to reveal God himself.

But under the clouds was reality.

At first it was difficult to see what was on the ground. They looked like boxes. Rows and rows of boxes, or perhaps cars parked in formation. As the plane got lower, it was clear that what looked like boxes were actually houses. Tiny houses, rows and rows of them in the black townships that surround Johannesburg. The area was criss-crossed by red dirt roads in a precise fabric. It was my first sight of poverty.

Welcome to Africa.

Ten minutes' drive from the box houses, rich families live in mansions. Children skip in and out of their parents' BMWs. Gardeners tend impossibly neat flowerbeds. White suburbanites put up boom gates to keep criminals out of the neighbourhoods.

Johannesburg is a city driven by money. Many who can only just afford a luxury car buy it at the expense of other things. They wear the worry of living at the frayed ends of their means, just to be able to show off their shining set of wheels.

South Africa has the largest market share for BMW in the world. The intersections of the wealthy suburbs look like a showcase for a game show. Sleek cars sit bumper to bumper. The occupants have lone conversations on their mobile phones as they ignore the beggars pawing at their windows.

Among the opulence there is a special breed of urban creature. The real estate agents, coiffured piranhas in high heels. They spruik their properties in manicured voices.

'Delightful home. Four bedrooms, maid's house, wendy house, armed response and razor wire.' 'Swimming pool, high walls, surveillance cameras and tennis court.'

It sounded like I was about to rent a time share in a luxury maximum-security prison.

I ended up choosing 'Cottage garden, lovely unit with electric fence, twenty-four-hour guard and remote controlled gates.'

Sensors blinked from the ceiling as I walked in. This would be my home for the next three years. There were panic buttons attached to the wall in the bedroom and the kitchen. And just in case I thought I would live on the wild side and go into the garden on my own, there were mobile panic buttons on a chain that I could wear around my neck. Just the accessory for the crime-wise gal about town. Press the button, I was warned, and the armed response team from the security company would be there before I could say 'South Africa's Most Wanted'.

The armed response teams are a suburban cavalry. They patrol the streets day and night, waiting to rescue a client in distress. They wear bulletproof vests, which make them look even bigger and more earnest than they already are.

The first I knew they were about to knock my door down was the screech of their tyres. It was three o'clock in the morning. The power had gone off and triggered the panic alarms. The response team was shouting outside, asking if I was OK, with their handguns at the ready. I was upstairs in bed, a little confused and completely naked. It was fashion or survival. I pulled a t-shirt over my head, a towel around my waist and not much in between. It was either that, or a startled confrontation with my hands up and my legs out like a starfish. I made it to the door, just in time.

Within my first week, I met the gaggle of other foreign correspondents based in Johannesburg. They had come here from around the world: Americans, Swedes, Brits and French journalists, all swapping tales across the dinner table. I didn't have much to say. I was yet to earn my own African anecdotes. I sat quietly.

My first assignment finally came. The Zimbabwean election. I was nervous. I didn't know what to expect, let alone what to do.

It began at a dusty football stadium in the township of Chitungwiza, outside the capital, Harare. Thousands of people were packed inside. It was loud, hot and crowded. There were two sound systems. One broadcast President Robert Mugabe's speech. The other rattled the determined voice of one of the President's enforcers, warning people not to leave the stadium. It was a conscripted crowd.

Interviews also happened in two parts. People spoke of their love for the President while the police were close by. Then in frenzied whispers they confessed their support for the opposition.

President Mugabe was shiny and animated. His arms waved wildly, as if someone else was in charge of his movements. He shouted and whispered in turn as he launched his speech into the crowd.

The rally ended in a blustering cloud of red dirt as President Mugabe's helicopter took off. The facade was over. The gates were opened. Those who had been forced to spend the afternoon in a mass audience with their President made their way home.

The 2000 general election was the first test of President Mugabe's hold on power. He was under challenge from the opposition Movement for Democratic Change (MDC), which had been formed nine months earlier. It was led by Morgan Tsvangirai, a former union official. Tsvangirai was a tough but distant man who was marshalling the energies of a new breed of Zimbabweans.

Zimbabwe is a mixture of genteel colonialism and brutal violence.

The locals have names like Cloud, Obey, Lovemore, Nomore, Learnmore, Gift and Innocent. In remote villages, policemen in British style uniforms keep guard. In Harare, schoolboys in shorts, long socks and shiny shoes play cricket on green ovals.

But, in the townships, riot police armed with batons and rifles keep watch. Residents peer out from broken windows. The poor neigbourhoods fester with discontent and disappointment.

Ironically, one of President Mugabe's greatest legacies is education. He schooled a generation, and then failed to build an economy to employ them. The townships are full of bright, articulate young men and women, happy to be interviewed and desperate to work. They still have hopeful faces … only just. But their clothes are torn and worn. They are A-grade students who have never had a job. They sleep on dirty mattresses in cupboard-sized apartments, where second-hand air hangs in musty corridors.

This was Zimbabwe's chance to vote for change. People queued patiently to cast their ballots at tents in the townships. Young opposition supporters waved red cards, their trademark signal to President Mugabe to leave office.

In the early hours of the morning, I was woken by the sound of singing. Deep Zimbabwean voices resonated from the street below. I hurriedly pulled some clothes over my pyjamas, picked up my microphone and recorder and went downstairs.

More than twenty young opposition supporters were crowded into the back of a ute. The tyres were bulging in and out as the passengers danced and bounced. They were celebrating. The opposition Movement for Democratic Change had won its first seats in parliament.

The MDC activists pushed their open hands in the air, in salute as they sang. But by dawn it was obvious that the celebrations were hollow. The opposition had won a record number of seats, but failed to take power.

It was the start of a new era of uncertainty in Zimbabwe. President Mugabe was facing a functional, aggressive opposition for the first time in his political life. The nation was about to slide into economic and political turmoil. Within two years, half the population would be in need of food aid. Banks would be running out of banknotes, garages would be out of fuel and inflation would be above 200 per cent.

We returned to Zimbabwe in February 2003 after having been banned during the Zimbabwean government's crackdown on the foreign media. It seemed like a different place.

The hotel in Harare, once full of reporters and business travellers, was almost deserted. I was the only person staying on the eleventh floor. It was eerie.

Outside, there were more police than before. Petrol queues clogged the streets. Sometimes the queues were so long it was difficult to work out which petrol station they belonged to. People left their cars in the queue, just on the basis of a rumour that petrol might be on its way. Some taxi drivers worked for three days until their fuel ran out, and then spent until the next week waiting to fill up their tank again.

On the footpaths, people stood in lines outside bakeries and grocery stores. Bread, sugar and maize meal were no longer on the shelves. Some people queued all day for something to eat. They went home hungry, and simply came back the next day. It was a display of desperation and unending patience.

Hotel and guesthouse operators saved their fuel to go on monthly grocery shopping safaris in neighbouring Botswana. They were forced to take their passports and cross the border in search of basic things like cornflakes and flour.

But for most Zimbabweans there was no easy way out. In two years the country had changed, almost beyond recognition.

I had also changed. I had returned to Zimbabwe with more

experience and caution. I had seen hunger, corruption, death, violence and hope. I had learned the smells, touch and emotion of the scenes that previously I had only seen on television.

I had found my own way to accept, and understand, what I saw. I realised that I couldn't stop the suffering around me; all I could do was to tell people's stories. To make sure that, if nothing else, someone would know what had happened. But sometimes it felt a bit trivial. As a journalist, I had little to offer people who really needed doctors or food or protection.

Sometimes just telling the story was difficult.

'That's the school, on top of the hill, over there.'

My translator Jean-Pierre pointed to a group of abandoned buildings in front of us. The school was surrounded by the beautiful hills of Rwanda's Gikongoro Province.

We were on our way to one of the most notorious sites of Rwanda's genocide. In 1994, more than 800,000 ethnic Tutsis and moderate Hutus were murdered by Hutu extremists in a hundred days of bloodshed.

Rwanda is sad and fascinating. The genocide was so cata-strophic, its remnants are everywhere. Millions live in half-families of brothers and sisters without parents. Teenagers without siblings. Grandparents without their adult children. People have regrouped into whatever leftover family they can make.

Nine years ago, this school was crowded with families. Tens of thousands of people came here when the killing started in the villages and hills. But on 21 April 1994 the killers came here too.

Now the classrooms are full of bodies. The remains of up to 27,000 people have been kept here as a chilling memorial. The bodies are stored on white wooden racks. The windows of the classrooms are covered with tarpaulins, which keep out the weather but keep in the smell.

The smell of genocide is unmistakable. It's a damp, sad scent. It smells like old fertilizer. It pushed its way inside my nose and mouth.

The room was full of death. I could smell it, touch it and see it. But I felt nothing.

I thought that, after almost a decade, the remains would be dusty skeletons, impersonal and sanitised. But the bodies were intact. All the skin had turned white. The flesh was dried and distorted. It looked like plaster.

I peered through the lens of my video camera at the mangled limbs of those who had died here. It was a terrible puzzle of arms, legs and torsos. Some of the rooms were mixed, others were just full of children. Tiny, chalky bodies, corrugated ribs, withered limbs, broken skulls. They looked out of proportion, like an unborn baby on an ultrasound.

The bodies were in the same position as at the moment of death. Some were clutching their head. Others were stretched out with arms reaching for help that never arrived. Some still had hair, others were wearing necklaces.

Up to 60,000 people were killed here. They were chased, shot, beaten and hacked to death. Names, personalities, talents and hopes, were cut to pieces. Whole families were wiped out in a day. The delicious, minute memories traded only between parents and children were gone. There was almost no-one left to remember.

The families sheltered at this Catholic school because they thought they would be safe there. They sought the protection of the clergy. But within fifteen days of the start of the genocide, most of the people were dead.

Emmanuel was one of only four survivors. He still has a bullet hole in his forehead. It's a deep indentation. His wife and six children were killed here. The attackers thought he was also dead. They took his clothes and his possessions as they stole from the bodies around him. Emmanuel hid among the battered corpses of his family until he took the chance to run into the nearby forest.

I walked behind Emmanuel. He unlocked the doors of the former classrooms, like a warden opening a cell. I could see that he tried not to look inside. The bodies held secrets for him. He knew many of these people, when they were his friends and neighbours.

I followed him in a controlled daze. My heart rate was steady. My mind was empty. My face was neutral. It was an unwilling feeling of nothingness. Something had shut down. All I could think of was my camera, the light, my filming. I felt nothing for what I saw. I was empty.

It had never happened before.

The only feeling that came was guilt.

The first time I saw the remains of genocide victims, a year earlier, I could hardly breathe. It felt as if my ribs changed size in my chest. It was a burning, breathless feeling as I looked at the skulls and bones of those who were killed. It was haunting.

But this time I was blank and clinical.

I sat in the car on the way back to Kigali. Jean-Pierre shook his head.

'Terrible, terrible. The killing,' he said. 'That's what happened to my family. My mother, my father, my six brothers and sisters were killed like that, in our village.'

Jean-Pierre was a genocide survivor. I couldn't tell him that I felt nothing for what I had just seen.

I was worried that I'd reached the point of overload, where I couldn't absorb any more. If I felt nothing, I could write nothing. I was robotic and detached.

I wished that the emotion would come.

Three days later, it did.

I watched the footage of the bodies in my hotel room. I stopped and started it, as I checked and logged the pictures, ready to write my television story. But, even after I turned off the camera, the pictures stayed in my mind. They crashed through my thoughts. They lingered and swirled as I tried to get to sleep. The body with the necklace, the body of the toddler grasping a hole in its temple. I couldn't stop the images.

It was a delayed return to normality. I started to feel emotion again, in bursts of sadness and dull contemplation. The next four nights were restless. Thoughts of the bodies were a constant interruption.

Africa has changed me. It's revealed a spectrum of life far richer, and yet more terrible, than I had known. The peaks of joy and sincerity are more precious than anything I have experienced elsewhere. But the suffering and the evil are on the very fringes of human existence. The killing, the greed, the brutality are almost beyond understanding.

I have slowly been rewired. Every visit back to Australia is a little more distant and unsettling. The luxurious calm of home makes me feel a bit uncomfortable. I watch the teenage surfers at the beach, the yuppies having long lunches, I listen to the friendly chatter of neighbours. I feel like I'm looking at my own country through a thick pane of glass.

The experience has been so profound, I can't undo it. Beyond its sadness, it has delivered pure delight, surprise and goodness.

I'm glad they sent a sheila to Africa.

TREVOR BORMANN has been travelling and reporting overseas for the ABC for fifteen years, and is now Supervising Producer of *Foreign Correspondent.*

He grew up in country South Australia, and began his career in newspapers and regional television before working in Melbourne and Sydney for the Nine, Seven and Ten networks.

Trevor joined the ABC in 1987, and later became Network Editor of television news.

He covered the 1991 Gulf War for ABC-TV, and found himself back in the region reporting on the Iraq war in 2003. Trevor was Middle East Correspondent in the early 1990s, and established the ABC's bureau in Amman, Jordan. From there he also covered conflict in Afghanistan, and war and famine in Somalia.

A Walkley award-winning journalist, he has also reported for the ABC from North America, South-East Asia and the South Pacific.

Money, Guns and T-shirts: The Somalia Tragedy

A smudged, handwritten sign at reception in the city's only functioning hotel beckoned new guests: 'Sahafi Hotel Mogadishu – comfort, safety, luxury. For business or discreet weekends'. For two hundred and fifty dollars a night the former school offered space on a concrete floor and cold water that didn't run. The gutted shell that formed the main wing of the complex had been occupied, evacuated and reoccupied by a procession of armed gangs who had each contributed to the anarchic chaos of this miserable country.

But in December 1992, Mohammed the smiling manager of the Sahafi had every reason to be optimistic about this establishment's relaunch as a hotel. His acumen and enterprise were about to pay off in Somalia's military and media-led financial recovery. After eighteen months of perverse tribal infighting and the most brutal civil war, it was famine that had ultimately drawn world attention to this desperate country. Television images of the starving had validated Africa's latest crisis. In a CNN-directed beach landing, the Americans had launched a military operation called 'Restore Hope' to extinguish the lawlessness and create an environment safe enough for the distribution of food aid.

I arrived in less spectacular style on a UNICEF flight from Kenya. American military air traffic controllers gave priority to a small plane ahead of us. I remember seeing its cargo unloaded later: one thousand T-shirts with an 'I restored hope in Somalia' motif on the front. Most of them sold in the airport. Others found their way to a new marketplace that had mushroomed outside the Sahafi Hotel. The small girl who sold them was competing with a one-legged child who was pushing 'Hard Rock Cafe Mogadishu' T-shirts from a neighbouring stall.

Inside the walls of the Sahafi compound, Mohammed could afford to charge two hundred and fifty dollars a night at his hotel only because arriving media could afford to pay it. 'Sahafi' means 'journalist' in Arabic: Mohammed knew his market. And as his hotel filled with media fired by the arrival of the Americans, his smile grew wider still.

I'd first come to Somalia five months earlier, after the BBC broadcast a series of alarming reports on an emerging crisis in the Horn of Africa. ABC Foreign Editor John Tulloh called me at my Middle East bureau in Amman, Jordan, to discuss a trip there, combining a shoot for *Foreign Correspondent* with a series of news stories. I agreed knowing that a calamity had to be covered – and then dived into the atlas to check out where exactly Somalia was.

In July 1992 Mogadishu was the most dangerous city on earth. The survivors of the ongoing civil war scrounged in the rubble for daily needs. There was no food, no water and no order. Rising from the chaos were the only organised entities in Somalia – the gangs of teenagers who menaced everyone in their cut-down 'Mad Max' cars with machine guns mounted on the back.

The desperate young men who roamed the streets held allegiance to no-one. Mostly orphaned and dispossessed, they formed predatory gangs with transient bonds. The gun empowered, but it also made survival more precarious in the complex turf war of Mogadishu. Suburbs and streets were divided into spheres of control for the gangs.

The Mad Maxes didn't quite know what to make of us. Television crews were still a rare and novel sight on the streets of Mogadishu. I was hoping if they were familiar with a Mel Gibson film they'd be well disposed towards a television crew from the country that made him a star.

If anything, they played to the camera, attempting donuts on the dusty streets. During one display of exuberance the gunner at the back of a Toyota flew off into the mangled remains of a statue in the city square. His embarrassment was excruciating. My great fear was that he'd open up his machine-gun to eliminate those who witnessed this indignity.

Mogadishu was also a city divided. One side was ruled by self-proclaimed president Ali Mahdi, a former businessman with a penchant for white suits. On the other was warlord Mohammad Aideed, who preferred darker, earthy tones. In my two trips to Somalia I managed to speak to them both about the misery they had created. Apart from their preferred attire, it seemed to me they had more in common than the world had given them credit for. They were equally responsible for the deaths of several hundred thousand people, and neither was sure how it had happened.

I interviewed the dapper Ali Mahdi at a dusty office with empty bookshelves. A Coca-Cola yo-yo and a Snickers bar sat on the edge of his desk, next to a photograph of the President himself with an Italian soccer star. The odd round of AK-47 outside played havoc with the soundtrack. But in between shots President Ali admitted to me that he was amazed at how ferocious his people had become.

'I never thought they could kill each other like this, and for no reason,' he said.

'But we have been fighting for thousands of years, it's part of our heritage.'

There were two ways a Somali man could feed his family in Mogadishu. Both of them involved carrying a gun. You could use your AK-47 to get a job guarding the aid shipments, or you could instead turn the gun on your mates and steal the aid. Many young desperadoes could claim both roles on their résumés – some faced a daily career crisis over whether to protect the food or run off with it.

I shared the scepticism of most in my generation about how much of your donor money actually gets to the people who need it. In fact, it's quite a lot. Peering into the warehouse at Mogadishu port, I saw bags of rice and wheat stacked to the roof, ready for distribution throughout the country.

Graeme Roberts was an energetic Englishman from CARE who claimed to be in charge of logistics at the Mogadishu docks.

But he knew he was as much a hostage of the gangs as anyone. CARE had hired seven hundred gun-toting guards to 'supervise' the movement of food aid. But on this day, the docks were silent.

'We've got an industrial issue,' announced Graeme. 'The boys are on strike.'

Upwards of five hundred Somalis were going to die of hunger on this day alone, but two hundred tonnes of donated grain would sit idle at the docks while CARE negotiated a pay increase.

Graeme introduced me to the shop steward. His name was Rambo, and a huge ammunition belt concealed the message on his canary yellow shirt. His chief lieutenant had a more recognisable T-shirt with the signature of a famous Australian label.

Terrific, I thought, Rambo and Mambo.

There were so many gangs on the wharves that even they were getting confused about who belonged to whom.

Graeme had six personal bodyguards, we had three. Another ten made up the Rambo–Mambo alliance.

'So who are the others?' I asked Graeme.

'Mate, they're either guards or robbers,' he said. 'And most of them won't make up their minds until the food starts moving tomorrow.'

When in Mogadishu, cast and crew used to stay at a former prison on the outskirts of town. The walled fortress had now become a Red Cross hospital receiving a constant flow of gunshot victims – most of them civilians caught in gang war crossfire.

A jail was a perfect place to stay. No one could break into a prison, we thought. The cells had once been occupied by political prisoners of the repressive Siad Barre regime.

Now they were bedrooms for Red Cross staffers and guests. The walls made interesting reading. Names of the incarcerated were cut into the brickwork. And on the wall above my bed, a reassuring 'Elvis lives'.

The Red Cross compounds in Mogadishu were just another piece of turf as far as the gangs were concerned. Staffers sought protection in the sanctuary of former diplomatic missions, and didn't leave without their own group of young gunmen–minders.

There was no good or bad in Mogadishu. The two dozen or so teenagers hired as bodyguards by the Red Cross had originally turned up at the headquarters on the southern side of the city to rob and kill everyone inside. The operations head persuaded them to accept jobs with the organisation instead, to protect Red Cross workers against all the other guys wanting to kill them

My producer, John Budd, sub-contracted three young gunmen to look after us on our travels through the streets. Add driver and interpreter, and the protection racket was complete.

I have no idea whether over that week our minders had any feelings for us; I suspected not. One morning as our entourage headed out towards the docks for filming, a cut-down truck clipped the front of our car and ran us off the road.

In a rare frenzy of excitement, our bodyguards jumped out to confront the four young thugs in the other truck. It shouldn't have surprised me that a nation racked by famine and civil war also had road rage.

But then interpreter Mohammed calmly explained that we were being robbed, and that we were about to find out whether our lads were worth the fifty dollars a day we were paying them. Our three minders introduced themselves to the offending carload of gunmen with weapons aimed at their heads. For the next ten minutes they circled each other with AK-47s held high. It was like a couple of roosters shaping up for a cockfight – although I'm convinced at one point our youngest minder Ahmed was so stoned he actually forgot who his mates were and where he should be pointing his gun. I recall he was wearing a bright yellow T-shirt that said 'Kiss me, I'm Italian'.

When the guns were lowered and the two gangs started talking, Mohammed grew tense and suggested we worry. He told us to stay in the car while he ran to join the negotiations.

Our young minders had refined their business skills since deciding to join the Red Cross rather than obliterate it. Now they were discussing another proposition with the four teenagers they'd been going to shoot ten minutes earlier. The deal was, they'd make peace with the other gang, then kill us together and spread the spoils – the wads of American dollars that filled our pockets, socks and underpants. For our lads, it was a business decision, whether it would be financially more worthwhile to stay employed, or take the money and run. They decided to keep their job. Ahmed was even smiling at me as he returned to the car.

Any newcomer learned very quickly who ruled the streets of Mogadishu. The Mad Maxes, commissioned by the clan rulers, were ever present, always menacing and often threatening.

On a drizzly morning I arrived at a walled compound like so many others I'd visited in the past week. A blue flag draped limply on a peeling flagpole. Within the security of the large whitewashed building, fifty-one immaculately uniformed soldiers sipped tea and ate perfectly formed triangular sandwiches. This was the outfit from UNOSOM, the United Nations' observers in Somalia.

They were soldiers of five countries who'd come to this broken nation to look but not touch. The problem was, the observers weren't seeing much because they hadn't actually left the compound. Their Pakistani general told me with a straight face it wasn't safe to do so. Until the security of his unarmed solders could be guaranteed, his men would continue to stand around and sip tea and limit their Somali experience to what they could see from a vine-covered courtyard.

Outside, the predatory Mad Maxes waited, hoping to pick up a contract. They knew there was money to be made from the United Nations – they offered 'protection' to every other UN agency in town.

The UNOSOM general conceded he would ultimately call on the gangs for protection, for there to be any hope of his unit doing its job.

'We're just observers,' said the general in a moment of candour. 'If my masters in New York want to make a difference, maybe they'll think about peacekeepers.'

Baidoa in central Somalia was the epicentre of the famine in mid-1992. It had been physically destroyed by civil war and then disembowelled by starvation.

I arrived on a chartered flight from Mogadishu. My knowledge of the place and what was happening there was contained in a series of clippings I'd read from obscure wire service sources.

Our aircraft touched down on a dusty strip of flat desert just after midday. A local Red Cross official, Ahmed, greeted me with a loose handshake and a correction. This wasn't usually desert, he said, the terrain was actually good agricultural land in normal rainfall years.

Behind him, in the midday glare, a formed line of cut-down trucks with gun-toting teenagers reminded me I was still in Somalia.

Ahmed explained that before we could do any television work in Baidoa we had to check in and do coffee with the local clan leader. His nickname was Captain Cucumber for some inexplicable reason – but Ahmed warned me to keep that to myself. I don't recall much about my meeting with the captain; I hope I wasn't too polite. My memory is of the only man I ever saw in Somalia with a beer gut.

Warlord Captain Cucumber was part of the protection industry. His network of cheerless, desperate thugs controlled the turf of Baidoa and gracefully allowed the aid agencies to conduct their work of saving the very people he had condemned to suffer because they belonged to the wrong tribe.

I actually thanked the captain for his time, and emerged from the meeting with the smell of damp carpet in my nostrils and the impression of a man overpowered with delusion.

The road to the food kitchen of Baidoa followed a shady tree-lined street of concrete box homes that had survived the ravages of house-to-house fighting. An entourage delivered us to the Red Cross food kitchen on the outskirts of the town, a stark, walled compound with a faded painted cross on a displaced placard.

The perimeter was smothered with recently tilled soil; four

men were on a patch near the walls, driving shovels into dirt loosened by earthmoving machinery. They were digging graves neatly six feet deep.

Growing up in country South Australia, I gleaned an impression of African famine from television news. As a child with ample food each mealtime, it seemed there was always someone starving somewhere on a dark continent. I remember hearing about and momentarily feeling sorry for people in far-off places like Biafra. The images on nightly new bulletins conveyed a grainy impression of thin, emaciated people looking sadly into a camera.

When you're raised on television you can see famine and you can hear it. But nothing prepares you for the smell of people dying of hunger.

The Red Cross called this place a 'food kitchen', but in a perverse kind of way I couldn't imagine how anyone could die of hunger in a kitchen. Hunger is a complex affliction, a very strange physiological process for a journalist to understand. Like most people, I thought of starvation as a slow, lingering demise. It actually happens very quickly.

The courtyard of the food kitchen was filled with skeletons in the dirt. Dr Said Moussa Aden took me on a grand tour and explained to me in more detail than I needed why he would channel his energies into saving some, and why he thought there was no hope for others.

Those lying in the dirt were teenage boys and girls. They were the most robust in a community that had been slowly strangled by the mechanics of famine. Tin cans had been placed at the mouths and backsides of each of the patients.

A utility arrived and the decrepit figure of a woman was helped to the ground. Her name was Awa Ali Abdi, and on the twenty-day journey to Baidoa she'd lost her husband, two young children, father and mother. Awa was in the final throes of malnutrition, and when she began to talk to me she seem to project something more than other starving people I'd seen on television from the comfort of a living room.

It seemed pathetic, but I didn't imagine someone about to die of starvation would have a conversation with me. Her quivering voice told me a tale of fatal desperation. Awa said she'd lost all hope in life. She'd arrived at the food kitchen for sustenance, but she felt so sick and depressed by the loss of everyone around her that she had lost the will to live.

Awa's chances of survival were about 30 per cent, explained Dr Said. She had passed a critical point in the starvation process where food couldn't be held down.

A boy no more than four years old, with a bloated stomach but a faint smile, appeared in a doorway. No one knew his name or could even remember how he came to be at the kitchen. Infant curiosity had him playing around the legs of the camera tripod.

Dr Said explained that about a thousand people a day were dying in Baidoa. Many of those only reached the kitchen after striking deals with gunmen for safe passage.

At the end of our tour we returned to a verandah where the young nameless boy lay, less agile now, on a squashed Sanyo television packing case. An extraordinary deterioration had overtaken his frail body. A bowel prolapse signalled the child's death throes. His insides were literally slipping out of his backside. In his final moments the boy raised his fingers to toy with the lens shade on the camera, inquisitive to his final breath. It occurred to me later, that child didn't make a single sound in the last ten minutes of his life.

Outside the food kitchen, the gravediggers were now placing bodies in the holes they'd just created. It struck me that no food was actually being served in the kitchen, because everyone who made the journey there was too ill to eat.

I felt somewhat miffed having to share my Somalia experience with dozens of other journalists on my return to Mogadishu five months later. The UNOSOM general and his tea-drinking observers had long gone. American troops in a 'peace enforcement' operation had become bogged down in clan politics. Ultimately it would lead to disaster for them.

The death toll of the famine had been revised down by aid agencies, but still, hundreds of thousands of Somalis had perished. The drought had ended – but in a cruel twist, heavy rains had cut the roads, hampering food distribution.

By Christmas, the world's media was keeping Mogadishu alive with a huge influx of foreign money. The American networks had taken over compounds, and were employing dozens of drivers and gun-toting Rambos. Teams of cooks worked around the clock to feed correspondents and crews. Chartered aircraft from Nairobi flew in fresh food each day.

We settled for the dining room of the Sahafi Hotel, and its bland menu of rice and lentils. One day 'Chicken Somali Style' appeared on the blackboard, but it was a joke – just like the Sahafi's claim as a place 'for business or discreet weekends'.

At least now we could feed our stories out by satellite: the networks and agencies were in town with their dishes.

But there's one thing guaranteed to make a foreign correspondent want to break furniture.

That's being on the end of a phone in Mogadishu and having someone call from Australia to ask 'What time is it there?' The response can be a colourful variation of 'if you don't know, don't call' or 'do you know, in some organisations that question's a sackable offence?'

Coming to terms with absolute deadlines on cruel time differences is one of the least appealing aspects of working in a war zone. Filing for the ABC TV's *World at Noon* program meant feeding our cut stories at one o'clock in the morning. Often, tight satellite schedules meant that we had little flexibility anyway.

No-one with any sense ventured out after dark in Mogadishu. A sizeable proportion of the population didn't even face the streets during daylight hours. But for several nights running I drew the short straw to ferry my cut story from the walled sanctuary of

107

the Sahafi Hotel through the pitch black to the Reuters feedpoint a dozen blocks away.

Khalid, my driver, would sit in his cut-down, beaten-up car from about eleven each night, just waiting for the moment when the steel doors of the Sahafi were flung open for our bumpy ride into dangerous darkness.

On one steamy night a couple of weeks after the launch of Operation Restore Hope, a burst of gunfire sent dogs two kilometres away into a barking frenzy. I had no idea what was going on. I recall Khalid jumping out of his revved-up Toyota to demand more money before we went any further.

Khalid insisted on negotiating the back streets to the satellite point with his car lights off. We shared an eerie ride through dusty streets illuminated by a full moon. In a sense I was pleased that his car was so noisy and unroadworthy. I couldn't hear a single shot in the fifteen minutes it took us to reach Reuters.

The gates opened, and Khalid attempted a high five on my sweaty right hand. Oblivious to our achievement of just making it to the feed point alive, a beer-swilling Reuters technician grunted and snatched our tape without even looking at us.

In the next room a party had attracted television types with no apparent deadlines. The remnants of a dozen lobsters littered a kidney-shaped coffee table, empty champagne bottles were scattered across the floor. A young woman I hadn't seen before was wearing a T-shirt that said 'Somalia 1992 – kickin' butt and feelin' good'. I asked a tall red-headed American what the party was for. Before he could answer they screamed, embraced, and broke into a drunken rendition of 'Auld Lang Syne'.

MARK CORCORAN, has been a reporter–producer for *Foreign Correspondent* for six years, filing reports from thirty countries, with a particular focus on South-West Asia. Since September 11 he has reported extensively on the regional impact of the ongoing war on terror.

In the Middle East, his reporting has included stories on sanctions imposed against Iraq, the rise of the pro-democracy movement in Iran, and a variety of features on social and political issues in the region.

Mark started his career eighteen years ago as a cadet journalist with Capital 7 TV in Canberra, before moving to Sydney as a news reporter for the Seven Network.

From 1988 to 1992 he worked for SBS TV's *Tonight* and *Dateline* programs covering regional diplomatic and defence issues.

In 1992 he joined the ABC as a producer for *Four Corners*. He produced the 1994 investigation 'Codename Mantra' on the alleged misconduct of Australia's overseas intelligence agency ASIS, prompting a Federal Government Commission of Inquiry into the accountability of the agency.

From 1994 to 1997, Mark was a Sydney-based reporter–producer on ABC TV's *Lateline* and was briefly ABC TV's Washington Correspondent before joining *Foreign Correspondent*.

Mark has received a Walkley Award for Best International Report (All Media) for his coverage of the conflict in Sierra Leone, a High Commendation from the Walkley Committee for his reporting on Afghanistan's Taliban regime, and the George Munster Award for Independent Journalism for his story on the US military's alliance of convenience with Afghanistan's biggest drug lord, Haji Bashar.

His international awards include Gold and Silver World Medals from the New York Television Festival for his reporting in Iran and Sierra Leone, and the Mohamed Amin–Reuters Award for an Outstanding Contribution to International Newsgathering for his investigation of the opium industry in Afghanistan.

Mark Corcoran is married with two children and lives in Sydney.

Sierra Leone: Gunship for Hire

'If we ever catch you, we'll cut out your heart and eat it!'

It is a very real threat, made by people to be taken seriously. The rebels of Sierra Leone's Revolutionary United Front (RUF). The intended victim is Neall Ellis. To those involved in his secretive business, Ellis is a 'private military contractor'. To the rest of the world, he is a mercenary pilot, dispensing death and destruction from the controls of a helicopter gunship.

Ellis has now lived with the threats for five years – not that he looks too worried as we meet in Paddy's Bar in Freetown, Sierra Leone. Paddy's is the watering hole of choice for mercenaries, spies, peacekeepers and aid workers: all the usual suspects who seemingly materialise at every third world conflict, now spill out of this noisy, sweaty, open barn, perched above the appropriately named Pirate Bay on Freetown harbour.

This port city was founded in the eighteenth century by freed slaves from America. The mood and look of the bullet-scarred streets seem more Caribbean than African.

It is a typical night at Paddy's, reverberating to dance music, war stories and bar girls on the make. All the clichés of airport fiction, straight from the pages of the Frederick Forsyth novel *The Dogs of War*. Except that here it is for real, and the patrons of Paddy's are all doing their best to intoxicate themselves against the horrifying reality that lies outside.

Ellis, a bespectacled, fifty-something South African, is totally unassuming, displaying none of the 'hard-man' qualities that make him a legend in mercenary circles. Short and heavy set, he has, like so many South African mercenaries, the social air of a rugby player on tour, or perhaps a Johannesburg dentist cutting loose for a couple of weeks away with the boys.

But his reality is quite different. Ellis is a former South African colonel. One of the world's most experienced combat helicopter pilots, he fought in apartheid South Africa's toughest and dirtiest battles. He flew combat missions in support of the feared 32 Battalion, a Special Forces Unit at the forefront of Pretoria's secret war against black Africa's frontline states. In Angola he became, reputedly, the only helicopter pilot to survive being targeted, simultaneously, by three surface-to-air missiles – fired by Cubans – who lived to fly another day.

When apartheid ended, most of the 32 Battalion quit the army, effectively privatising to form the nucleus of Executive Outcomes, which quickly established a reputation as perhaps the most ruthlessly efficient private army in the world. Ellis also resigned, at first trying his hand at farming and commercial fishing before succumbing to the lure of 'the job', signing on as a soldier of fortune in Bosnia and the Congo. He then landed in Sierra Leone to work for Executive Outcomes and, later, the British outfit Sandline International – the big names of the mercenary world, although these days they prefer to be called Private Military Companies.

To paraphrase one mercenary executive, 'The dogs of war now live in a corporate kennel.'

Ellis agrees: 'The job, I think, is the same, but the image has changed. Now it's suits and briefcases. You are more professional. I think the days of Congo and Angola when you had the image of mercenaries as drunken guys going around shooting up the place, you know, having a fine time, has gone – the people you find now, generally speaking, are well-trained, professional soldiers, special forces trained.'

Nursing a large beer, Ellis explains that his opponents in his latest dirty little war are best described as Africa's Khmer Rouge, without the ideology. The RUF's only clear objective seems to be controlling the country's fabulously rich diamond fields.

Even by the brutal standards of African civil wars, this conflict is terrifying. The RUF's trademark punishment is amputation. Out in the darkness that night, just beyond the bright lights of Paddy's Bar are the camps and slums, home to thousands of men, women and children who've had arms, legs and even lips hacked off by teenage rebels. RUF commanders enforce a deliberate policy of drug use among the ranks to fuel aggression and obliterate any mercy or compassion for their victims.

Through such savagery, the RUF has defeated the national army and confounded two peacekeeping forces in the course of a nine-year civil war. Now, in mid 2000, the guerrillas fear only one thing – what Neall Ellis calls his office – a Russian-built Mi-24 Hind helicopter gunship which he flies under contract to the Sierra Leone Army.

Ellis talks about it all in the dispassionate tone of the professional pilot – much the same way as he reflects on the country's unpredictable tropical weather, which can be just as deadly to a helicopter.

He's keen to display the 'new professionalism' of his calling, and a few days after our drink at Paddy's, we're on the helipad at Cockerill Barracks, the Freetown HQ of the Sierra Leone Army. Cameraman Geoff Lye and I have been invited on a combat mission.

With flying helmet in one hand and assault rifle in the other, Ellis strides towards the Hind helicopter which squats on the tarmac, a large, menacing camouflaged bullfrog.

Ellis boasts: 'The RUF call this aircraft "Wor-Wor Boy". *Wor-Wor* means ugly, so it's "ugly boy" to them. They fear it, they are very frightened of this aircraft. When we'd get overhead, they used to shoot at us quite a bit – small arms fire. They used to shoot at us – but now they duck for cover, they run, they scatter all over the place.'

His nine-member team was recruited from around the world – a veritable United Nations of mercenaries. The mechanics scrambling over Wor-Wor Boy making last-minute checks are Ethiopian. Loading a machine-gun is 'Fijian Fred' Marafano, a grim hulk of a man in his late fifties who served in the British

SAS. He was highly decorated for his part in the dramatic 1980 hostage rescue drama, when an SAS team stormed the Iranian Embassy in London – but that is a story told by others. Fijian Fred is unwilling to talk about that incident – or anything else. Wary of the outsiders who've abruptly entered his secretive world on Ellis's orders, he communicates through subtle shrugs or hand gestures. The other door gunner stacking ammunition is Christophe, a short, wiry Frenchman who insists that he's holidaying in Sierra Leone. Everyone wears flying suits except Christophe, who flies to war in jeans and T-shirt.

They've run out of ammunition for the big nose-mounted cannon, so there's no need for a co-pilot gunner on this mission. Ellis gestures that this vacant front seat should be occupied by Geoff and his camera. I'm to ride in the back with the door gunners.

Fuelled, armed and strapped in, we lurch off the helipad for a heart-stopping 270 kilometre an hour ride, just metres above the jungle canopy. 'It makes it harder for them to hit us with a missile or rocket,' offers one of the crew as reassurance. The rebels have just overrun an army-held village. Ellis has been called in 'to sort it out'.

Rice paddies and coconut trees flash by, so close that I flinch – to the amusement of the crew. The margin for error is zero. Our lives are in the hands of pilot Ellis. If he flinches, it will be all over in an instant.

The back of the helicopter is stacked with rifles and grenades. If we are forced down in a rebel area there will be no prisoners. The crew will fight their way out, or die. Ellis' view: 'If you do this job and worry about dying then you should go home and do an eight-to-five job back in the first world.'

The RUF's vow to cut out the hearts of captured mercenaries is no idle threat. In 1995 the rebels ambushed a mercenary force of ex-Gurkhas, led by a former American colonel, Robert Mackenzie. According to eyewitness reports, the wounded Mackenzie was dragged back to the rebel base, and tortured in the presence of seven Roman Catholic nuns being held hostage. His heart was then carved out and eaten by his captors. In a sense it was a mark of respect – his killers believed that by their actions, they would absorb Mackenzie's power and bravery.

'Five minutes to target,' warns Ellis on the intercom. Time enough to briefly ponder the ethical issues. If I survive a crash landing, should I pick up a weapon in self-defence, sure in the knowledge that, as a European, the rebels will assume me to be a mercenary? Or will I maintain my non-combatant status to the end, hoping that some drugged and dread-locked teenage rebel, going by the name Commander Superhero, will make the distinction between media and mercenary?

I need not have worried. Later, Ellis reveals that if Geoff and I were facing imminent capture, he'd given orders for the crew to shoot us. He smiles when he says this – I'm still not sure he was joking.

Smoke from burning houses marks the target village. 'Are you going to fire?' asks Fred on the intercom.

Ellis: 'I see them. I'm not sure if they are civilians or not – there are not supposed to be any civilians here. It's all supposed to be a rebel area.'

Seconds later, he unleashes hell. A volley of 80-millimetre rockets shreds a row of houses. 'These rockets were used very effectively in Chechnya,' Ellis remarks. Now they very effectively shred a row of houses and anyone hiding inside. 'You can tell the difference between a rebel and a civilian. You get the feeling, you can tell the difference,' he insists.

Arbitrary decisions of life and death at 270 kilometres an hour.

The door gunners open up, picking their targets with slow deliberate aim, tracer rounds arcing towards the ground like the stream from a deadly garden hose. There's no Hollywood bravado, just a cold clinical efficiency to it all. This is the business of contract killing.

To many, it's morally reprehensible. Human Rights Watch accuses the crew of indiscriminately killing civilians by targeting marketplaces. Ellis says the RUF use villagers as human shields. If he's fired at, he shoots back. 'Rebels are carrying guns. Civilians aren't carrying guns. If a civilian is carrying a gun he is a rebel, so he is a target.'

But the rebels are also armed with shoulder-fired missiles. Ellis takes no chances, throwing the aircraft around the sky. The floor is awash with hundreds of expended machine-gun shells, a sea of brass, rolling from side to side as the gunship lurches at high speed.

The crew spots figures huddling under a river bridge. The cabin shudders as another deafening rocket salvo is fired, the barrage sending sheets of water high into the air. 'The rebels are terrified of this aircraft – when they see it, they just run,' says Ellis. From my position in the back of the gunship it's impossible to determine what they're shooting at. All I see is the occasional flash of movement through the tree canopy below.

Then it's all over, and we're tree-hopping back to base, over villages where the people don't run away. They recognise Wor-Wor Boy – smiling, waving, cheering as the unlikely saviours of Sierra Leone scream overhead.

Fijian Fred, hunched over a still-smoking machine, is transformed. Minutes ago he was wild-eyed with controlled aggression. Now he's a laughing, grandfatherly figure waving to the kids below. The other door gunner, Christophe, remains expressionless, staring blankly at the passing scenery. I wonder what these men dream about at night.

In one sense this is a mission of redemption for men more accustomed to being vilified. In other parts of Africa mercenaries are, with considerable justification, accused of perpetuating rather than ending conflicts. But here in Sierra Leone they are, for many, heroes who stood and fought when everyone else had fled.

Ellis and his crew first landed in Sierra Leone in 1995. Like so many other mercenaries, he came for the money. Hired by the South African outfit Executive Outcomes, his crew joined a force that in just a few weeks drove the RUF out of the diamond fields and to the brink of defeat.

Then the soldiers of fortune were forced out of the country themselves, after allegations they were receiving diamond-mining concessions, dubbed 'blood diamonds', as payment. Ellis says this wasn't true. They'd demanded, and received, cold hard cash for their efforts.

'It was pressure from the international community for using a private military organisation,' Ellis says. 'I think the World Bank had some input on that. Executive Outcomes had just about achieved their aim when they were forced to leave.'

Eighteen months later he was back, this time flying for the UK-based mercenary outfit Sandline International, providing air support to a West African intervention force, ECOMOG. That contract also crashed amid political uproar in Britain, when it was revealed that Whitehall had tacitly approved Sandline's involvement while publicly supporting a UN arms embargo on Sierra Leone.

Yet when the pay cheques stopped, Ellis and Fijian Fred kept flying and fighting. At one stage, Ellis says he and his crew were owed more than a million dollars – twelve months' worth of back pay and costs. These soldiers of fortune realised they were fighting for a cause they actually believed in.

With the rebels in the suburbs of Freetown, and the West African peacekeepers in disarray, it was Ellis, at the controls of a lone helicopter, who is widely credited with saving the capital – evacuating nearly a thousand civilian refugees to safety.

He finally drove the rebel columns from the city in desperate strafing runs – but not before the RUF had slaughtered thousands more: mainly women and children. Many of the survivors wished they too were dead, left bloodied and limbless after encountering their would-be liberators.

After the smoke cleared in Freetown, and the rhetoric in Whitehall ebbed, Sandline quietly gave Ellis the helicopter, an aging Russian transport that they had nicknamed 'Bokkie' – aviation's equivalent of a flying dump truck.

It was intended as payment in lieu – but Ellis says Bokkie's flying days were over. He simply parked the disintegrating, battle-damaged chopper on the tarmac and walked away.

The West African peacekeeping debacle was in turn replaced by broader international concern. 'Something must be done,' declared the United Nations, suddenly horrified by the bloodbath. First world nations provided the angst, but it was left to the developing world to send the peacekeepers: a poorly equipped, faction-ridden force with no clear mandate which rapidly found itself bogged in the mire of a civil war with no peace to keep.

Early in 2000, Sierra Leone's tragic cycle repeated itself. The rebels took five hundred peacekeepers hostage and, with the UN mission in chaos, were once more at the gates of Freetown.

A UN convention bans the use of mercenaries, yet Ellis, at the controls of his newly acquired Wor-Wor Boy, came to the rescue of embattled UN units on several occasions, buying valuable time until Britain could land paratroopers to defend the city.

As one of the new breed of 'corporate soldiers', Ellis insists he only works for legitimate governments. But down in the jungle below us are others who work for the highest bidder. The rebels control most of the diamond fields, smuggling out up to US$100 million dollars worth of stones a year, so there's plenty of money for hired help.

'An Israeli guy and a Russian guy were arrested – they were giving assistance to the RUF,' he admits. A couple of Ellis's old comrades from South Africa are training the rebels. If they get in his way during a day at the office, 'It's just bad luck.'

While the Sierra Leone government is willing to hire 'private military contractors', God help any foreigners caught working for the other side.

A senior Sierra Leone police intelligence officer later tells me that during a rebel assault on Freetown in 1999, his men captured six Ukrainians acting as combat advisers to the RUF.

The senior officer reveals that the Ukraine government was formally notified, but denied any responsibility for the men. The officer says there was no hearing, no trial. The six were simply taken outside and shot. Being a mercenary pays well – but only if you are on the winning side.

I raise this story with Neall Ellis shortly after we've landed safely back at base, but it's not something on which he wants to dwell. 'I don't know that it was six ... I don't think anyone was actually arrested. I don't know anything about that ...' Ellis stumbles; his quiet, assertive manner momentarily fails him.

Uncomfortable with his local hero status, Ellis acknowledges the moral ambiguity of his calling. Working for Zaire's President Mobutu Sese Seko in 1997, Ellis found himself on the losing side, his employer overthrown, and his helicopter grounded by lack of spare parts. He and two others spent a week fleeing through the jungle on foot, outwitting a posse of rebels in hot pursuit. They eventually escaped across the Congo River in a stolen boat – having been robbed of everything but their underpants. This adventure reinforced his legendary status among mercenaries, but perhaps also explains why he is so reluctant now to accept the mantle of Freetown's local hero. Mobutu was a murderous despot, and Ellis was being paid to keep him in power.

As he shuts down the aircraft, and the ground crew sweep out the bullet casings, another helicopter with civilian markings lands nearby. Two Europeans dressed in polo shirts and chinos stride towards us, beckoning Ellis over for a chat. They also exude the purpose and manner of white Africa's social rugby set. It finally dawns on me why a group of mercenaries attempting to mount a coup in the Indian Ocean state of Seychelles tried to infiltrate the country posing as a touring rugby team. But there's no sporting bonhomie today. For the first time since we met, Ellis waves the camera away, warning us, for our own safety, not to film his mysterious visitors.

There's a brief discussion, they shake hands, and Ellis returns to tie down his helicopter. The pair are South African, recruiting for an upcoming 'job' in a nearby African country. Ellis has declined the offer of work. From such casual meetings are born so many of Africa's coups and wars.

There's another revelation in store as we walk back into Ellis's operations room, wallpapered with maps, buzzing with radio chatter. The Sierra Leone government regards this mercenary helicopter operation as the country's only effective defence against the RUF. So too, apparently, does Whitehall.

Across the room, I spot a figure in a British camouflage uniform, with the rank of Royal Air Force squadron leader, issuing orders down the phone. We both do a double take. My surprise, only matched by his instant recognition of a journalist. At this point I'm about as welcome as an RUF guerrilla.

There's a flicker of dismay on the face of the British officer, before he decides to ignore me. Perhaps he has a premonition of what inevitably follows my reporting of his involvement here – the heated questions in the British Parliament on yet another covert entanglement with mercenaries, and the London tabloid headlines screaming 'Britain Backs Aerial Killers'.

Neall Ellis finds it all mildly amusing. 'He's technically an adviser, but he's basically running the show,' he laughs.

Apparently the British had tried to stop Ellis from taking us on the mission. An order he ignored. No-one is going to argue with the man who saved Freetown.

Back at Paddy's bar that evening the crew, still in flying suits, are propping up the bar, ignoring the spectacular tropical sunset. Only Christophe, the self-professed tourist, has changed into evening leisure wear. It's another *Dogs of War* moment.

Fijian Fred no longer glowers at us, he's all backslaps and smiles. We now have the bond of shared adversity. I laugh out of relief that I'm still alive. But Fred seems to need the adrenalin surge of combat to come alive. 'I enjoy this job,' proclaims Neall. Fred nods in agreement, still a man of few words.

Now, out in the darkened jungle, there probably lies the mangled human wreckage of their 'good day's work' – but there are no regrets. I'm told the RUF are vermin, who can never be trusted. What jars is that this is the private view of UN officers and foreign aid workers who come over to pay their respects to the crew.

In Sierra Leone, compassion and neutrality died a long time ago.

The mission had taken barely an hour. One crowded hour, as the saying goes. Tomorrow the crew of Wor-Wor Boy will be back at the 'office' to do it all again. But for Neall Ellis, this is the last campaign. The mercenary who arrived on a contract, but found a cause.

'We're earning some money to keep ourselves going, but I want to stay here. I like this country, I believe there is a lot of potential here. I'm intending to make this my country, where I'm going to stay, where I'm going to retire.'

JILL COLGAN is a senior foreign correspondent with the ABC based in Washington DC.

She has more than twenty years' experience as a broadcast journalist, working in television and radio. Washington is her third posting as a foreign correspondent for the ABC – she has previously held positions as Bureau Chief in Tokyo and Moscow.

During her time with the ABC, Jill Colgan has worked extensively for Radio and Television News and Current Affairs, holding senior reporting positions at the *7.30 Report* and *Four Corners*. In recent times she has been the ABC's correspondent in Afghanistan in the lead-up to the military campaign against the Taliban and in the post-Taliban era. She has reported extensively from the Middle East, covering the *interfada* from both the Israeli and Palestinian perspectives. She has covered the war in Chechnya and was reporting live from outside the theatre siege in Moscow in October 2002.

More recently, Jill Colgan has reported on the build-up to the war in Iraq, providing coverage from the US for the duration of the war and analysis on the aftermath of the conflict – economic, political and social.

A Baby in Bethlehem: Palestine

It's stiflingly hot. The two of us are loaded down with camera gear and waiting for an Israeli soldier to arrest us, or worse.

Our interpreter tells us the booming loudspeaker from the nearby mosque is warning that anyone caught out on the streets during this curfew will be shot.

I knock on the door of a small, cream-coloured sandstone apartment block, hoping desperately someone answers. Within moments I'm looking up into the round, brown face of Issa Daboub.

'Hello?' He says it as a question, peering down from an upstairs window. We explain we're Australians, we're with the media, can we come in? Seconds later he is at the front door of the block, quietly murmuring and smiling, 'Please, please, come in. Come in – welcome to my home.'

The place is Bethlehem – one of the most holy places in all Christendom, the birthplace of Jesus Christ the Saviour. A town inhabited by Palestinian Muslims.

The date – April 2002. Around Israel and within the Palestinian territories, scores of men, women and children are being killed as Israelis and Palestinians tear each other apart in a religious and territorial war – Muslims killing Jews and Jews killing Muslims.

Suicide bombers from extremist Palestinian groups are randomly killing dozens of people as they detonate their explosives-packed bodies in crowded markets, on busy thoroughfares and on rush-hour buses. They do not differentiate between man, woman, child or infant. In turn, Israeli soldiers are killing militants and innocent civilians alike as armed units pour into Palestinian towns, to hunt down and exterminate the terrorists in the streets and homes where they live – and to flush out their well-hidden ringleaders.

It is a time of horrendous bloodletting.

On this day, 18 April, all of Bethlehem is under curfew. The sun is blazing down – surprisingly hot for this time of year. At the town's heart, heavily armed Israeli soldiers and tanks surround the sacred Church of the Nativity where nearly two hundred people are holed up. A tense siege is underway – the aftermath of a firefight days before when Israeli troops swept into the town to flush out wanted terrorists. Local police and militants resisted but as the overwhelming might of the Israeli force bore down on them, a group of militants grabbed their wounded and took refuge in the church. They also took dozens of monks, nuns and civilians hostage.

Now there is an impasse, interrupted only by sporadic gunfire between the Israeli troops and the men in the church. The Palestinian gunmen know the Israelis will not storm the 1600-year-old church – it is sacrosanct. Deep within lies the very site where Christians believe Jesus Christ was born. For centuries, pilgrims have travelled from all over the world to visit this simple grotto. Religious leaders around the globe are watching, fearful this holy place may come to ruin.

Just out of firing range of the church, dozens of local and international journalists and camera crews have taken up vantage points on nearby rooftops to film the gun battles and explosions that burst from and around the church. Gophers ferry water and supplies as the media watches, waiting for the conclusion to this bloody siege. From time to time there is a temporary truce as militants send out hostages and the wounded, while the Israelis send in supplies and mediators.

It is a siege that will continue, day and night, for more than five weeks. On this morning, the tension has heightened with Israeli soldiers forcing all the media down from the rooftops and away from the church. There is a feeling another violent clash is coming. Down below, the streets are crammed with stinking rubbish, burnt and crushed cars, debris and damaged buildings – all torn apart by Israeli tanks. Cameraman, Mark Slade packs the equipment and together we carry it down, clambering around the rubble below and pulling back with the rest of the media.

No-one doubts the warnings from the Israeli troops and we need to find somewhere safe. But we still need a vantage point, and our Palestinian fixer, Samir, is trying to find someone in town he knows. He remembers Issa Daboub and soon I'm knocking on the door of Issa's apartment block. Within minutes we're inside, deeply appreciative of the cool, dim interior of the white plain-walled block.

Issa is gracious and welcoming at this sudden intrusion, treating us like honoured guests – constantly smiling and waving his hands to encourage us up the stairs to his home. He shares the apartment block with his extended family. No-one has ventured out for days though – the curfew has kept them indoors. Issa then, is dressed for indoors, wearing his house slippers and socks below pale grey, light canvas trousers and a dark-blue striped shirt. His hair is shaped like a monk's tonsure and is black but greying at the sides. His belly is rounded, his cheeks full – and he has one of the kindest faces I have ever seen.

We've explained we need a vantage point from which to safely view the church and Issa is able to take us up to a high window at the top of his stairwell. The small space will hold the two of us with our equipment and we can see the church. Just a few steps further up, there is a door leading onto the rooftop. There is still no sign that the shooting has resumed so we make a quick, furtive foray onto the roof.

Issa takes us to the edge of the building and quickly points out the different parts of the Church of the Nativity.

'This is the Greek Orthodox part,' he says and then swings his hand across. 'This is the Catholic part, and the white roof over the grotto (where Jesus was born) is in the middle of the church.'

He has lived his entire life in Bethlehem. The Palestinians are his people, but this is not *his* religious war. Caught in this conflict between Muslims and Jews, Issa and his family are Christians.

'I am forty-six years old, and always, I go to this church' he tells me in stilted English. 'Almost every Sunday and on every occasion – deaths, marriages, baptisms, etcetera. I feel this church is part of ourselves. My grandfather and my father, when I was young and small and was a baby, used to take me to church and pray with me, to teach me how to pray, how to have peace and love towards each other and people outside our home. His church – His place is under siege right now. I'm distressed, I'm disappointed.'

The terrible drama unfolding around him casts a cloud over his face and he becomes anxious and upset. Every now and again a 'popping' sound has us ducking as we speak – it sounds like a gun firing but it's hard to tell. We've spent enough time on the open roof he decides – it's time to go back downstairs.

In their small apartment two stories below, we meet his wife Elena, in her late thirties, and their exuberant four-year-old daughter Juliana, a small dark-haired delight who swings her talking 'Grover' doll by one arm, chatting incessantly. Grover wears a set of white rosary beads.

For weeks they have been prisoners in their own home. Issa was last able to go to work three weeks ago. They cannot sleep for the gunfire and movement of tanks. The warnings boomed out from the mosques by Israeli soldiers constantly remind them of the danger outside.

When they do dart out – it is a brief respite – to get food or to check on nearby relatives. If it's quiet, Elena will go to the rooftop and hang out washing on a rope line in the sun. Now – with the area around the church still silent, Elena cannot resist the temptation to take Juliana upstairs for some fresh air and the chance to play in the sunshine.

The top of the stairwell is housed in its own concrete walls and ceiling – standing behind it, they are afforded some cover on the otherwise open rooftop.

'For the last two or three days I would never come up here – it was too dangerous,' Issa says. 'I was afraid I would get shot.'

Juliana laps up the sunshine, running back and forth with her doll. She has grown increasingly restless, unable to play outside or see other children.

All the residents of Bethlehem are being worn down by this standoff. They cannot leave their homes. They cannot go to their jobs, schools and community centres. If they are ill, no ambulance will be allowed in to attend them. The militants have used the ambulances to hide in before, and the Israelis are taking no chances.

'I'm very concerned, very concerned … concerned about the future of my people and our national dignity' says Issa, stumbling over his words in anxiety. 'We feel that we are hurt, we are hurt very much. Christians and Muslims, we are hurt very much – too much, we are hurt. We are treated like animals – not like the human species.'

Issa is worried about his family and friends who have been out of contact. He is afraid he will lose his job and be unable to feed his family. But most of all, he is fearful for Elena. My first glimpse of his Russian-born wife showed me she is heavily pregnant.

Elena's face is broad and without make-up – her dark hair swept up and held with a bold blue alligator clip. Stray strands are pinned back with big, practical hair clips. She's dressed for comfort in a roomy blue Adidas windcheater and red track pants. Now, out of the cool apartment, she is looking tired in the heat and weary from worry. For all the problems her homeland Russia faces, nothing, she says, could have prepared her for the daily fear and anguish of living between two warring sides.

At eight months pregnant, neither Elena nor Issa knows how they will get to the hospital beyond the checkpoints when she goes into labour. I, like them, have heard the many stories of civilians caught outside during curfew, being shot or injured. An Australian doctor working in the hospitals here told me of a Palestinian teenager who was rounded up by soldiers. He was released after dark, during curfew, and was shot on his way home.

Another child was shot in the doorway of his home – his father risked being shot to get him to medical care.

Young Israeli soldiers, nervous in this hostile territory and waiting for a bullet in the back, will open fire at a sudden movement – be it child or adult, civilian or militant.

The couple become increasingly fretful as they go over the potential problems in getting to hospital. I've heard the other stories too, of injured or ill people dying before their families can get help. An ABC colleague filmed a shot man bleeding to death right before the eyes of the family whose home he'd staggered into. They were unable to get him medical assistance.

Issa and Elena know they are having a baby boy – a brother for Juliana. But they don't know the health of their unborn child – Elena had an appointment with her doctor a week ago but was unable to go because of the curfew.

'God forbid,' says Issa, 'if something happens to the baby. We cannot go to the doctor, we cannot go anywhere. It has been impossible to get doctors or ambulances in for three weeks. No-one can get in – even if you are dying, no-one can get in.'

Standing on that rooftop, surrounded by history, it is almost impossible to believe that in this, one of the holiest sites in the world – such violence reigns. That a town so symbolic of hopes for peace among men, is so mired in bloodshed. That in the town where Christians hail the birth of the Son of God, a mother is left desperately fearing for her unborn son, in a conflict she cannot escape. In 2000 years, it seems, mankind has not travelled far.

The heat and the lack of safety drive Issa, Elena and Juliana back downstairs to their apartment, leaving us to maintain our vigil on the church from the stairwell window.

A short time later, this family with so little – unable to replenish the meagre stocks they have until the curfew lifts – brings us a meal. Bread, vegetables, meat, cheeses and juice. It is enough to feed four people, let alone two. They insist Mark and I eat the meal ourselves – they do not share it.

When we have eaten all we can, they insist on giving us fresh fruit – dates and other stone fruit. It is unexpected hospitality and civility in the midst of something so very inhospitable and uncivilised.

In the hours that follow, Issa's sister and her husband, living in the same apartment block, come up to talk and spend time with us. They don't condone the use of violence by either side. They want the conflict to stop. They want their lives to return to normal. They want to live freely.

As the afternoon wears on, our deadline for returning to our Jerusalem office approaches. There is no sign of any breakthrough at the Church of the Nativity and, although we do not yet know this, it will be weeks more before there is an end to the siege.

As we leave, Issa and Elena refuse to take money to pay for the use of their rooftop or for the food. It is only when I make Elena promise to buy a present for her baby that she will accept a few notes pressed into her hand.

It is quiet outside – the expected clash at the church has not yet materialised. But we move quickly, knowing we're breaking the curfew and risk the wrath of the Israeli soldiers. We head away from the direction of the church ... distance means safety. Finally we reach a small hill, where a car has been scheduled to wait for us on the other side to take us back through the checkpoints and into Jerusalem.

As I climb into the vehicle I realise how easy it is for us to leave it all behind. But one thought remains constant on the drive back: the small Daboub family remains captive in the streets behind us.

Postscript: I have since contacted Issa and Elena to find out about the birth of their child. Elena went into labour in the middle of the night. A neighbour, an Algerian man working with the French Consulate in Jerusalem, agreed to take them in his car, at 2 am, through the checkpoints. With his international passport, he was able to get Elena past the soldiers and to hospital where their son Jonathan was born around 8 am. Both mother and baby were fine. When I spoke to them, months after the birth, Bethlehem was again under curfew and Issa is the only one in his extended family who has been able to keep his job. He is trying to support them all, not knowing what the future holds.

CHRIS CLARK has over twenty years' experience in television and radio news and current affairs, covering politics, international affairs and business for the ABC, ITN and the BBC.

Chris is currently presenter of *Midday News and Business* on ABC TV, having most recently been the ABC's Middle East Correspondent in 2001 and 2002. Before that he spent six years as an ABC correspondent in London and Moscow.

As Europe Correspondent in London from 1995 to 2000 and Moscow Correspondent in 1994 and 1995, he covered the major regional stories of the time including assignments in Northern Ireland, Bosnia, Kosovo, Serbia, Albania and Chechnya. And while he was based in Moscow, Chris travelled widely in the former Soviet Union.

In the late 1980s and early 1990s, Chris worked in London for the BBC and for two years as a Foreign Editor for ITN, working on *The Channel Four Daily*.

His earlier career with the ABC includes time as presenter of the national radio current affairs program *The World Today*, as National Business and Finance Correspondent for ABC Radio, and as National Political Reporter for ABC TV.

Chris has been a Walkley Award finalist.

Chechnya: A Cautionary Tale about Food and Guns

I have no idea if Aslan, my Chechen fixer, had ever heard J K Galbraith's remark that 'modesty is a vastly overrated virtue' – in any event, he had no need of the advice.

Who, I asked, was intelligent enough to run a place like Chechnya, if not Djokar Dudayev, then President of the tiny region?

'Well, there's me,' replied Aslan without missing a beat. Fair enough. In fact, when I thought about it, this former English Professor at Grozny University, regular contributor to the BBC World Service and A-grade 'fixer' was more qualified than most.

Aslan spoke an English that belonged to the BBC of the 1950s, what could be described as a 'civilised tone' – all rounded vowels of great precision. It was, of course, how the BBC once sounded and, like many who grew up in the Soviet Union, his pronunciation was a copy of the English he'd heard on the BBC World Service, listening on short-wave radio.

By contrast, life in Chechnya was becoming less civilised by the day.

Late 1994, and Chechnya was crazy and deadly. People wandered around the streets of the capital, Grozny, with AK-47s. While the rest of the world was about to chuck out the Filofax and snuggle up to the Palm Pilot, the smart Chechen man-about-town had his Kalashnikov assault rifle. Another modern classic. Don't leave home without it.

There were nightly gun battles between rival gangs fighting turf wars over everything from petrol supplies to cigarette smuggling. Trying to separate the criminal from the political was almost impossible when half the politicians were making their money from crime too.

But there was already a more formal conflict between forces loyal to Chechen President Djokar Dudayev and an equally gruesome bunch of desperadoes bankrolled and otherwise encouraged by Boris Yeltsin's Government in Moscow.

The issue was independence. After the collapse of the Soviet Union there were plenty of Chechens asking why they shouldn't have a country of their own, just like the tiny Baltic states, Latvia, Estonia and Lithuania.

Chechen resistance predated the Soviet era. It was subdued – with great difficulty and bloodshed – only after decades of effort by tsarist armies.

But the Chechens never gave up. They supported Hitler's invading army during World War II, and Stalin had them deported, en masse, when the war ended – around half a million of them were packed off to Central Asia. It was decades before most could return.

Feelings of injustice and betrayal on both sides were still raw and deeply felt.

And now Moscow was worried that Chechnya's self-declared independence would have dozens of other small republics following suit. If the Chechens got away with it, then who next?

And after months of economic and political pressure from both sides, the push for Chechen independence looked like descending into war. Our analysis was, immodestly, spot on.

Yet the place still functioned, after a fashion. You could buy fresh food at the market, cars were still on the streets, people went to work in their offices, children still trotted off to school.

And despite their reputation among Russians as little more than savages, Chechens still had time for life's courtesies.

The women who ran the little hotel where the few journalists who ventured here stayed were not from this tradition, however. We were given eggs for breakfast on the first morning, but for the next couple of days there was only bread and a bit of cucumber. We asked for eggs. There are none, came the answer.

Later that morning at the central market I was struck by the number of fresh eggs for sale – as though Grozny had suddenly become the fresh egg emporium of the north Caucasus. The only thing missing was a huge billboard declaring this the Chechen 'Festival of the Egg'! So we bought some eggs and returned triumphant to our hostess.

… And watched as they were turned into carbon, with the sort of malevolent satisfaction that only comes after a lifetime's practice.

Chechens are fond of a barbecue, and the addition of lighter fluid directly onto the uncooked meat is an innovation which has caught on big-time in these parts. It gives a sort of petroleum nose, a little like an aged Clare Valley riesling – but only a little.

Dining alfresco at one of Grozny's finest street restaurants one evening, the peace was disturbed by the arrival of two young Chechen men in a car, blaring music with enough bass to make an elephant's ears bleed. The blast, appropriately enough, was the work of another endangered species, the ageing Australian heavy metal band AC/DC.

As our evening meal flamed merrily away, illuminating the night sky and presenting a hazard to hot-air balloonists, the two young men came over and started making conversation.

It was the birthday of one of them, and were we really from Australia? Yes, and of course we enjoyed the fabulous sounds of one of Australia's most successful rock exports.

The charred remains were eventually brought to our little table as we were treated to another rendition of 'Highway to Hell' while chatting amiably about music, football and Kylie Minogue, more or less in that order. The Budgie, all agreed, was a fine talent.

Strictly speaking, Grozny by then was under dawn-to-dusk curfew, so our (by then) hosts insisted on escorting us back to our digs. Too risky without a local to look out for you, they said, with the automatic sense of duty which dictates that as their guests our safety was now their responsibility.

I sometimes cynically believe that the tradition of hospitality in this and other parts of the less developed world is all about creating obligation – which it is, but it's about more than *our* sense of obligation.

We see a sense of obligation almost always as a burden. Others are capable of seeing it as one of the essential ingredients of human affairs, without which, the terms *society*, let alone *civilisation*, don't really mean much. And in my experience, the more chaotic a society becomes the more individual courtesies matter, particularly to strangers. It's as if people are saying: 'I can't stop the war around me, but I can still be civilised as an individual. *I'm* not one of the barbarians dragging us to hell.'

But don't think I'm going all starry-eyed about Chechen society and behaviour. Read on.

When Aslan, our fixer and late of the English faculty at Grozny University, arrived for work the next morning he was carrying a gun – no, he was wearing a gun – like Dirty Harry wore a gun, in a shoulder holster, with a light jacket over the top.

I tried to ignore it at first, as if to say: 'Well of course, in Tasmania where I come from we don't even start the day without shooting a couple of close family members.' But it was no good – I had to ask. After a few kilometres of bumping along towards the hills to the south I expressed my surprise.

'I know,' he said, looking embarrassed. 'When I told my mother we were going up into the mountains today, she told me I had to take my gun.'

I tried to picture a woman in her mid sixties, absently looking up at her son as he left the house, going through the checklist: bus fare, handkerchief … 'Have you got your 12-shot automatic pistol, dear? Bye, don't be late – we're having a barbecue tonight. The boys with the AC/DC tape are coming over.'

Aslan explained: 'You have to understand that a Chechen man assumes that every other man will be carrying a weapon, and that if there's an argument or a fight he might be killed. So there are fewer arguments and fights if everyone is armed, because every man knows he might be killed if he starts one.'

So much for the theory. I'm not sure Aslan was wholly convinced by his own explanation, but Chechen thinking on the topic runs deep.

Practical application of this notion had already turned Chechnya into a lawless patchwork of gangs squabbling for control of what few assets there were – routinely shooting each other and murdering and maiming other innocents in the process.

And amid this mayhem some people were making money, a lot of money. You only had to look at the cars on the roads. There was a strong rumour that week that someone had just arrived back in town with a new Porsche, but so far there'd been no confirmed sightings. I was starting to think it was nonsense – I still think it was nonsense – after all, who would be stupid enough to drive a Porsche around Chechnya's rutted goat tracks? What you really need here is a Rolls-Royce to smooth away life's troubles.

It was sort of cream or off-white, not my favourite shade, and it was parked outside the sort of house you wouldn't give a second glance to unless it had a Rolls-Royce in the driveway.

We stopped, reversed and knocked on the gate. Eventually a man appeared. Sultan el-Mazayev told me the Roller belonged to his nephew – bright kid – who lived in the States and had various businesses. Sultan was just looking after the car. With his AK-47 resting against the wall, we chatted about events. Sultan was convinced that Dudayev, the Chechen President, was a disaster. These days, he said, you answered the door with a gun in your hand. And a war with the Russians would last a lifetime. Madness.

Time for lunch, and I piled far too much onto my plate – then couldn't eat it all, couldn't hide it under anything either, huge embarrassment. Sultan doubtless wondered why he'd invited this otherwise well-presented oik into his home.

Then we went for a spin in the Rolls, a fairly gentle spin, at least until the cows got off the road, then he opened her up a bit and the big tank leapt away. We cruised around for a while, then thanked our host and went on our way. Only later did I realise that I'd forgotten to listen for the clock ticking. Damn.

My one and only ride in a Rolls Royce and I forget the clock! Idiot.

We wandered up into the foothills of the Caucasus, towards the border with Dagestan. It was late summer and the green slopes were sprinkled with people scything pasture, a landscape dotted with the business of living. Donkey carts trundled past at regular intervals piled impossibly high with freshly-cut grass, all of it to be squirrelled away for the winter.

Aslan, trusted fixer, called in to see one of his aunties. 'I'm glad to see you carrying your gun,' she said. (You're right, she didn't say that, I made that bit up.)

But she did introduce us to her near neighbours. The grandparents had been exiled to Kazakhstan; now they were three generations under one roof, back home, proud that Chechnya was trying to go it alone, proud of their President, Djokar Dudayev, proud to have a little pocket handkerchief of a country to call Chechnya.

This was the problem. Chechen nationalism wasn't something dreamed up out of nowhere by Dudayev – though it was being used by him and others for, at times, utterly cynical purposes.

Chechen nationalism was an observable fact. What Chechens perhaps hadn't examined closely enough was how, exactly, it should be expressed. Did they really need their own state? Couldn't they cut a deal with Moscow?

And what of Yeltsin and the Russian political and military establishment? Shouldn't they compromise a bit more? Now both sides were acting without thinking first of the consequences. If war started, how would it finish? Hubris, as usual, on both sides …

It was late in the day, and we had a long drive back to Grozny in the dark. Not ideal. But it would have been the height of ill manners to refuse food. And I was starving.

We sat at the big table. All of us. There was Aslan, the man of culture, with his absurd pistol and shoulder holster. What would happen to him if Chechnya descended into war? And our hosts, a family who'd endured exile and might now lose their home once again.

A large pot was brought forth. As a guest, I was given first dibs. Naturally. I was hungry. I piled a large spoonful of steaming, stewy goo on my plate and put some in my mouth. I nearly threw up. Surely there'd been some mistake? Were my hosts trying to poison me? Dreadful! Did they really think that I should put this in my mouth? Exactly what part of the sheep were we talking about here? You call this hospitality? Never.

I struggled through one mouthful, but I still had a huge pile of gizzards in front of me and I couldn't just leave them there. To do so would have been the height of rudeness. I had to force them down.

There was a brief moment when reaching for Aslan's pistol seemed the only honourable course: 'Just popping outside, I may be some time …'

Instead, I ate – and learned a lesson.

Postscript: Russia invaded Chechnya in late 1994, and although I returned to report some of the conflict, I've not seen Aslan or any of the other people mentioned in this story again. The war – which has claimed around one hundred thousand lives continues, despite various ceasefires and political deals.

GREG WILESMITH is the Executive Producer of *Foreign Correspondent*, the ABC's award-winning international current affairs television program.

In 2001 and 2002, Wilesmith was Head of Policy and Program Development for ABC News and Current Affairs and Executive Producer of Elections and Special Coverage.

He was one of the ABC's Europe correspondents, based in Brussels between 1997 and early 2000. He covered the Kosovo guerrilla war, and reported from the Yugoslav capital, Belgrade, during the entirety of the NATO bombardment of Serbia and Kosovo for eighty-eight days in 1999.

Wilesmith was the ABC's Middle East Correspondent between 1987 and 1991. He reported the Gulf War from Iraq and Saudi Arabia, entering Kuwait as it was 'liberated' by Coaltion forces.

He began his international reporting career freelancing for ABC News and Current Affairs (Radio) from East Africa in the late 1970s.

He is a Walkley Award winner and lives in Sydney with his family.

A Resident of Montenegro

There are few things more ludicrous than trying to push an armoured vehicle weighing several tonnes. Accordingly, I left my colleagues heaving and puffing and strode off to what I hoped was the nearest petrol station, swearing silently and plotting revenge on the bastard who had caused us to be stranded.

We'd flown into the Serbian capital, Belgrade, in 1998 and picked up our white four-wheel-drive Land Rover, specially plated with armour and strong enough (it was claimed) to provide protection against mines and snipers. Collection point was the car park in front of an enormous dark glass box called the Intercontinental Hotel. The black plastic and chrome lobby was a favourite hangout of the thugs of the Slobodan Milosevic regime and appropriately enough was the scene, less than a year later, of one of the most spectacular assassinations in Belgrade in recent times – of which there have been not a few – of the creepy war criminal, Zeljko Raznatovic, generally known as Arkan.

The armoured vehicle's owner, a Croatian entrepreneur with whom I'd been in telephone contact from the ABC bureau in Brussels, had boasted of its specially fitted extra petrol tanks. But petrol, I reflected on that hot, frustrating walk to the garage along the main southbound highway from Belgrade, must be an optional extra. Not to mention a faulty fuel gauge which, when we'd set out less than half an hour previously, had shown more than half full.

By the time I returned bearing a can of petrol, Katy and Tim, strong willed and strong limbed, had done a mighty job in advancing the expedition to Kosovo by several hundred metres. There were, however, another four hundred kilometres ahead if we were to reach Kosovo by nightfall. At least I was in the best of company. Katy Cronin, also based in Brussels for the ABC, was cheerful in almost all circumstances, as was Tim Bates, camera operator and editor, who was in the habit of asking with irony, as we'd set off on our treks around the Balkans, 'What can go wrong?'

It had become obvious, before running out of petrol, that our vehicle was top-heavy, inclined to slew and slither even on the straight. By the time we'd turned off the main highway onto the back roads leading to Kosovo, arms and backs were aching from the strain of keeping Son of Heffalump on the road. (The original Heffalump, named after a large, blundering cartoon character then much favoured by my children, was an even more difficult beast to drive. It had been wrangled earlier in the year on our first visit to Kosovo, just after a massacre of ethnic Albanians – known as Kosovars – near Drenica.)

A Serbian army convoy of tanks and trucks slowed progress in the valleys outside Priština, the dusty and far-from-pristine capital of Kosovo. On that night, though, the ethnic Albanian guerrillas of the Kosovo Liberation Army, known as the UCK and (pronounced *oo-cha-ka*), left us well alone and we headed for the doubtful delights of the Grand Hotel.

Overstatement is a Serbian trait. My Serbian friends would proclaim that they were, as of course I knew full well, 'the strongest, bravest, smartest people in the Balkans' if not in Europe – a strength of opinion seemingly undiminished by the disintegration of Yugoslavia through the 1990s as Slovenia, Macedonia, Bosnia and Croatia separated from the overbearing Serbs. Kosovo was just the latest in a long line of wars of independence.

The lobby of the Grand was dirty and dingy, occupied by black-leather-clad oafs with bad haircuts and sunglasses stapled to their ears. Entire days were spent hunched over tiny cups of vile black coffee, watching the comings and goings of the visiting hacks, diplomats and aid workers whose movements would be reported to various – and competing – Serb intelligence services.

As a rule, I quite like shabby hotels, which – given an unhealthy interest in mad, bad regimes in Africa in the late 1970s, the Middle East in the 1980s and 1990s, and now the final death throes of Yugoslavia – was just as well. Yet I never warmed to the Grand, with its slovenly staff who seemed never able to remember a reservation, let alone find a telephone number, not to mention the unmade dirty beds, the scabrous carpets and the windows that faced the rising sun with rarely a tatty blind to shield it.

Apart from a few graceful old mosques, Priština was a squalid, garbage-strewn, smelly dump – the product of the previous decade during which the Serb minority, at the instigation of Milosevic, had throttled the largely autonomous province of Kosovo and imposed a form of apartheid so calculated to produce misery that even the Boers of South Africa would have been ashamed of it.

After years of forbearance and the creation of a parallel, Kosovar-run state within a state, with its own schools and medical clinics and even a university (in which one day we filmed a class, conducted in English, on British property law), young Albanians were finally arming themselves and rebelling against the Serbs.

Our job was to saddle up Heffalump Junior every day and head off into the wild west of Kosovo, searching out the guerrilla war. Leaving Priština involved negotiating a series of Serbian checkpoints. They were manned by square-headed, so-called special police, clad in camouflage uniforms, with bulletproof vests and clunky helmets or occasionally woollen balaclavas. Quite why the Serbs had chosen blue as the dominant colour for camouflage I could never quite figure out, since the landscape was basic Balkans – muddy greens and browns or foggy grey.

Invariably, as we drove the byways in preference to the highways, we'd find the war, or more often the effects of this hit-and-run conflict – burnt-out Albanian villages, Serbian villages under siege, weeping widows and orphans on both sides. The challenge was to make these intensely human stories of loss and despair relevant to Australians halfway around the world.

Finding the rebels took patience. But one day, after our Albanian translator had made the right connections, Son of Heffalump was rammed up a muddy track. Light arms fire was crackling in the distance. In a crumbling walled courtyard UCK guards armed with Kalashnikov submachine-guns checked us over.

As with the Serbs, there was deep suspicion of foreign journalists and camera crews. Finally we were escorted down a tree-lined slope. The trees offered some limited protection against snipers up in the hills.

The UCK had made a discovery and were keen to share it with us. In a sheltered glade was a well and in the well was a body. Cameras rolling, it was pulled to the surface, bloated and distended. The story, as told by a Kosovar doctor conveniently on hand, was of an innocent villager abducted by Serb soldiers, interrogated, tortured, dumped – another life snuffed out in the name of maintaining Serbian control of Kosovo.

Several weeks of reporting these atrocities, day in, day out, had left us weary and dispirited. Serbian military tactics weren't working. The UCK were growing stronger and more daring. We could see the Kosovo civil war spiralling out of control. Yet our visas would soon run out and we had little confidence that another one would quickly be forthcoming from the Yugoslav Embassy after we returned to Brussels.

Over burnt meat and beer, pretty much standard Balkans fare, we heard from a British colleague that there might be an option on the visa front. It seemed that in Montenegro, the other constituent but disaffected republic which, with Serbia made up Yugoslavia, it was possible with a wink, a nod and hefty fee to become a resident. And with residency came the prospect of a multi-entry visa to Yugoslavia.

To test this theory the ABC team took no time at all deciding that a few days on the sun-drenched (we hoped) Adriatic coast were urgently required. In order to save the ABC the vast costs involved in filling up old Heffie with petrol and trundling over the mountains (Montenegro translates in Italian – for it was once a Venetian colony – as black mountain) it was felt that a much more satisfactory form of transport would be a red BMW that just happened to be available for hire.

So we drove in relative style to what all the signs on the outskirts of the Montenegro capital described as Titograd, named in honour of the great partisan hero who'd managed to hold fractious post-World War II Yugoslavia together. He'd achieved this ironically enough by (among other things) giving Kosovo and the ethnic Albanians a modicum of autonomy. Titograd had now been saddled with the less evocative name of Podgorica and was the worse for it.

We began the paper trail in various government offices. 'Were we planning to buy property in Montenegro?' 'Well, no, not exactly.' I secretly doubted that the ABC budget would quite stretch that far. 'How about a long-term rental of a room in the Hotel Crna Gora, would that suffice?' Our translator, Marko, communicated the proposition. It seemed it just might, but would take a few days.

Clearly, there was time for lunch. Wanting to show off the delights of Montenegro, Marko offered to drive; and as he knew the way to the Adriatic, this seemed sensible. It was not. He took our automatic buckling of seatbelts as an insult to his ability as a driver. After all, he said, during the Bosnian War he'd escaped to London to work as a taxi driver.

We'd been scared numerous times in the previous weeks in Kosovo, but Marko at the wheel of the BMW was like a man possessed, passing other cars on blind corners on the coastal cliff road. Katy took charge, ordering half-speed. Shaken *and* stirred, we fetched up at the port of Kotor. After throwing down a round of calming brandies, splendidly fresh fish and salad was consumed with relish. Gazing onto silvery lake-like waters with towering mountains all around, the slopes dotted with Italianate villas, we felt a collective sense of peace noticeably absent in Kosovo.

The problem with breaking away from covering a war and enjoying the normal pleasures of life, like eating, sleeping and reading, is that it seems close to crazy to go back. However, with the first part of the Montenegrin residency process accomplished, there seemed little justification for hanging about, so we headed the BMW back up the hills to Kosovo, and yet more stories of conflict, before returning to the relative sanity of Brussels.

Early in the new year we landed in Belgrade again on a *Foreign Correspondent* shoot. The subject was the struggle of a charismatic newspaper publisher, Slavko Curuvija, to have his newspaper *Dveni Telegraf* distributed in Serbia. Milosevic had done his best to close down critical media. Curuvija sought to exploit Montenegro's more liberal climate by publishing his paper in Podgorica and smuggling tens of thousands of copies by road, rail and air back into Serbia. The battle of wills between Curuvija and an increasingly desperate and draconian government seemed a good vehicle by which to tell the broader story of the crisis in Yugoslavia.

Mass murder in Kosovo forced a temporary abandonment of our assignment. Late one night in Belgrade, word filtered through that there'd been significant killing in the village of Racak. Some hours and many telephone calls later, another Heffalump was located. Early next morning we were off again to Kosovo, and twenty-four hours later we drove, in convoy with other media, through the fog into the freezing village. It was spookily quiet. Hundreds of Serb paramilitaries were on the outskirts, armed and dangerous, but none seemed to be in the centre.

Finally a villager came out of hiding and took us to the mosque. There, laid out in neat rows on the cold marble floor, were row after row of bodies. Rigor mortis had set in. Sun shone through the windows, causing steam to rise from the thawing bodies. There were old men, and some young, a woman and a child. A young girl, perhaps twelve years old, came out of the mosque with tears streaming down her face. 'Mother, mother,' she cried, 'I saw my father in there.'

In the interviews that followed, it emerged that fifteen villagers had been shot in the fields, lined up in a row and executed; some others had been shot where they stood in the village. The death toll was more than forty. As we left the village the sounds of a Serbian advance were evident. They were coming back to collect the bodies and to begin an 'inquiry'.

After filing our stories overnight in Priština, we returned to Racak and found it blockaded. After a time it became clear that as many as six hundred people had fled into the hills. The only way to establish what had happened in Racak was to follow them. Donning flak jackets and lugging a camera and tripod, we climbed up towards the snowline. In the shelter of a valley was a group of about fifty survivors, predominantly women and children; some were wrapped in blankets and shawls, but most were ill-prepared for freezing temperatures. They had horrifying stories to tell.

Through our translator, one of the leaders of the group, Amina, fixed me with a look and said, 'I would be so happy if someone would just shoot me and kill me so that I wouldn't have to run, so I wouldn't have to think about my children without a father, so I wouldn't have to think about the bodies in the mosque that I can't even go and bury.' As we were leaving a woman asked if she could come with us. With several sick children she hid in the back of the armoured car, and we smuggled them through the Serbian checkpoints to a village where relatives could care for them. We wondered how the Racak survivors would fare in the mountains if there was another snowfall.

William Walker, the American head of the OSCE (Organisation for Security and Cooperation in Europe) delegation in Kosovo, declared that what had happened at Racak was a massacre. It was what finally forced open the closed eyes and ears in Washington and in European capitals. Not so in Belgrade. As we resumed filming for *Foreign Correspondent,* it became clear that even relative liberals such as Slavko Curuvija had failed to recognise that Racak was a turning point. The world would no longer allow Serbia to continue its ethnic cleansing.

Fast forward to 23 March 1999. We were standing in a snaking queue at Belgrade airport. One of those times when it was important not to show one's nerves. Would the passport control officer accept that we were indeed genuine residents of Montenegro or would we be packed off on the next plane out? It seemed to me there was a glimmer of a smile from the officer at the gate as with a thump the passport was stamped. A few hours later Tim, Katy and I were staking out the marbled lobby of the Hyatt Hotel, along with other reporters and camera crews, jostling for the best spot. The sign, reminiscent of wild west movies, which politely asked visitors and guests to 'Check Your Weapons' with security, had been tucked out of sight.

Into this media maelstrom strode the square-jawed hitman of US diplomacy, Richard Holbrooke. His title, at that time, was Assistant US Secretary of State. But he carried more weight than that principally because he'd bullied Milosevic, several years before, into signing the Dayton Peace Accords which halted the Bosnian War.

On this day, Holbrooke had come direct from yet more hours of verbal head-butting with Milosevic. The US envoy had delivered an ultimatum that Serbian police and Yugoslav army units should end their terror campaign in Kosovo. Now in the lobby he looked as though he'd been coshed. His usual bravado had drained away. He didn't need to tell us: Milosevic was obdurate. The time for talking was over, war was inevitable.

Waiting to be bombed is not pleasant. There were echoes of Baghdad. We'd been in the Iraqi capital just before Christmas the previous year as US and British bombers had plastered it. We'd stood on the roof of the Iraqi Ministry of Information and filmed the missiles striking government installations, hoping all the while that our building wasn't on the target list.

A similar preoccupation with personal safety niggled as we climbed onto the roof of the Hyatt about thirty hours after the US delegation had swept out of town. Tim set up the camera, envious of our better-equipped colleagues with their nightscopes. Surely NATO had a good map of Belgrade. And why bomb the Hyatt? After all, if it was destroyed where would Holbrooke stay when he came back for the inevitable peace negotiations? It was the only five-star hotel in town.

All around us reporters were talking on mobile phones to colleagues stationed near Italian air bases. Bombers were taking off. It was just a matter of time. The air raid siren blared out shortly before dull thuds sounded in the distance.

Most interesting were the 'smart' missiles; from our vantage point they seemed to be not so much streaking across the sky as wobbling towards their pre-set targets. As expected, among the first targets was the Batanica air base, about twenty kilometres away.

I left Tim on the roof with his gear, where some of the crews had ordered sandwiches and coffee from room service – 'roof service' they joked – as though waiting for a football game, and descended to my room. Miroslav, an archaeology student and our translator, was waiting to see what lies the state television service would tell us tonight. Up on the roof, though, the Serbian police in their baggy blue camouflage were rounding up the hacks, confiscating the cameras and bundling them into buses.

Fortunately Katy was off the roof and filing for the morning radio bulletins. But Tim was caught. It was his second arrest within twelve hours. The first had been in dramatic style, atop a hill in a wooded park that just happened to be near a military base. Plain-clothes cops in their battered old Yugo careered in front of our car and emerged with pistols drawn. Out of the vehicle, hands in the air in true Hollywood fashion. 'What were we doing up on this hill? Didn't we know there was a military installation down there?' 'Of course not, we were just enjoying the park, seeing the sights.'

After a twenty-minute journey in which we were told not to talk or to ask questions, it was a relief to be taken to a police station where there were many questions. Fortunately, Tim hadn't shot a frame. Eventually, a police apology: we had to understand how sensitive things were. We did. They were going to be bombed – and the next time we were found in the wrong place they would throw away the key.

Later, after we'd heard about the roof arrests, I pondered this possibility as Miroslav and I bolted for his father's car and headed off through blacked-out streets on a tour of the city's police stations. Had they, by any chance, arrested a tall, brown-haired, bespectacled Australian cameraman? A surly sergeant at one pre-dawn stop suggested our problem wasn't exactly a top priority. After all, they had a war to fight. It was a fair point.

Tim and the others were released a few hours later. It could have been worse: the hotel had sent an employee to travel in the police bus with the media to ensure their welfare. Moreover, they'd delivered sandwiches and coffee to the station. It was, Tim thought, the ultimate in room service.

Not much sleep was had that night. It was to prove a pattern. Bombing, at least in the Belgrade area, rarely began before midnight. Most often the NATO bombers struck between two and four in the morning. We'd try to get a few hours kip before the inevitable *ka-boom*. It became a routine to stumble out into the corridor, checking all windows (the roof being by now a no-go zone) to try to get a fix on the target. The dilemma then was whether to charge off into the night, risking arrest (or worse, having the camera confiscated) or to wait until first light.

Early on in the conflict, hotel staff had roused us out of bed, pleading that we go, immediately, to the bomb shelter. They feared, they said, that NATO missiles had struck a chemical factory, releasing clouds of poison gas. We gathered, grumbling, in the cavernous lobby, the Italian reporters, as usual, outshining all the others in immaculate robes and slippers. Cursing NATO, we tried to telephone contacts in London and Brussels who might know what had *really* happened. Re-opening the bar seemed a sensible option, but the managers declined.

Belatedly it became clear that the hotel security people had used the poison gas scare to search our rooms. The Serbian secret police took the view that all foreign journalists were spies, that we must be hiding sophisticated beacons in our rooms, guiding NATO bombers to their targets! The hotel spooks were to be disappointed. We didn't prove to be a nest of spies after all – though a few carefully hidden portable satellite phones were seized.

At breakfast, BBC TV's veteran correspondent John Simpson confessed over scrambled eggs and toast, and to general laughter, that rather than be herded down to the basement he'd hidden, stark naked, behind the curtain, while his room was done over. The hotel staff had realised, after a time, that he was there, but had been too good mannered – or probably embarrassed about their searching – to end the charade.

Simpson led something of a charmed life. When we found ourselves in a muddy field north of Belgrade, inspecting the wreckage of an American stealth bomber (supposedly invisible to the Yugoslav air defence system), an old woman from a nearby house clumped up in her rubber boots and presented him with a small pitcher of *rakija*, a home-brewed plum brandy.

Despite the bombing, most Serbs demonstrated remarkable hospitality. Being Australian helped; so many uncles and cousins had done well in Sydney and Melbourne and elsewhere. I tried to exploit this tenuous connection – in particular with the staff of the government television station – to try to get our stories sent on their satellite uplink.

In the first few days of the war, when hard-liners of the Serbian Information Ministry were expelling media representatives from NATO countries, we found ourselves cast in the accomplice category, banned from feeding our edited stories from the television station. We weren't on the approved list, which comprised Russians, Chinese, Japanese, Greeks and a bunch of other odds and sods. So I'd rise at about 6 am and thrash together a script, and then spend hours trying – and mostly failing – to get a decent quality telephone line to file (given the time difference) for the evening news.

It was one of the most frustrating periods of my professional life, matching more than a few periods during the Gulf War. Our comfort level, though, was considerably superior to that of ABC staffers like Chris Clark and John Benes, who were deep in the mud, covering the Kosovo Albanian exodus to Macedonia and later in Albania. All the while we were banned from leaving Belgrade, without a government escort, to visit the latest bridge that had been bombed or building destroyed. I thought often of the Kosovars I knew and wondered whether they were being herded out of their homes by the Serbian special police, inspired to greater acts of cruelty by the NATO bombing. Thoughts also of Steve Pratt, of Care Australia, whom I'd met briefly before the bombing, and Peter Wallace, whom I knew not at all, cooped up in their cells, hearing the explosions and wondering what would become of them.

As always things improved. Eventually the censors agreed to view our stories and mostly passed them and allowed them to be sent by satellite, although every now and then – and for no apparent reason – they'd erase an image that was somehow thought to be a danger to national security. This would leave a black hole in the story, which needed to be edited in Sydney.

As the war settled into a pattern, the people of Belgrade spent less time in bomb shelters. I telephoned the newspaper publisher Slavko Curuvija in mid April. We agreed to catch up the following week. On the Sunday he went out to lunch with his wife. As he returned home two assassins were waiting. They didn't miss. The war had provided convenient cover to take out a political critic.

In due course NATO, angered at the reports coming out of Belgrade of missiles mis-targeted or going awry and killing civilians, demonstrated its commitment to free speech by bombing the television and radio station. As we watched firemen trying to dig a dying civilian technician out of the smoking rubble in the pre-dawn, I reported on a scratchy mobile telephone for the midday radio and television programs that it was a classic case of 'killing the messenger'.

On another long, black night I broached a wire fence with our long-suffering driver, Zoran, to watch the Chinese Embassy burn. The shriek of another missile overhead caused a stampede as people feared a second stage attack. In fact the target was a few kilometres away, a casino and hotel part-owned by the aforementioned Serb war criminal known as Arkan. He told me later that morning, indignantly, that he blamed the CIA. (The intelligence agency later claimed it had selected only one target in the entire war; unfortunately their map was outdated, and the Chinese Embassy had been struck by mistake.)

In abnormal times it is important, when possible, to do normal things. One night Katy and I went to the movies. *The English Patient*, set in World War II Egypt and post-war Italy, seemed a suitably weird choice of subject matter. We walked back to the hotel through darkened streets and across the Brankova Bridge, trusting that it wasn't on NATO's target list for the evening.

Occasionally, as the weather warmed and to relieve the boredom of war, there was time for lunch. Two floating restaurants were moored close together on the Sava River. Their names, *Dialogue* and *Argument*, represented typical Serbian humour. In spring sunshine one day Katy and a BBC reporter, Michael Williams, and I looked up from the desks of *Argument* to see flecks of white floating down. Retrieving several from the water, a waiter translated the dripping leaflets – NATO propaganda, he laughed, screwing them up and tossed them back.

We'd come to Belgrade expecting a short war. Almost three months later, the ABC's indefatigable International Editor, John Tulloh, who'd generally been in daily contact, had pleasure in telling us that we'd set two records. One was for sheer endurance, for the longest continuous coverage of a story, at least since the Vietnam War. The other was for spending the most money doing it. The news budget, it seemed, was shot to hell!

Postscript: The endurance record didn't last long. It was broken by the ABC's Middle East staffers Mark Willacy and Louie Eroglu during the Iraq War in 2003.

MICHAEL BRISSENDEN has been a foreign correspondent with the ABC for most of the past decade.

His first posting was to Moscow in 1994 where he reported on the chaos and excitement surrounding the disintegrating empire and the vast social, economic and political transition occurring in the former Soviet states and eastern Europe in the aftermath of the Cold War.

His most recent posting was as Europe Correspondent in Brussels from 1999 to 2003.

Michael has also covered the fall of Suharto's regime in Indonesia and reported from the Middle East many times, including from Afghanistan, and from other areas in the region during the Iraq war.

He was part of the team that covered events in New York immediately after September 11, and he has reported on every war in the former Yugoslavia from Bosnia to Kosovo and Macedonia.

In 1998 he won a Walkley Award for his series of reports on corruption at the highest level of politics in Papua New Guinea.

Before seeking the excitement of a life as a foreign correspondent, Michael worked for many years as a political reporter in the press gallery in Canberra. And he has now returned to Canberra as the Political Editor for the *7.30 Report*.

Berlin: The Wall in the Mind

It's 31 August 1994. I'm standing on a wooden platform watching the last few thousand Cold War foot soldiers goosestep around a memorial to fallen Soviet troops. They're kids, teenagers most of them, the third generation of Soviet occupation. As they march, they sing a specially composed song, 'Farewell to Berlin'. I've no idea what they're thinking. Are these eighteen-year-old conscripts burdened at all by history? Have they reflected on the significance of this final parade-ground duty? I'll never know, but it's a moment Rudy, our twenty-year-old East German sound technician, has been waiting for all his life.

Rudy's been busy the past few hours rolling out the flex cable for the camera positions on this side of the park. Now he's chain-smoking and taking in the show. He's wearing a heavy metal T-shirt, an unfashionable haircut and a scowl. He looks like any other detached, angry young man. But like almost everyone in this city, Rudy's a philosopher and a student of history.

'In a symbolic way this is freedom,' he says, 'physical freedom. They're leaving, and that's not just freedom in your head or your mind – it's physical freedom, and that's important.'

Berliners, as I was set to discover over the next few years, are like that. This is a city obsessed with its past and its future: the seat of power for two world wars, HQ for the world's most evil political fanatic, a symbol of Cold War division and now the face of a new united Germany. History blows in the construction dust that still settles around the now-smart shops lining Friedrichstrasse. Berlin wears its politics, its passions and its hopes on its pavements, and since the wall came down in 1989 it's been the most interesting, the most engaging and the most energised city in Europe.

The day before the parade I came into the city with a busload of Russian journalists. We'd flown in from Moscow on Aeroflot and landed at Tempelhof Airport. Extremist politics and architecture have a symbiotic relationship. In its day, Tempelhof was a technical wonder: a piece of engineering genius, the longest unsupported concrete canopy ever built. Today, as airports go, it looks small and somewhat severe. But I like it. It works. It's not trying to be a shopping mall, or a restaurant or a travel agency. It's an airport. A huge hangar of a space greets the traveller. A few airline and rental car counters line up almost apologetically against the perimeter walls, and just one baggage carrousel sits unmoving at the far end underneath an old-style ticking arrivals and departures board and a locked room with the word *Restaurant* written in 1930s go-fast lettering above it. Templehof has a sort of brutalist charm, but it's the sort of structure only totalitarian regimes can build. It was constructed by the Nazis, but it could just as easily have been built by the Communists. My Russian colleagues that day probably felt quite at home.

And for them nothing would have seemed too much out of place as we turned into Karl-Marxstrasse and rolled past block after block of Soviet Central Planning and the Kino International, a movie theatre built straight from the Central Committee architectural model. Exactly the same building can be seen in Khabarovsk in the Russian Far East, in Vilnius or in Warsaw. Many of them still sport exhortations to keep building for a better communism or glorifications of collective achievements of one sort or another. Up towards Alexanderplatz there's still a wonderful example of the genre: a classic constructivist style mosaic depicting the superiority of socialist science. In one panel a scientist in a white coat inspects a test tube, in the next a collage of futuristic buildings rise up pointing the way to a better communist future and next to that another scientist brandishes the plans for a no doubt ever expanding space program as a rocket blasts off above his right shoulder.

Then there's the Forum Hotel, a towering square block of a building. Back then it was an early example of the trend to 'Westernise' existing Eastern Bloc hotels. It's a fairly simple formula: leave the basic structure as is, put in new lifts, remove the cheap aluminium beds, install new carpet, a shower cubicle and cheap prefab plastic-and-chipboard furniture, double the price and try and make the staff smile. We checked in at a sparkling new reception desk. The staff wore new suits and corporate badges, but they still had the surly, indifferent attitude. Some things take longer to change.

This trip to Berlin was my first outside the former Soviet Union since I'd taken up the Moscow posting four months previously. I'd arrived hoping for a break from the sensual assault of socialist monumentalism. I was bitterly disappointed. Back then everyone seemed caught up in the euphoria of the changes and I had little appreciation for what was being left behind. The process that's now lamented by many East Germans as the colonisation of their country by the West was pushing relentlessly ahead. But Germany, and even more so Berlin, can never leave its history behind.

There were once 350,000 Soviet troops in the East. One of the great ironies of the years after the wall came down is that while the soldiers left their military bases — taking with them everything they possibly could, including the wiring, the toilets and the door knobs — thousands of Russian exiles flocked in to replace them. Berlin, the workshop of the final solution, is now the fastest-growing Jewish city in Europe. Most come from the former Soviet Union. For the first time since Hitler there are more than 100,000 Jews in Germany. Some see this as a final moral victory over the Nazis, but it's a Jewish renaissance that's tinged with apprehension, guilt and violence. The symbols of fascism are still displayed, even idolised, by the beer-can Nazis on the radical right-wing fringe of German politics. Proof that even as Germany tries to remake itself in the twenty-first century it remains shackled to the stains it left on the twentieth. The capital, though, has gone to extraordinary lengths to come to terms — publicly — with its terrible legacy. The city is dotted with Jewish memorials. A confronting Jewish museum designed in the shape of a shattered Star of David has now been opened and the city still plans to build the biggest monument of all over the top of the underground bunker where the architect of the Holocaust finally took his own life before the Russians over-ran the city. The two thousand headstones will take up an entire city block.

There are so many memorials now that even many Jews speak of holocaust fatigue. At one of the less monumental, Salomea Genin, one of Berlin's most remarkable Jewish re-émigrés, told me she was ambivalent about most of them and angry about what she sees as the official hypocrisy that they represent.

'Sure, they put up memorials,' she said. 'But most thirty-year-olds today don't know what their grandparents did during the Nazi time, and what's really happened is that the grandparents haven't talked about it. They've kept silent about it, and not only that, they've made a taboo of it. So the grandchildren think the Holocaust has nothing to do with them, and they can't imagine that their grandparents had anything to do with it. But, I mean, the Nazis didn't come from Mars, and they *were* the grandparents of today's German grandchildren.'

Salomea is a small, serious woman with a remarkable story. She has the well-manicured grey hair and cultured middle-class Australian accent that suggests membership of the Melbourne intelligentsia. Her German–Jewish family fled to Australia in 1939. She came back in the 1950s as an idealistic twenty-one year old, drawn to East Berlin not by her heritage but by her politics. She came as a committed Communist, but as her political idealism crumbled over the decades her own cultural and religious rediscovery took place. These days she lives in a little street in the Mitte district that was once called Tolerance Street. It's a small Jewish area that in the past had a Catholic hospital and a Protestant church as well as a Jewish cemetery, old people's home and schools. In the Nazi years the old people's home became a deportation centre.

As we walked around the cemetery Salomea told me how she'd left Australia to escape her Jewishness, but that once she was back she found the East Germans' efforts to forget the Holocaust forced her to confront her own religious identity. She got to the stage, she said, where she *insisted* on being Jewish, defying the organised atheism of the Communist regime. Every three weeks she held a service in her living room and threw open the windows to let the songs drift out so that everyone knew what was happening inside.

'Here, in the area where they tried to kill them all. That was our triumph.'

She's now turned her life story into a musical and performs it to small audiences in a local theatre.

'These days,' she says, 'every German is a Jew on Saturday night.'

But while there are confronting reminders all over Berlin of Germany's most shameful chapter, there's virtually no sign of the city's other defining historical period. There are precious few remaining Socialist monuments, and almost all traces of the famous wall have been scrubbed away. Near the Brandenburg Gate – once stranded in the no-man's-land of the Cold War – a path of bricks laid in the road is the only reminder. There are a couple of crumbling small sections on Bernaurstrasse but even they are gradually being obscured by bus shelters and other urban trappings of unification. The only significant section can be found standing in an industrial area down by the River Spree. It's called the East Side Gallery. The Berlin government invited about a hundred artists to paint murals on it. At one end there's an entrance to a scrap metal junkyard. About a mile away at the other end there's a run-down little tourist shop that sells postcards and dubious pieces of concrete to the tourists who pour off coaches and take photos of each other standing next to the most recognisable of the painted images – the famous kiss between the East German leader Erich Honecker and Leonid Brezhnev.

In 1999, ten years after the wall was breached, Helmut Kohl, George Bush senior, Mikhail Gorbachev and various other politicians came to pat each other on the back and recall their part in history. It was more a victory celebration than an anniversary.

Not one East German was included on the original speakers' list at the Reichstag. Only Gorby acknowledged the omission.

'There are some things I still find difficult to understand here,' he said. 'For example, the way some former politicians of the DDR are treated by the new country. It's strange that some of them who ultimately decided to open the wall are not here today.'

The fact that the long-despised concrete barrier had come down was proof to the rest of their own convictions. The wall was gone, and it could no longer impede their world view. By 1999 all that was left at the former border crossing point on Bornholmerstrasse were a few of the old lamps and the lane markings painted on the ground. On 10 November 1989, tens of thousands of East Berliners streamed across this checkpoint with tears in their eyes. They were met on the other side by West Berliners with champagne and fireworks. Ten years later a caryard had set up shop where the attack dogs and the border guards once ruled – a supreme irony for East Berliners, many of whom had had to wait up to fifteen years for a new car.

Now almost everyone can buy cars, but many in the East still resent the steamrolling of their history. The euphoria of freedom quickly gave way to the realities of the occupation. Almost overnight the social structures they'd lived with were replaced. Everything, from the economic system to education, social security and the law was absorbed by the West. What good was a lifetime's study of Marxist economics any more? What use was a collective factory manager to anyone? The young and the old both fared reasonably well. Twenty-year-olds now had the chance to chart a course to a profitable career, older workers found they were retiring on generous pensions. But the thirty- and forty-somethings, men and women my age, became the lost generation. University professors in the East found their departments scrapped. Second-rate academics from the West took all the positions in the new ones. Former state workers quickly found they couldn't compete for scarce jobs with CVs that were meaningless in the new market economy.

In 1989 Juan Roer and Roland Steper were both in their thirties. Juan lived east of the wall. Roland lived on the west side. They are both architects – educated, intelligent men. But when I met them ten years later their experiences of a unified country couldn't have been more different.

When he was just eight years old Roland saw his own backyard cut in two as the first barbed-wire coils were rolled out to mark the course of the wall. When it finally came down, he was one of the many West Berliners who seized the opportunity to move to the cheaper and, for them at least, more exciting atmosphere of the East. Berlin has always been one of Europe's most bohemian cities. The once decrepit streets of the East quickly became the new Mecca for movers and shakers like Roland. One night we drank too many beers at one of the eclectic bars in Mitte and watched the young and the beautiful, the wild and the grungy parade around us: a passing menagerie of sharp-suited money men, fashion extras and anti-globalisation protestors on a day off.

'Everything's changing all the time,' he said with obvious enthusiasm. 'This is unique. If you love this you can love Berlin. I love it.'

Unification opened up enormous opportunity for Roland. The reconstruction of the city was an architect's dream, but it depended which side of the wall you came from. Roland worked for a big West German company.

Juan on the other hand was an East German academic. By 1999 he had established his own restoration business in an old warehouse complex in the East. The office was basic to say the least – a big drawing table, a computer and a small electric heater. Juan said he was starting to do well, the business was bringing in some money. But he was still bitter about how hard he'd had to fight. He had tried to get work with big companies but always lost out to West Germans with more relevant qualifications. He tried to get a start at a number of universities, but again lost out to academics with West German teacher training. In the end, starting his own business was the only way out.

Juan's story wasn't unique. He didn't want the wall back, but he planned to vote for the old reformed East German Communist Party.

'At least,' he said, 'they are one of the East's last surviving institutions.'

In a way Juan was lucky. He had the skills and the motivation to start out on his own. Hundreds of thousands of others haven't been so fortunate. Like Juan, few of them would say they want the wall back, but equally not many of them have seen the 'blossoming landscapes' that former chancellor Helmut Kohl promised, and most yearn for what's been lost. So much so that enterprising individuals have even started to capitalise on the nostalgia. In a rundown building near one of the East's main railway stations, someone's opened a shop called 'Intershop 2000'. It takes its name from the communist-era hard-currency stores and it sells only products made in the East, like 'Club Cola' and 'Karo' cigarettes. These formerly popular Eastern brands still have consumer recognition, and they have attracted Western investors with a keen eye to a free market opportunity.

The city has tried hard to present a new face for the future, but in many ways Berlin has entered the twenty-first century as a city still divided. The old no-man's-land has been filled in with sparkling new buildings. Potsdammer Platz has become a concrete-and-glass wind tunnel much like anything you could find in the central business district of any modern capital. The Brandenburg Gate has been cleaned; fancy shops and hotels have reclaimed Unter den Linden. The Reichstag, the most important building of all, has been given the most successful and powerful reworking of any postwar building in Europe. Graffiti scrawled by the victorious Red Army soldiers has been left on the walls inside, a glass dome has been thrown over the top, and every day hundreds of German and foreign tourists line up to get the chance to look down at their city and their politicians who sit in full view beneath the feet of those climbing up the circular walkway.

Some critics have suggested parts of the city should have been left in ruins as an example to the nation and the rest of the world. Few Berliners would see it that way. But then again, few Germans would honestly say they feel like one nation. The wall in the mind is still standing, and Germany has a long way to go before the concrete and render of reconstruction truly unifies the people.

MICHAEL MAHER is the ABC's Asia–Pacific Editor and has been covering on Australia's neighbouring regions for over fifteen years. He is the ABC's longest-serving Indonesia Correspondent, having reported from the Jakarta Bureau from 1993 to 1998.

His reporting on the world's fourth largest nation and the fall of its dictator, Suharto, made him a winner, finalist or medallist in a range of industry awards including the Walkley and Logie Awards, the United Nations Media Peace Awards, the New York Film and Television Festival, and the Australian Human Rights Association Awards. He is the author of the book *Indonesia – An Eyewitness Account*; a contributor to *Diplomacy in the Marketplace: Australia in World Affairs*, a book on Australian foreign policy; and has written for *The Bulletin* magazine on Asian affairs.

Michael is an honours graduate in Asian studies. His interest in Asian history and politics first developed while growing up in India, Thailand and Burma.

Vietnam: Between Deadlines

The spell was first cast … by the tall elegant girls in white silk trousers, by the pewter evening light on flat paddy fields, where the water buffaloes trudged fetlock-deep with a slow primeval gait, by the French perfumeries in the rue Catinat, the Chinese gambling houses in Cholon, above all by the feeling of exhilaration which a measure of danger brings to the visitor with a return ticket.

GRAHAM GREENE ON VIETNAM

Every year from 1951 to 1955, the English writer Graham Greene escaped Europe's frigid winters for the alluring sultriness of Vietnam. There, this occasional correspondent for London's *Sunday Times* gave himself up to French Indochina's intrigues, its wars, its beauty and its vices. Especially its vices.

These were more languid days for foreign correspondents like Greene, days during which it was possible to appreciate the 'slow primeval gait' of a water buffalo or the scent of perfume on the rue Catinat without a mobile phone going off every five minutes with head office on the line.

In Greene's day, of course, there were no mobile phones let alone phones of the satellite and video varieties. Back then the lumbering telex machine was the medium of communication, and it had a calming, even civilising influence on the pace and temper of journalistic endeavour. The concept of 'on the hour, every hour' deadlines or 'live crosses' would have had Greene and his colleagues choking on their sundowners in bars across the Orient.

'So the war goes drearily on its way,' wrote Greene from the frontline. 'Lunching at Nam Dinh, I was asked by the general commanding whether I had ever had so good a soufflé before to the sound of gunfire.'

Alas, fifty years on, no-one has ever offered me soufflé to the sound of gunfire. The lot of the foreign corespondent today is to feed rather than be fed – to feed a voracious beast with an insatiable, twenty-four hour a day appetite.

But there are still occasions when the beast can be crossed. There are still days when it is possible to escape. These are days when you're on the road to Asmara, Bukittinggi or Makassar; days when beyond each mountain bend another startling vista beckons, when cooling breezes waft off the rice paddy stirring palm fronds and sweeping away lingering thoughts of looming deadlines. These are days when, out of mobile phone range, you allow yourself a quick, self-satisfied smile and quietly marvel: 'I can't believe I'm getting paid to do this!'

One such occasion involved Graham Greene and his beloved Vietnam. *Foreign Correspondent* commissioned me to retrace Greene's footsteps – to discover what it was about Indochina that had so captivated the English writer and provided the grist for one of his most celebrated novels, *The Quiet American*. Published in 1955, the novel was a work of remarkable prescience, staring down the future and foretelling the terrible tragedies that awaited the United States in the hamlets and jungles of a nation it didn't understand. It told the tale of jaded English journalist Thomas Fowler, a character shaped from Greene's own personal experiences in Indochina, and the zealous young American spook Alden Pyle who's hell-bent on saving the Vietnamese from the grips of communism. The two clash ideologically. And, of course, they clash over a girl.

For a fortnight I travelled the length and breadth of Vietnam, visiting the cities, the battlegrounds and the haunts that so fired Greene's creative energies. It was a journey which took me through Hanoi's boulevards lined with tamarind trees and gracefully fading colonial villas; to the Red River delta where Greene watched the French army slowly sink into the muddy plains under the weight of Ho Chi Minh's dogged Nationalist forces; and to Saigon where Greene availed himself of all the sybaritic pleasures this freewheeling river city had to offer: good French food, the boutiques, *patisseries* and cafes of the rue Catinat, the brothels, gambling houses and opium dens of the Chinese district of Cholon and the boozy camaraderie of the bar at the Continental Hotel.

It was in the bar – known to all its patrons as the 'Continental shelf' – that I met a Frenchman who once, under the same slow rotations of the same ceiling fans, had a drink with Greene. Philippe Caron came from a long line of distinguished naval officers. As a young navy pilot he had been sent to Indochina to fight in the war. For bravery on the battlefield he was awarded his country's coveted *Légion d'honneur* and now, in his seventies, he had returned to Saigon to reclaim some of the vestiges of his youth.

'I came here again to live out my fantasy,' Monsieur Caron told me as he examined the melting ice cubes in his pernod. 'I came to meet a dream creature to go on with me for the last period of my life. But it's now another country. What I have discovered is that it has nothing to do with the country I knew fifty years ago.'

In his worn, blue serge jacket, collar, tie and cufflinks, Caron appeared out of sorts with today's Saigon, admitting that the frenetic South-East Asian metropolis that is modern-day Ho Chi Minh City failed to match the fond memories of his youth. 'The best advice we can receive,' he confided, 'is that you should never again taste the waters of the past.'

But for a few hours that day, Caron let the waters of the past wash over him and drifted back to 1951, a time when France's colonial empire in Indochina was in its death throes. The French never conceived of it then, recalled Caron, but a crushing blow to Gallic pride was just three years away on the battlefield of Dien Bien Phu, and a cocksure United States was positioning itself to take over the fight against communism. It was into this cauldron of intrigue and instability that both Caron and Greene immersed themselves.

Greene was already a famous writer and was treated as a celebrity within the French colony. Aware that he had worked for

British intelligence during WWII, however, the French authorities also suspected that Greene might be spying on them.

'I was a very shy midshipman and he was already a celebrity,' Caron recalls of his fleeting encounter with the English writer. 'Greene was at the bar with his friend Lucien Bodard, who was also a war correspondent and very well known. Both were drinking very heavily before going off to Cholon to maybe have a few [opium] pipes.'

Throughout his life, Graham Greene was driven to escape. As a youth he escaped the demons urging him to commit suicide. Later he would escape a string of failed love affairs. Tellingly, he even named a volume of his memoirs *Ways of Escape*, musing '... sometimes I wonder how all those who do not write, compose or paint can manage to escape the madness, the melancholia, the panic fear which is inherent in the human situation.'

Opium was also an escape for Greene. 'Of those four winters which I passed in Indochina,' he wrote in his memoirs, 'opium has left the happiest memory.' It was in the crowded streets of Cholon, Saigon's Chinatown, that Greene discovered the balm to soothe his torment. Now, we are told, the opium dens have all gone. But walk the alleyways of Cholon today and you can almost hear the touts luring passers-by towards assignations at the House of Five Hundred Girls – and imagine that behind the mildewed facades of the shop-houses lie dimly lit *fumeries*, their prostrate patrons giving themselves up to the reverie that Greene once described as the 'white night of opium'.

Monsieur Caron enjoyed his pipes as well, assuring me: 'If you can stay moderate, [opium] puts you in great intellectual and psychological shape and you can carry on with your duties being a civilised man.'

Beyond the hedonistic distractions offered within the confines of French Saigon, however, Vietnam was a country at war.

It was in the Red River delta, in the north of the country, that Greene travelled to witness the fighting. A land where Gothic spires loom out of the iridescent paddy, this was once the heartland of Vietnamese Catholicism. On a visit there in 1952, Greene observed: '… in every village there rises up a church as big as a cathedral. From the plane you can count more than twenty of these big churches at the same time … One might imagine oneself in Europe seven centuries ago.'

Fifty years on from Greene's visit, I made my own way to the delta during the holy month of Lent. Despite their depleted numbers, the Catholics of the area could be seen observing the Stations of the Cross, worshipping in the ornately devotional manner borrowed from Europe centuries ago. As we filmed, worried looks were directed our way. The government of the Socialist Republic of Vietnam has been at pains to present itself as a champion of religious freedom. But the imprisonment of priests and the unwillingness of Vietnamese Catholics to talk openly about their faith are sure signs that such freedoms are far from guaranteed.

In Greene's day, however, the bishops of the Red River delta wielded the power of feudal kings. They were an integral part of Vietnam's unruly political patchwork, making enemies of both the French and the Communists. And later on, when the Americans arrived in force, it was to back the Catholic strongman Ngo Dinh Diem who had spent a good part of the so-called 'French War' in a monastery in New Jersey.

Greene's memoirs in hand, I travelled to the district of Phat Diem to climb to the top of the bell tower of a sullen stone basilica where Greene once sought refuge to watch combat on the surrounding plains. It was literary tourism at its best. Little had changed since Greene's day. With the massive bell behind me – described in the Lonely Planet guidebook as making 'Quasimodo's famous chimer at Notre Dame' appear pale in comparison – I looked out to the horizon, allowing Greene's words to set the scene.

'From the belltower of the cathedral at Phat Diem,' he wrote, '… I could contemplate a panorama of war that was truly classical, the kind that historians or war correspondents used to describe before the era of the camera … howitzer shells exploded in little clouds, hanging motionless for a moment in the calm air above the plain, as in a painting.'

But there was nothing picturesque about the ugly, unrelenting struggle then underway down in the monsoon-churned quagmires of the delta. French losses were rising sharply and by 1952 about a thousand officers had been killed, the equivalent of two entire graduating classes at the prestigious army academy Saint-Cyr. For most it was a lonely death in the turbid waters of a paddy field or a jungle thicket half a world away from the comforts of Paris.

Like many other foreign correspondents, Greene was torn by his morbid attraction to battle, writing: 'I always have a sense of guilt when I am a civilian tourist in the regions of death: after all one does not visit a disaster except to give aid – one feels a voyeur of violence.' Voyeur or not, Greene was attracted to danger. Some have suggested that this was an expression of his own sense of Catholic guilt, that he wanted to punish himself for his sins, as so many of his characters do, by constantly courting death as a means of seeking redemption.

Shortly after climbing down the dank stone staircase of the belltower, I came across an old man who had fought in those battles Greene described. For Luu Huan Tran, escape was never an option. As for redemption, that would only come when foreigners were no longer running his country.

I first saw Luu Huan Tran riding towards me on a rickety bicycle. In a remarkable balancing act, one leg rested on the handlebars while the other deftly rotated a pedal. His wispy Ho Chi Minh beard, pith helmet and green fatigues marked him as a veteran – as did his handshake, which might have crushed a man's throat. Rolling up his trouser leg, Luu showed me the battle scars inflicted on him all those years ago, the scars that accounted for his unique cycling style. 'I was wounded when I was helping to lead a squadron,' explained Luu. 'My men and I were trying to capture a French submachine-gun and I was throwing a grenade when I was shot.'

Luu Huan Tran's story lay at the heart of what Greene was writing about in *The Quiet American*. Luu was first of all a peasant farmer, then a Nationalist. Communism came a distant third. The battlegrounds on which he and Ho Chi Minh's other soldiers fought two foreign armies were their fields and their homes.

With the light fading on that afternoon in Phat Diem, Luu, now surrounded by young spectators who had the great good fortune not to have lived through the travails of their forbears, recalled that giving up was never a consideration: 'We were fighting with nothing in our hands,' he said. 'We didn't even have a gun – only swords. But we triumphed over our enemies who were so strong and powerful. If we are united together we always win in the end. It doesn't matter how strong the enemy is.'

Tragically, the truth of Tran's words had to be learnt twice over. First by the French. Then by the Americans.

Graham Greene visited Vietnam for the last time in 1955. By then the French had abandoned the North, and Greene claims to have drunk the last bottle of beer left in Hanoi. Feeling ill, tired and depressed he again resorted to a few pipes of opium to steel himself for an interview with Ho Chi Minh, who was about to prosecute yet another protracted war.

It was also in 1955 that *The Quiet American* was published. Tragically, little was then known about the Nationalist struggle in Indochina, and in the United States Greene's novel was dismissed as 'anti-American'. Had more of the politicians and generals who waged this war read this prophetic book, their eyes might have been opened to the impending nightmare into which their nation was about to descend. But nearly half a century on, the anti-American tag still attaches itself to Greene and his seminal work – as film director Phillip Noyce was to discover after filming the second celluloid version of *The Quiet American*.

I met Noyce in a charming Hanoi neighbourhood, surrounded by girls selling bunches of gladioli, outdoor butchers lopping the heads off ducks, chickens and frogs, and stalls festooned with red lanterns to usher in the lunar New Year. The Australian director was a picture of jagged intensity, puffing furiously on cigarettes and consuming draughts of black coffee as he marshalled his army of actors, cinematographers, gaffers and make-up artists. As we sat down to discuss *The Quiet American*, Noyce's passion for Greene's work spilled out of him:

'Graham Greene was able to describe the fundamental principles of American foreign policy that have existed from 1950 right up to the present day,' Noyce said. 'The question of whether the means are justified by the end – if you are right in doing anything to achieve what you consider to be a goal that is for the good of mankind or the good of another country. Basically, whether America should play puppeteer in other people's business …'

Phillip Noyce spoke to me just months before the shocking events of September 11. He was soon to have first-hand experience of just how contemporary and controversial Greene's work remained. The film – with its theme of American meddling in international affairs – tested badly in pre-release screenings in a nation shaken to its core by the terrorists attacks on New York and Washington DC, and the film's distributors threatened never to release it in the United States. Only after a year and much cajoling by Noyce and the film's star, Michael Caine, was *The Quiet American* eventually screened in a limited number of US cinemas.

There are no such sensitivities about *The Quiet American* in today's Vietnam, however. The novel is read in schools, and street urchins do a flourishing trade in photocopied versions of the book. Having spent months filming throughout Vietnam, Noyce concluded that: 'The novel is much loved because it explains something to the Vietnamese people themselves – that is, why they were bombed and napalmed to death in so many millions for so many years.'

For me, apart from being a remarkable novel, *The Quiet American* also opens a nostalgic window on a time when the trade of foreign correspondent was plied differently. During those few weeks spent following in Greene's footsteps through old Indochina I was transported back to a less frantic era: an era when interviews were recorded in shorthand scratched out in ring-bound notepads with a fountain pen; an era when officers may well have served you soufflé, instead of hermetically sealed starch, to the sound of gunfire; an era in which the time between deadlines could be measured in days – even weeks – instead of minutes and hours. And as luck would have it, a Saigon pickpocket helped prolong my reverie by plucking my mobile phone from the breast pocket of my jacket. For days I was incommunicado, out of head office's reach and free to fall under the spell cast '… by the tall elegant girls in white silk trousers, by the pewter evening light on flat paddy fields, where the water buffaloes trudged fetlock-deep with a slow primeval gait …'

TONY EASTLEY began his career at *The Examiner* newspaper in Launceston, Tasmania.

He has been a journalist with the ABC for 23 years, working as a reporter in news and current affairs in both radio and television.

He has also been Television Chief of Staff, presenter of the radio current affairs program, *The World Today*, and presenter of a range of television programs including *Asia Focus, First Edition, World at Noon*, the weekend television news bulletins, and, most recently, the main weeknight ABC Television news bulletin at 7 pm. In 2004 he will take up the role of presenter of ABC Radio's current affairs flagship program, *AM*.

Tony was Bureau Chief of Asia and a foreign correspondent for five years. He has twice been a finalist in the Walkley Awards, winning a special commendation for his work in China during the Tiananmen Square crisis, and he won a Television Logie Award for best news story for his coverage of the bloody confrontation between students and troops in the Bangkok riots in 1991. He has also won the New York Gold Medal for best series of television news reports in the same year.

Cambodia: 1988

The view across the rooftops of Phnom Penh was singularly depressing. What was once described as a beautiful and charming city was now grey and drab, its wide boulevards potholed and strewn with putrifying rubbish.

Pol Pot had long gone but his bloody spectre hung over the city; the memory of his frightening years etched in the faces of those who had been touched by the mad cadres of the Khmer Rouge. The intervening years had done little to erase his legacy. Even people who openly smiled – those happy to see Western reporters in town – bore traces of a deep melancholy.

It was as if a vast deadly tide had washed over and wasted the country, and then retreated, leaving Cambodia and its people exhausted, still gasping for breath and seeking some semblance of a life they once knew. People had an air of wistfulness, a detachment that left them in a state of limbo, as if they were waiting. In fact the majority of them could only wait and hope, cling to what they had and see what else was in store. Cambodia was weak and vulnerable, and waiting for someone else to come along – God willing, a benevolent hand.

A vast and rich Khmer Empire once stretched across Thailand, Laos, Vietnam and Malaysia. In the ninth century Jayavarman the second, a Khmer prince, sat at the head of what is generally known as the Angkor kingdom. For more than two centuries it dominated life in the region, but by the late twelfth century it had begun to decline.

Thai and Vietnamese powers then held sway alternately until the 1800s, when France extended its colonial control over Vietnam and Cambodia. By 1884 Cambodia was a full French colony, albeit a reluctant one.

World War II saw Japan in power, and ruling Cambodia with the help of the pro-Vichy colonial administration. After Japan's surrender the loyalist French returned, but nationalism had taken root in Cambodia and, under mounting pressure in Indochina, France conceded the independence of the kingdom of Cambodia in 1953, under the rule of Prince Norodom Sihanouk.

Cambodia performed a balancing act through the years of the Vietnam War, bombed by US planes for giving refuge to Communist and Vietcong troops. The aforementioned Pol Pot seized power in 1975, renamed the country Kampuchea and commenced his brutal regime. The world watched in horror, but did nothing. It was Vietnam that invaded Cambodia and ousted Pol Pot. The United States led the way in imposing sanctions and the group of ASEAN countries was keen to do Washington's bidding. Vietnam installed a puppet regime with Hun Sen as prime minister. The United Nations eventually negotiated a tenuous coalition between Sihanouk and Hun Sen.

But the young country struggled, and this was to be a recurring theme.

It was early in 1988 that I first visited Cambodia and I had no idea what to expect. Correspondents I'd spoken to had said it was a broken country, still struggling to come to terms with the murderous Pol Pot years. The crops had failed, the cities were full of starving people and there were 300,000 refugees living in camps along the Thai border.

My Air Cambodia flight into Phnom Penh from Ho Chi Minh City (Saigon) was like any other third world flight, and the over-officious military men at the airport were like many I'd seen elsewhere.

On the short road trip into the city it was immediately noticeable how few vehicles there were. This was Asia, so where were the ubiquitous two-cylinder motorcycles? For an Asian country, even a desperately poor one, this was unusual. There were some vehicles on the outskirts of town but they were just shells. They'd been attacked and burned by Pol Pot's zealots. (Anything remotely Western, even spectacles, became a target for the mad purges.)

All that was on the road at the moment were some small army jeeps and the odd large military transport. Ordinary people walked or rode bicycles. If they could afford it they hired a cyclo – Cambodia's pedal-powered taxi.

Phnom Penh was full of people who didn't belong. Many of them were country folk who, after seeing another crop fail, had packed up the little they had left and made for the city. Some squatted in half-ruined buildings while others lived on the streets, hoping their luck might change.

But the city didn't have much to offer, especially to the destitute. There was little or no sanitation, and to top it off, a civil war was draining precious resources as well as killing and maiming more of the population. Electricity was intermittent and there was a shortage of cooking fuel and most essentials. It was obvious Phnom Penh could not cope with the sheer numbers of people – with more arriving from the countryside every day.

In 1975 Cambodia had a population of around seven million. The number who died in the course of Pol Pot's Maoist-inspired reforms is put at somewhere between one and two million. Most perished through malnutrition and disease, but at least 300,000 are thought to have been executed by the Khmer Rouge.

I soon discovered Cambodia was a land of ghosts and rumours. For a new reporter it was confusing. Realising I knew very little about the place, I latched onto someone who did – in this case a burly producer from the American CBS network who'd spent time in Cambodia during the Vietnam War.

'I know bugger-all about this place,' I pleaded, offering to pay for another of his beers. Perhaps out of allegiance to other Australians he'd worked with, or just out of pity, he pointed me in the right direction, and I began to absorb how Cambodia had suffered and to appreciate the enormity of the struggle ahead.

A trip to the local hospital shocked me. The camera crew and I walked among the crowds to find people on makeshift litters in the overcrowded rooms and out in the hallways. It was barely a hospital as such: more a dumping area for the sick and dying.

The damp crept up the walls and formed vast dark patches in the plaster. The fetid air inside was stifling, and the open windows simply allowed the free flow of flies and mosquitoes. Relatives spent hours hunched over their loved ones, fanning them and feeding them from small bowls of food they had prepared and brought in themselves. I felt dearly for the children. They seemed so small and fragile, yet they suffered mostly in silence, their large, brown, uncomprehending eyes staring out on a confusing world.

The local doctor began to tell me what was being done for the patients, but he soon made it perfectly clear there was precious little he could do. Western embargoes on supplies had starved the hospital. Vietnam's invasion, while ridding the country of Pol Pot, had earnt the wrath of the United States. An American-led embargo was soon in place, denying Cambodia of so much of what it needed. When he told me that they were so short of hypodermic needles they had to re-use them, and they were now so blunt that they bruised the children's arms, he began to cry. The tears trickled down his cheek. The camera caught his pain. But it couldn't record my shame that, as an Australian and a close ally of the United States, we were somehow part of the problem. It was some consolation that my story was aired at home ... not that it did much for those kids in the hospital.

Filing stories from Cambodia was a nightmare. Without any telephones it was almost impossible to verify any of the 'Chinese whispers' that coursed the country. Attempting to distill and analyse information was nigh on impossible – you couldn't telephone or telegraph anyone for confirmation.

There were two telephones in the entire country. One was at the Post Office in the capital, where the solitary line was guarded by a bevy of flirtatious, heavily nail-polished telephonists. But beneath the smiles and long lashes there were hearts of steel, and heaven help anyone who upset the orderly – and long – process of waiting in line.

The second telephone, and by far the more important line, was into the home of Hun Sen, a former Khmer Rouge commander who had defected to the Vietnamese side and then been installed as Cambodian leader by the Communist government in Hanoi. His phone was guarded by a lot of men with guns who stood outside his Phnom Penh home. With only one of the lines open to reporters we would hire cyclo drivers for the night, and they would dutifully move their bicycle cabs along the queue outside the Post Office. A runner would be sent to fetch the reporter when the odds of making a call had shortened.

With the Khmer Rouge still a formidable force in parts of the country, various reports would filter through to the journalists in Phnom Penh. Checking anything was difficult enough for the handful of wily journalists stationed there – even more difficult for visiting correspondents.

Regularly, reports circulated about where the Khmer Rouge had struck, or were likely to strike. The more hysterical reported on the likely atrocities to be carried out by the Khmer Rouge.

The northern city of Battambang, a large regional centre, was a choice prize, and the Khmer Rouge forces were staging spasmodic attacks on outlying areas. In the summer of 1989 a headline in a Thai newspaper screamed 'Battambang on Fire'. For the correspondents and crews in Phnom Penh, this was an important development. Wire services began to run stories that the government's tenuous control was slipping. The Khmer Rouge had amassed large forces and were on a major, and seemingly successful, offensive.

Harassed ministry officials wrung their hands and repeatedly assured the correspondents: 'The city is not under Khmer Rouge control and nothing is on fire, nothing.' Desperate to allay fears that government forces had been routed, the Foreign Ministry hastily arranged for reporters to be flown to Battambang to see for themselves.

It was to be an early morning flight from Phnom Penh. Correspondents and camera crews arrived, more bleary-eyed than usual, shading their eyes against the long, low rays of the rising sun that swept the tarmac and the modest building of the city's international airport. Already the heat was beginning to rise from the concrete and tar, mingling with the heady scents of aviation fuel and a typical musty Cambodian morning. On the edge of the airport, squatters' cooking fires had been started and the smoke rose in lazy spirals.

Among the assembled throng was a Russian cameraman with what had to be the heaviest 16-mm camera known to man. Its incredible weight was only matched by the noise of its agricultural innards. Its cogs ground and rattled so much they threatened to drown out just about everything else.

The only thing older on the tarmac was the plane which we were about to board. DC-3s have been around since Moses was a boy, and they are still flown all over the world. They began service in the 1930s, and the one that greeted us on this day must surely have been among the first off the assembly line. But don't get me wrong – the DC-3 is a proven and admired workhorse. Twin-engined and broad winged, they're slow but reliable.

Not so reassuring was the pilot – a large, fleshy, red-faced Russian whose stained white shirt was fighting a losing battle against the bulge of his belly. We were told he had flown in Afghanistan during the Soviet occupation. Indeed at that time it was common to find Russian pilots around Phnom Penh. Most of Cambodia's aid came from the Soviet Bloc. A good number of them were helicopter pilots. One, known as Vlad, took great delight in flying fuel drop missions at low altitudes down the Mekong River. He was everything a movie director could possibly want. A mad glint in one eye was only outshone by his string of gold teeth, which were on permanent display as he flew his missions, his lips peeled back in delight as he frightened the daylight out of new correspondents.

The flight to Battambang was smooth enough until we got near the city. The burly pilot, driven either by old habits of dodging shoulder-launched Stinger missiles fired by the Mujaheddin around Kabul, or by fear about reports of the Khmer Rouge, put the old plane into a steep, gut-wrenching, spiralling dive. It's what they call strategic flying – making the DC-3 a difficult moving target. As uncomfortable and frightening as it was, we could hardly complain.

On the ground we made for the city to see for ourselves what the fuss was about. Khmer Rouge units were nowhere in sight. There were some signs of a minor attack, and there was some nervousness about just how close they might be, but Battambang certainly wasn't burning. The Foreign Ministry officials seemed almost surprised, certainly relieved. The camera crews got their shots, brief interviews were conducted and it was time to return home.

Everyone jumped aboard the ageing aircraft. The cabin door was shut tight and everyone waited – and waited – in an almost airtight metal box on a shadeless runway in Battambang in the hot season. Rivulets of sweat coursed down foreheads and dripped off noses. It ran down hands onto notebooks, blurring the ink and leaving the notepaper a sodden pulp. It ran down the back of pants and pooled in crotches. This was a sauna on a grand scale. The air, already thick with the smell of dozens of perspiring correspondents and crew, grew staler by the second.

From the old tin and wire hangar that passed for the airport building emerged the Russian pilot, his arms full of shopping. Obviously Battambang's markets were operating.

Minutes passed as he loaded his curios into the cockpit.

By now the lack of air and the heat in the passenger compartment had become unbearable. The Russian cameraman, who had shown such patience throughout the flight and on the ground, burst from his seat. He launched himself up the ascending, narrow aisle to the steel cockpit door. 'Comrade ... you are killing us back here,' he shouted as his fist thumped on the door.

A moment later the aircraft's main passenger door opened. There was a rush of cool air, and a perceptible sucking sound as the atmospheres compensated.

Moments later the engines kicked into life ... but the view out the fogged windows was not pleasant. The starboard engine was on fire. This trip was getting hotter by the minute!

The airport fire crew sprang into action. A string of Cambodian youths carrying buckets of water attacked the overheated engine. It was a sterling display of fire fighting, and with the flames extinguished the pilot taxied and took off. He put the old plane through a similar daring set of spiral manoeuvres – this time on the way up – but no one seemed to mind. We were finally out of Battambang, and our plane was the only thing to have been on fire.

The Keen Cameraman

We had been negotiating for weeks to go on patrol with the Sihanouk forces. Our main purpose was to find out more about the strength and morale of the soldiers loyal to Prince Norodom Sihanouk. They were a key part of the opposition troika which appeared to be making gains in some parts of the country.

The patrol was a drudge. We walked in single file through scrubby terrain in stifling heat. After a brief stop for lunch the patrol continued. There wasn't much life in the soldiers, but I could hardly blame them for that.

The only sign of excitement came when Sebastian Phua, my ever-keen cameraman, decided to get some cutaway shots of the long line of soldiers. A cutaway is normally a wide shot of the action at hand. In this case Sebastian stepped off the side of the track to get pictures of the long line of soldiers passing by him. No sooner had he started than there was a shout from the captain leading the patrol, and everyone stopped abruptly. Sebastian, keen to get a natural, moving shot, didn't take his eye from the viewfinder on the camera, just waved us on with his free hand. But the troops remained frozen.

'Keep moving, guys, just walk natural,' shouted Seb.

Still the soldiers remained where they were. By now Sebastian could see the frozen looks on the soldiers' faces – and they were all looking at him! There were some shouted words in Khmer from the captain ahead of me. Our interpreter, normally a happy, smiling man, looked a little ashen as he said in a grave, almost whispered monotone: 'The captain wishes to tell you your cameraman has stepped into a minefield. He must come back onto the track and be very careful to come back the same way he got there.' Sebastian did.

There were no more cutaways.

WALTER HAMILTON was the ABC's North-East Asia Correspondent, based in Japan, for three postings over a total of eleven years. He reported on the oil shocks of the 1970s, the expansion of Australia's energy trade with the region, the 'high yen' era of the 1980s, the success of democratic movements in South Korea and Taiwan, and the growth and collapse of Japan's 'bubble economy' in the 1990s.

He reported from China in the aftermath of the Tiananmen Square protests in 1989 and, when he was based in Singapore as the ABC's South-East Asia Correspondent, covered the fall of President Ferdinand Marcos of the Philippines in 1986.

He has also worked in London for Australian Associated Press, Visnews and the BBC.

He took up a position as Head, National Coverage for ABC News and Current Affairs in 2001.

The Kobe Earthquake: Japan

In myth, it's said that a giant catfish, or *namazu*, lies beneath Japan, and every time it moves an earthquake results.

Many are too faint to be noticed, but often enough, usually around once a week, the catfish whips its tail and somewhere in Japan feels the tremble.

Modern seismic mapping shows why. The country sits near the meeting point of several continental plates, at the top of a Pacific 'rim of fire' that stretches up from New Zealand and around to the Californian coast.

Nearly ten percent of the energy released by earthquakes worldwide is concentrated in and around the Japanese islands. That's produced thirteen major quakes in the last century, each with a death toll exceeding one hundred.

The worst, the Great Kanto Earthquake of 1923, devastated a wide area of Tokyo and Yokohama and killed 140,000 people. Tokyo awaits the next 'big one' which, seismologists calculate, is now overdue.

Yet, however much science has learned about the 'how' and the 'why' of this age-old menace, nobody can predict exactly where and when the giant catfish will lash out again.

*   *   *

Every year, on 1 September, the Japanese practise earthquake survival. The anniversary of the Great Kanto Earthquake is a day for showing off the country's much-vaunted capacity for mass mobilisation.

The Prime Minister, in grey tunic and cap, presides over a committee of experts, calmly directing the mock earthquake response; office workers evacuate buildings in orderly lines, as fire crews run up ladders and ambulance officers treat 'victims' smeared in fake blood; schoolchildren dive for cover under their desks on a pre-arranged signal; volunteers set up booths in riverside parks to supervise boisterous teenagers hurling water bombs at kerosene fires.

I once lined up to try the 'Earthquake Simulator': an open-sided, furnished room, built on a mobile stage that gyrated like an amusement ride.

Every time Japan experiences a real tremor, within seconds television stations flash details of the location and magnitude – another reassuring sign of everyday readiness.

When I first arrived in Tokyo in 1979, I inherited a homemade 'earthquake survival kit' from the previous correspondent. A bag containing instant noodles, bottles of water, a torch and warm clothing sat in the cupboard near the front door. Though my rather flimsy wooden house would swagger alarmingly whenever a minor quake struck, I became used to it, and the cockroaches got to the instant noodles before I did.

Then there was the time an earthquake hit while I was eating dinner at the Correspondents' Club, on the top floor of a city skyscraper. Our group instinctively braced, hands pressed on the table as in a séance, while the steel structure swayed to and fro, showing off its flexible design. Afterwards, people seemed more impressed than scared.

They have an old saying in Japan: *Jishin, Kaminari, Kaji, Oyaji* or Earthquake, Thunder, Fire, Father – 'the four frightening things'. I came to think it was mainly about Japanese fathers. I had grown complacent, and it was a while before I learnt my lesson.

Towards the end of 1994, I happened to be in northern Japan when there was a swarm of minor earthquakes. Tsunami warnings were issued almost daily. We were driving at night, approaching a railway level crossing, when a tremor started up. Though we slammed on the brakes, the car we were in kept bouncing like it was going over potholes. Up ahead, the red flashing lights of the crossing swung menacingly from side-to-side.

I sat up that night, monitoring the television because of a 'severe tsunami' warning, but it passed without further damage: another false alarm.

So, back in Tokyo a few weeks later, when I awoke to an early morning telephone call from my assistant, bearing news of an earthquake in Kobe, I was prepared for the least, not the worst. 'Kobe doesn't have serious earthquakes; it's the wrong part of Japan,' I thought. 'Here we go again.'

As soon as I switched on the television these thoughts quickly retreated. The urgency of the announcer's voice accompanying an aerial shot of flames rising from a city still in darkness: this was the real thing. It was the Tuesday after a holiday long weekend, 17 January 1995. My dash to the office began an odyssey that would permanently alter my view of Japan.

The first day, we watched and reported as the disaster grew in proportions, buffeted by every new image of destruction, every leap in the toll of dead and missing, every new alarm: 'What about the temple-city of Kyoto? That's not far from Kobe. Has the destruction spread there?' Suddenly it felt the country was no longer whole. This feeling was more than just the sense of unreality of an event witnessed through the media. Crumbling before our eyes was a nation's trust in its own strength and preparedness.

Once we had cleared our television reporting commitments for the day, my assistant, Kumiko Sakamoto, the camera crew, Joe Phua and Hiro Muramoto, and I loaded the ABC van for the drive to Kobe. It was midwinter, and our destination, if we could get there, was 550 kilometres away.

Kobe has a reputation as a comfortable, international city. It was one of the first ports opened for trade in the 1860s when Japan reluctantly emerged from centuries of seclusion. The city is centred on a narrow strip of land, about thirty kilometres long and two to four kilometres wide, between the Rokko Mountains and the Inland Sea. One and a half million people live there. The cities of Osaka and Kyoto lie just to its east.

Kobe was firebombed during World War II and had come through its fair share of typhoons, but there hadn't been a severe earthquake for centuries.

As we drove through the night, my thoughts went back to my first visit there in 1980, in the midst of a construction boom. The second of two colossal, man-made islands was taking shape in the bay.

'We get the soil from the mountains,' a proud city official had explained. 'But instead of carting it by truck through the city and disrupting traffic for a year, we built a tunnel underneath and pumped the soil through to the harbour.

'Our mayor is a man of ideas.'

We were taken for a ride in an automated train (no driver in sight) to Port Island, where tourist hotels and fashion houses, we were told, would transform Kobe's image from a place of steelworks and shipping.

Now, as we entered the city, the day after the earthquake, I witnessed a very different Kobe emerge out of the predawn gloom. We were crawling along in a monster traffic jam. Ahead of us sat a dozen fire trucks, emergency lights flashing, but also going nowhere fast.

There are four main highways into Kobe, sharing the same narrow strip of land with conventional railways, the Bullet Train route, power, water and other utilities. This 'lifeline' had been shattered. The one passable highway was choked, and nobody seemed to have foreseen the risk; nobody was even controlling traffic.

Lining the road, houses, small shops and factories lay in ruins.

The traditional house in this part of Japan is two storeys, built of wood, with a roof of heavy ceramic tiles and mud inlay. The tiles are designed not to blow off in a typhoon; the mud helps absorb the summer humidity. But, like a top-heavy sumo wrestler, many had come crashing down or were knocked wildly askew, defying gravity. There were no lights, no signs of life out there. Incongruously, my mobile phone worked, and I was able to report directly into ABC Radio's AM program.

192

We were still somewhere in the suburbs of Kobe, but decided to leave the van and set off on foot, carrying the camera gear. Down a side street, we immediately encountered the unexpected. In the middle of the road was a group of men sitting around a fire, frying eggs and sipping sake. Even after a freezing night in the open, they greeted us cheerfully:

'Come along, have some eggs.'

'Yes, the firewood is what's left of our houses.'

'Can't be helped.'

One man, a rough bandage covering a broken nose, grabbed my arm. 'I was sleeping on the top floor,' he said, pointing animatedly to his home, now missing its lower floor. 'It knocked me out of bed, and when I climbed out the window I found I was already on the ground.'

Another led me around the corner to where a three-storey apartment block had once stood. 'Many died here,' he said, surveying the jumble of concrete and metal. The real sights and sounds of a disaster greater than anything I had imagined were now rushing at me.

We went to the end of the street. A railway overpass had crashed down, blocking the way. We clambered up the stairs of an apartment block that was tilting at a crazy angle, but the roof might offer our first overview of the city. Turning at each floor, I passed rows of doors flung open, with the lifetime's possessions of unknown people scattered about.

When I stepped out onto the roof, I gasped with amazement. We could see as far as the mountains, and what lay below: railway lines twisted like ribbons thrown across the ground; whole neighbourhoods tumbling into each other, no property boundaries left; plumes of rising smoke; distant sirens coming through the haze. More disturbing than any one thing, however, was the sense this scene conveyed of vast energy spent, of human endeavour nullified.

Down the road we came across a patrol from the Ground Self-Defence Force, Japan's carefully named army. Their daunting search for survivors consisted of yelling, 'Anyone there?' at the piles of rubble as they moved past. The scale of the thing was too great, and there were too few of them.

Later, it was revealed that the city had hesitated for many precious hours before asking for national assistance, and the authorities had restricted the army call-out because of old post-war taboos. This wasn't the well-oiled emergency response we'd seen played out in Tokyo each year. Japanese people were discovering that surviving such a disaster would largely depend on individual effort.

We began to encounter more people: clutching futons around their shoulders, one lot pushing a pram loaded with possessions, moving along in shocked silence. Many would join a stream of refugees heading for Osaka, thirty kilometres away.

By now the earthquake had a name, in fact two official names. Reflecting how rigid jurisdictions contributed to the flawed rescue effort, the government dubbed it the 'Great Hanshin-Awaji Earthquake', while the Meteorological Agency called it the 'South Hyogo Prefecture Earthquake'. It recorded magnitude 7.3 on the Richter scale.

Lightning had appeared out of a stormless sky just before the quake struck at 5.46 am. The epicentre was under Awaji Island, southwest of Kobe, where rice fields were ripped open as though by a giant zipper, causing land displacements of up to three metres. It tore through the length of the city with a great roar, as one survivor recalled: 'It continued [for] about twenty seconds. Then silence. It was so strange – I have never heard the sound of silence like that.'

In the Kobe newsroom of NHK, the national broadcaster, a staff member was asleep on a couch. A remote video camera, activated by the first shock, captured his nightmare as it was thrown about like a doll amid the chaos of lurching filing cabinets and smashing glass.

A cafeteria manager, arriving at work, had just stepped off his bicycle. He described the streets as 'trembling like waves'.

Such was the force that, cleaning up later at Kobe University, they found a heavy safe which had bounced off the floor onto a sofa. It took four people to lift it back down.

After the stillness came the inferno. Broken gas pipes triggered hundreds of fires, and broken water mains prevented fire fighters putting them out. The city had installed a thousand underground cisterns for an emergency, but each had only ten minutes' supply of water. Natural streams might have provided an alternative source, but they'd been lined with concrete 'for more efficient land use'. Had a wind been blowing, the whole city would have gone up.

Mid-morning, we started walking back towards distant Osaka to get to a satellite feed point to send our story. Even with eight hours up our sleeve, I seriously doubted we would make it.

We passed long, orderly queues of people waiting to use a rare working phone or buy the last supplies from a shop still in business. A mysterious knot of people squatting in the middle of a freeway turned out to be a watering party, filling saucepans from a broken main.

Along the way, there were many reasons to stop. We came upon a middle-aged woman in great distress. 'There, just in there.' She pointed, hardly able to look herself. 'Please, somebody help.' At first we couldn't see anything in the rubble, but then some long black hair drew our eyes to the body of her teenage daughter, firmly in the clutches of their collapsed home. We could do nothing, though just paying attention seemed to comfort her.

The earthquake killed many asleep in their beds. But how many more would have died had it struck a couple of hours later, during the commuter rush?

After trudging another three hours, we managed to flag down a driver and ask for a lift to the nearest functioning railway station.

'He says all right, but we have to take off our shoes,' Kumiko explained.

This was stretching Japanese decorum, I reckoned, but I was in no position to argue. We rode to the station in a primrose-scented Nissan four-wheel drive, complete with white plush upholstery and carpet. It was a sharp re-entry to the strange reality of undamaged Osaka: satellite feed points, soft hotel beds and restaurant meals –

always knowing that, down the road, an altogether different existence was being endured.

For a week, we travelled each day between these two worlds.

Evacuation centres in Kobe were not coping with the 300,000 homeless. We found 1,500 people crammed into a school gymnasium, desperately short of water.

Others had spent a second bitter-cold night outdoors: 'When is help coming?' they asked us. I sensed rising anger. Many continued the search for kin. A young woman, surveying the silent remains of her parents' home, still had hope: 'Somebody told me my mother survived, but I don't know where they've taken her.'

There were moments of elation: an old man dug out of the rubble after forty-five hours. But, at a morgue, we saw the bereaved kneeling beside row upon row of unpainted wooden coffins, struggling in the Japanese manner to restrain their grief. Half the city's dead were aged over sixty, many living alone in those traditional-style homes, built just after the war.

In the gap left by the faltering official response, help appeared from unlikely quarters. A *yakuza* gangster boss earned kudos by setting up neighbourhood soup kitchens. At the other end of the social scale, Japan's biggest supermarket retailer, on first news of the earthquake, diverted delivery trucks from all over western Japan towards stricken Kobe. And a big brewery switched its bottling lines from beer to water, and gave away thousands of cases.

But with so much of the city's infrastructure gone, there was frighteningly little means of delivering help. Nearly 180,000 buildings were destroyed or badly damaged, including 90 per cent of hospitals; electricity was cut for a week, and it took up to two months to fully restore water and gas. The elevated expressways, which fell when their massive concrete pillars snapped, would take much longer to clear. Japan's biggest shipping container terminal, built on reclaimed land, was also in ruins.

We began to notice strange phenomena, such as buildings that had buckled halfway up, and places where an invisible line sharply divided the destroyed from the undamaged.

Answers to these puzzles emerged later. An older building code had allowed a weaker superstructure beginning at the fifth floor, and that's where many gave way. Also, beneath Kobe, lay an ancient sandbank that marked the border of a marshy delta, long since filled in. This was the invisible line that, for instance, marked the exact point where an elevated expressway had been cleaved off. On the section still standing, a commuter bus hung with its front wheels suspended in the air; its good fortune decided by nature's hidden footprint.

It took us several forays to penetrate to the west of the city where some of the worst fires had been. The Nagata district was home to most of Japan's synthetic leather shoe factories. They burnt fiercely. Many ethnic Koreans were living here, and I wondered how they had fared, mindful that after the 1923 earthquake in Tokyo large numbers of despised of Koreans were killed by vigilante mobs. But there was nothing like that in Kobe: part of a pattern, including the absence of looting and the extraordinary public order.

We stood in the midst of a blackened wasteland where a market, the size of several football fields, had once been a bustling centre of commerce. You find them in every Japanese city: criss-crossing alleyways, simple awnings to keep off the rain, and dozens of stalls selling everything from pickled radish to straw thongs.

I met an owner picking through the ashes: 'They won't let us rebuild in the old way,' he said. 'It'll never be the same.'

Some residents were ready to give up, like the woman who came back to find her restaurant still standing, but a 'condemned' notice already fixed to the doorpost. In common with most Japanese, she had no earthquake insurance because the available schemes provided limited payouts. 'After such an earthquake,' she wept, 'I don't want to live here any more.'

But even in the midst of the worst, I had a feeling Kobe would bounce back. By now, on the fifth day, the human tide was turning. Friends and family were descending on the city, walking for hours, bringing comfort and provisions. Volunteer groups were helping feed the population. The city was knocking together prefabricated housing. Bitumen was already being poured on new roadways.

In many places among the ruins, offerings of flowers and incense were placed in memory of the dead. Hand-written notes stuck on lamp posts sent out messages of hope: 'We have come through and are staying with friends.'

The Great Hanshin-Awaji Earthquake killed 6,430 people and injured another 43,782. The cost of rebuilding was estimated at US$150 billion. It was Japan's greatest post-war disaster.

I realised my view of the country had changed for good. I could look up behind Kobe, and recall how the tops of the mountains had been 'cleverly' lopped off to provide landfill for man-made islands. But the islands were now sunk under geysers of mud, and many people had died in landslips on those denuded mountains. And while most modern tower blocks did withstand the quake, that was of limited comfort because some other structures enjoying the benefits of the latest designs did not, such as the new subway station that collapsed, leaving a huge crater downtown.

But if I could no longer have the same faith in, and admiration for, the country's engineering prowess and efficiency, I had gained a new respect for its people. Behind their polished courtesy, Japanese can often seem cool and selfish: focused exclusively on their family or group, and indifferent to strangers. Here, instead, I saw a community that shone during its greatest test, and a people imbued with humour, openness and caring.

On our last night in Kobe, an assignment that I thought could no longer shake me produced one last haunting face.

We were sitting in the van catching our breath before the long drive back to Tokyo, when she appeared out of the darkness. I suppose she was about seventeen. There was something unnatural in her manner, overly eager, as she enquired who we were, and where we were from.

'Thank you for coming, thank you for coming,' she repeated over and over, her eyes wildly alight.

She stood there, in the open doorway of the van, like an apparition.

I hadn't noticed a young man who now stepped from the shadows and quietly explained that she wasn't herself, she had lost her entire family. 'I'm taking care of her,' he said.

I wondered who he was, and how long and how far they had wandered. He trailed after her into the night, a gentle custodian, sure to catch her before the fall.

PETER LLOYD has been the ABC's South-East Asia Correspondent based in Bangkok since mid 2002. His field of coverage includes Thailand, Burma, Laos, Cambodia, Vietnam, Malaysia, Brunei, Singapore and the Philippines.

He has been part of major ABC coverage elsewhere. In October 2002 he reported on the Bali bombings and returned to host the ABC's live coverage of the Bali anniversary service in October 2003. Peter also covered the US-led war against Iraq in early 2003, reporting from the US command centre in Qatar.

A working journalist since 1985, Peter has reported for Australian audiences from the UK, Europe, Africa and the United States.

He joined the ABC in 1988, working in the Sydney television newsroom for three years before moving to Britain to work for the BBC and British Sky News.

On his return, Peter spent a decade in commercial television news and current affairs in various roles including reporter–

presenter, program executive producer, and North America Correspondent.

In 2000, Peter returned to the ABC, taking up a senior reporting role with television news and later with the national radio current affairs programs *AM*, *The World Today* and *PM*.

He is married with two children.

Two Weeks in Bali

Don't bother reading this if you're easily given to fits of rage and anger at the media. If publications sometimes offend, then the processes that lead to print or broadcast may drive you over the edge. Don't read it if you're squeamish, either. To be blunt: Bali was a bloodbath. And don't read this chapter if you're anticipating some previously unheard insights into the motives that drove those madmen to commit the Kuta Beach bombings. After seventeen years working as a journalist I know only this: bad things happen to good people for absolutely no reason. And a *really* bad thing happened to two hundred people in October 2002 that will defy explanation for ever.

The following account is not a template for how every journalist goes about their business. But it is how *I* do it. That said, let's confirm a few long-held suspicions of my profession by airing some dirty laundry, for being raised a Catholic means I have an urge to confess a thing or two.

To be perfectly frank, journalists despise normality. Good is bad. Quiet is boring. Your up is our down. Generally speaking, the worse it is for you, the better for us. It makes for good copy. Perverts? Tick Yes/No. Read on.

Another secret: we 'get off' on our job. Not in a creepy 'mummy, there's a man in a trench coat at the school gate' kind of way. It's more the thrill of the chase, the thickening of the sinews as we do battle (against each other and deadlines) for truth, justice and – unspoken bragging rights for having another lead story. For some people adventure sports will do it. Others enjoy high-wire pursuits like parachuting or scuba diving. Honestly, those kinds of pastimes scare the life out of me. But day to day scandal, death, destruction and tragedy – baby, that's a real turn-on. Bastards? Tick Yes/No. Move on.

Finally, we embrace sweeping generalisations, even about

ourselves. Black and white is so much more interesting and easier to comprehend than endless shades of grey.

None of this is to suggest journalists enjoy pain, suffering and public humiliation (although in cases of hypocritical, venal politicians it's a bonus). Quite the reverse. Ours is the high-minded, vocational pursuit of the holy grail of truth and meaning. We're in it to shine light where others would prefer it to remain dark, delving the whys and wherefores, motives and prejudices, causes and effects. It's about all that, and more. Of course this is easily dismissed as hippie claptrap of the highest order, but even the most hard-faced, cynical old hack secretly believes it to be true. Otherwise they wouldn't still be doing the job.

Big stories like Bali are to journalists what a hit is to a junkie – a big, fat rush. In my case the physical signs are always the same. Usually it begins with an increased heartbeat. The blood starts pumping faster and harder. My stomach tightens. My mind zooms in to focus tightly on the unfolding event. Of course I can't see it yet, but I'm at periscope depth and the news radar is up and searching for a target. In a split second my mind shifts up to top gear. Being drawn into a big, breaking story is like being in my favourite 1970s television show *Time Tunnel*, where the two scientists are forever spinning forward into a new location for another adventure.

In these split-second moments I fall into a rhythm that has evolved steadily in a career working in radio and television. First, I 'clean house', which is to say that all those crappy bits of 'non-news' thoughts, plans and information are flicked from the mental diary. It's a bit like an end-of-season 'everything must go' sale. Lunch with a friend at one o'clock tomorrow? Can't do. Pick up dry cleaning today at four o'clock? Leave it. Go to bank? Forget it. Ask for pay rise? Reschedule again, you chicken. These are the golden rules of breaking news, crisis management: defer, delete, ignore. All items-of-no-further-use-until-after-filing are jettisoned from my head like a loose newspaper being sucked from a speeding car.

This process is what women mean when they claim men can't walk and chew gum at the same time. It's a bit unfair, because in my experience it's a profession-wide characteristic that afflicts the female of the journalist species just as much. In work and life, media folk tend to follow the core principle of news writing known as K-I-S-S: Keep It Simple, Stupid.

So with all that in mind, let me tell you about the Bali bombings. The call came at 4 am. Not to harp on the kinky 'turn on' factor – but there's nothing quite as edgy for a news junkie as the 'phone-call-in-the-middle-of-the-night'. It's the journalistic equivalent of 'follow that taxi'. Truly sad? Tick Yes/No. Move on.

I'm not much of a morning person, but since it was still technically the middle of the night some primitive story alarm went off straight away. My heart was racing before my feet touched the floor. This might have had less to do with my imagined nose for 'breaking news' than the shock sensation of being shoved in the back by my wife mumbling something like 'honey, the phone'.

Oddly enough (you may think) our first thoughts are just like those of other human beings. Is it a call from home? Has someone amongst our circle of family and friends died, had a car accident, suffered a stroke? Instead, the words coming down the phone were an escape – at least from personal tragedy.

'Australians. Bali. Fire. Nightclub. Many dead. Not sure how many. Go!'

No doubt my assignment editor has a far more composed recollection of the conversation. Like the rest of the ABC news team, she'd been awake for hours and at her desk at the ABC's head office in the inner Sydney suburb of Ultimo.

Bad news peels like an onion. Each layer brings more detail, usually more ghastly than the one before. It always happens the same way in the news business. The most historic event in retrospect was almost certainly born as a fragment of information. World War I? Man shoots bloke in carriage. World War II? Bloke named Hitler elected Chancellor, details page thirty-two. Marquee events in history start out small and grow larger and larger, just like that creepy slimeball in the 1960s movie, *The Blob*.

The Bali onion peeled in a sequence that went something like this.

Fire in club district, several injured. Then: Bali police say several patrons dead. A few minutes later: Authorities say fire in Bali caused by explosion. Some time after that: Bali hospitals report many dead, more injured being treated. Then another layer: Australians may be among casualties, say police. And another: Fire caused by big explosion. And yet another: Car bomb suspected. In the middle was the rub: Devastation. Hundreds missing. Many victims Australian holidaymakers. The big, bad news onion kept peeling all night long.

After I got off the phone the mind-zoom took me to the special zone reserved for 'the big one'. Remember, what's bad for you is good for us. And what's really, *really* bad is very, *very* thrilling. Really callous bastard? Yes/No. Tick the box. Read on.

Inside the 'zone' I experienced a series of simultaneous, instan-taneous, super-charged chain reactions. These could be called the Ready, Set, Go impulses. I wiped the calendar, put out the mind trash, prepared the 'must-do' inventory list, packed a bag in a very big hurry and climbed aboard the Time Tunnel express from Bangkok, City of Angels, to Bali, Island of the Gods.

Now this might sound a little like a Hallmark greeting card, but being a television reporter means never being alone. There's always someone with you, and in Bali that someone was David Leland, cameraman, confidant, friend. We're similar ages and had similar upbringings, though on separate continents. Almost from the day we began working together we formed a close bond. We're cut from the same cloth: share a love for the job, a black sense of humour and a star sign (Scorpio). We're so familiar with the other's moves that ours is a dance of instinct. Rarely do we need to say it, we just do it. It's almost telepathic. This combination made Bali professionally possible and personally tolerable.

We watched the bad news onion peeling on the TV monitors in the airport lounge, guessed how it was developing on the plane and got the shocker update on arrival. The number of dead, injured and missing was incomprehensible. Less nightclub explosion, more plane crash. I recall David coming up with the poignant comparison: that this was Australia's 'September 11'. It wasn't a surprise. Like other Americans, he took the attacks of 2001 on New York and Washington DC as a deep personal insult, and he was always on the lookout for signs of fanaticism's spread.

During the three-hour flight David regaled me with 'war' stories. He'd been sent to Pakistan during first phase of the US war on terror in neighbouring Afghanistan and he took great delight at the American victory. He carried the outrage of September 11 with him into the crowded streets, privately mocking locals who mistook him for an Arab simply because he was unshaven, and softly cheering at the sight of B-52 vapour trails overhead on another mission to destroy the rule of the Taliban.

David Leland is famous for ruminating and making glass-is-half-full predictions – a Scorpio trait if ever there was one – however he was remarkably prescient arriving in Denpasar: this is the work of the 'bad guys', Islamic extremists, he predicted. 'Just wait and see.'

I've learned during my time in the trade that the way to manage 'the big one' is to treat it just like any other story and follow the 'recipe' of making TV. It's just like baking a cake. Put together the basic ingredients of pictures and people, and out comes a piece that answers five fundamental questions of journalism: who, what, when, where and why. In journo-jargon these are known as the 'five Ws'.

For Bali, the essentials were pictures of the remains of the Sari Club and Paddy's Bar. On that score, two surprises awaited us. For starters they were just too easy to get to. I'd imagined roadblocks, police guards and forensic teams sifting for clues under arc lights. Instead, our progress was unhindered by anyone in authority.

What actually slowed us down approaching 'Ground Zero' was the passing parade of holidaymakers who'd come to take a gander.

Crowds of people in surf clothes surged past with cameras and video recorders in hand. Legian Street was in darkness because the power had been cut, but you didn't need electricity to illuminate the weird feeling. The mood was positively jaunty. An excited, carnival atmosphere had developed as the blast site just down the street became a macabre new attraction on the Kuta strip. The living had come to gawk at the dead.

Brief snatches of conversations floated over, like pieces of a jigsaw puzzle: 'I was just there last night', 'I was there today', 'All I heard was the boom', 'I came running to have a look', 'The guy was definitely dead, mate'.

I was so focused on the crowd that I failed to notice the obvious and almost fell into the crater caused by the car bomb. It took a few beats to adjust to the darkness, and the dawning realisation that I had not only arrived at Australia's 'Ground Zero' but was standing right in front of the smoking ruin of the Sari Club. The Sari was an internationally infamous watering hole. Lonely Planet and other guidebooks had put it on the map as *the* place for a beer or ten, especially if you were an Aussie or Kiwi.

As it happened, this fact had also been noted by the fascist-minded lunatics from Jemaah Islamiah. It was their now famously monstrous proposition that blowing the place sky high would help boost their ill-conceived campaign for an Islamic mega-state across most of South-East Asia.

Just across the street, Paddy's Bar stood as another beacon of Western licentiousness. Loud music, cheap beer and local hustlers pretending to be sexy made Paddy's another well known international landmark for decadence. It was tailor-made for those who believe in committing mass murder in the name of Allah.

Standing before the ashes of both clubs, David and I had an almost simultaneous reaction. It wasn't horror or shock, but rather a professional frustration. 'It's too dark to film anything,' we said almost in unison. And so it was. Too dark to film any kind of night-time pictures. Too dark to notice that we were stepping on crucial bits of exploded car that later led the forensic experts to identifying the vehicle and its owner, and making an arrest. It was too dark to see pieces of charred bodies in the rubble. And *mea culpa*: we absent-mindedly kicked around a piece of a wrecked car while we discussed our next move. None of this was deliberate or self-conscious. And we weren't alone in such disengaged behaviour. Several groups of Bali police officers stood nearby idly kicking similar pieces of debris, smoking cigarettes, flicking butts and making small talk. It was so cosy I wondered if anyone had considered putting the kettle on.

We were all like VIP visitors on a movie set where the actors were between takes. Nothing about the scene seemed real. Was that a smoke machine over there? This is not to suggest that we were unaware that a couple of hundred people had perished on this spot. But awareness was distorted by our proximity. In most cases authorities keep media crews as far as possible from crime scenes, especially one so large. But in Bali we had intimate, peeping-tom access, a backstage pass to horror. Soak it up, suck it in. It was a once-in-a-lifetime experience. And isn't that what the cheery punters with cameras had come for too?

Had we wanted, David and I could have walked deeper into the wreckage and begun our own personal search for interesting clues or maybe a memento or two. Indeed, had we abandoned all sense of dignity we could probably have persuaded the coppers to take our photograph – capture the grizzly moment. Civility, respect for the dead, law and order, simple commonsense; they were all missing in action that night. The closer you looked, the more blurred the bigger picture became, and the bigger picture was – you had to remind yourself – mass murder.

Gawking aside, there was no point hanging about. After calculating that the 'TV recipe' called for accounts of survivors and witnesses, we made our way back through the crowds and drove towards the main hospital. Oddly enough for a Sunday night, the streets were chocked with traffic.

Our driver explained that word was out that the bodies of the dead were piling up at the mortuary. The facility was intended for a maximum of eight or nine bodies at any one time. This disaster was causing overload in the extreme. Not knowing what else to do, hospital workers were carrying the dismembered, burned and broken corpses outside and leaving them to rot in the open air. At first there were a few, then a few dozen and then a hundred. By Sunday night the mortuary grounds had disappeared under a blanket of the dead.

The road outside was gridlocked by Balinese who had pulled over and leapt onto the fence to watch the unfolding spectacle of death without dignity. According to one distressed Australian nurse we ran across later, some of the locals had gone over the top, literally and figuratively, by climbing the fence into the compound to play a game of 'soccer' with a severed head.

I didn't see it happen so I can't swear by the story but the woman who sought me out to tell it seemed distressed and sincere, and didn't want to make mileage of the issue in front of the cameras. She just wanted to tell someone. Her story reminded me of the Joseph Conrad classic *Heart of Darkness*, which I'd read during my last year in high school. The grotesque violence and cruelty that I sometimes come across in my job brings back the Conrad line about how a civilised man may succumb to 'the fascination of the abomination'. Not to suggest moral equivalence; but isn't the urge to become a mortuary spectator (certainly not a player) just the same as the urge which makes any of us slow down to catch a glimpse of a routine traffic accident? Aren't we all sometimes tempted to take a look? In different degrees, it is a garden-variety 'fascination of the abomination'. In Bali, mine was as just as acute as anyone else's. What makes reporters different is that professional necessity makes looking *obligatory*. How else does one summon up the words?

Guided by our driver, David and I went in search of the living. Arriving at the hospital, I recalled my theory that doctors and journalists respond to disasters in a similar fashion. For both it's about process and outcome, never the victim. Both empathise and move on. But for both professions, that night, the rule was put to the test. There's something breathtaking about the way one is struck by horror and revulsion. In Bali it hit in waves. It started at the blast site but the absence of the human casualties made it seem less real. It was tragedy in sepia, devoid of blood and gore. But there was no escaping the 'realness' of the disaster at the hospital. I quietly gasped for air like a drowning man, drawing in ballast to keep me steady on my feet.

First stop was the emergency room, by now twenty-four hours into a crisis that was never envisaged by the planning department of Indonesia's Ministry of Health. The hospital was small, ill-equipped, under-lit and soiled from a constant bombardment of unspeakable bombing injuries. Exhausted medics moved about deliberately but slowly, fatigue eating at them. In a corner of the emergency room I noticed a basket of green bed linen that had been soaked dark by blood. On the floor there was more blood, displayed like a Pro Hart canvas – here a neat drop, there a big splash, over there a wild gush, probably from a recent arterial burst. Footprints smeared and spread bloodstains across every square inch of the floor.

Under one occupied gurney it was oozing rich, thick and fresh, bubbling as each new droplet arrived. I raised my gaze to find the source: a semi-conscious European man in his mid-thirties, lying flat on his back and wincing in excruciating pain. My first thought: he's OK, from the top at least. I scanned down the torso and waist. Still OK, I thought. Then the man came to an abrupt end at the knees, where I came across a pair of bandaged and bloodied stumps where his legs used to be. He'd just had a double amputation and was telling the nurse through a flood of tears that he didn't want his mum to see him this way.

I didn't need to tell David to stop filming, and I was overwhelmed by the urge to turn and run. The only thing that stopped me fleeing was the sound of an angel. Her name was Jen Fitzgerald, a nurse from Perth, who saw my revulsion and wanted to explain the chaos.

'Most of the patients had legs ripped off, like the gentleman here,' she explained. 'Their limbs are missing. Also common were head injuries, chest injuries, and burns. Most of the ones that have died had been burned.'

The urge to turn and run was gone. Instead the journalist's instincts kicked in with this: 'How bad is it?'

'I'd say most had limbs burned, their whole body burned. They're unrecognisable, even whether they're male or female.'

Jen was not a regular hospital employee, just a holidaymaker who had volunteered. She breezily dismissed suggestions that there was something heroic about her contribution, but I'd argue that she's dead wrong and to this day I believe she is deserving of a medal, *just for being there*.

'I've just been following them [patients] around like a little puppy dog and because I'm registered I'm able to look after their drips and drains and whatever they have,' Jen went on. 'It's been very satisfying work. I'm astonished that I've been able to do this sort of thing. Really, I don't feel – I feel dismayed, but I can do it.'

Twenty-four hours after the injured started arriving, the hospital wards remained a scene of barely managed chaos, with the Australian walking wounded and those still fighting for life kept in a long dark room that became known as the 'ANZAC ward'.

In spite of that, not one person there allowed themselves to complain about themselves – least of all Laurie Kerr who had seventeen stitches in the back of his head from where the roof fell on top of it.

'I've got 30 per cent of burns to my body,' he told me. 'But I can honestly tell you that the injuries pale to insignificance compared to the fear that you get in a situation like that, where you know it's either life or death. And quite frankly, I didn't think I was going to make it.'

Kerr was one of the now famous Kingsley Amateurs, a Perth football team which became emblematic of the appalling loss of life. The suburban footy team had come on end-of-season holidays to celebrate with a large party of young players and officials. Seven of them died that night. Laurie told me a vivid story about his role in saving a total stranger in the ruins of the Sari Club.

'There was only one way to get out, and there was a young girl trapped in front of me – and she wasn't strong enough to get the rubble off her. It took a lot of time because there wasn't a lot of room to work in. I managed to get her out and it was pitch black. The air was full of smoke. You couldn't see anything. You followed the voices of other screaming victims.'

Across the room, David and I found a trembling grandmother from Perth. Her name was Val, and she hovered over the bedside of her injured daughter and two teenage grand-daughters who'd been inside the Sari Club when the bombs went off. Val's sad expression of profound bewilderment and horror goes everywhere with me. It was a face that summed up so much of the grief, shock and confusion in that room. And it was contagious. During our brief encounter I dug my fingernails into the microphone and asked my questions but what I really wanted was to reach over and give her a hug of reassurance.

With his greying hair and ponytail David Marsh looked like an advertising executive from a fashionable Italian city. He was in fact a general practitioner from Melbourne who hadn't practised trauma medicine since the West Gate Bridge collapsed during the 1970s when he was a young doctor in training.

'You name it, we've done it,' he told me as he described his sleepless twenty-four hours patching together the wounded and comforting the dying.

'We were doing some very basic first aid and treating very severe injuries, some very severe burns patients, putting in drips, doing surgery on some patients, putting in catheters. It's taken me back twenty-five years.'

These angels of mercy were everywhere we turned. And to think – it almost went unrecorded.

When David and I first arrived the local nursing staff was adamant that no television cameras would be allowed inside. But an Australian ex-pat volunteer overheard my pleading. On our behalf he gently canvassed opinion, after which it was decided that the story of the ward needed to be documented, and that Australia's national broadcaster ought to be allowed to do the job.

So we met them all, the injured and their guardians – doctors, nurses, flight attendants – Australians in Bali who had rallied around their own. I was filled with admiration for each and every one of them. I've always cringed at the word 'hero', thinking it *the* single most overused cliché in the kingdom of journalism. But these people were authentic, three-dimensional heroes, the ordinary performing the extraordinary. If the bombing was an act of conventional 'evil', then the response of the hospital helpers I saw in Bali was a great counter-display of 'goodness'. They tipped the balance in favour of humanity.

So, too, the teenagers who helped with the most ghastly clean-up tasks at the mortuary. It had taken the best part of several days for the Indonesian authorities to come to grips with managing the number of bodies and body parts that were still lying exposed under baking Bali skies. Truckloads of ice were eventually brought in to keep the bodies from decomposing totally. Local seafood refrigeration wagons were also hauled in to store corpses until the forensic team could get around to performing the identification rituals. By the third day, the last part of the courtyard cleanup was all that remained, and the authorities left that to a group of Balinese schoolgirls.

The exercise commenced like a routine school excursion. The girls arrived in crisp blue uniforms in the company of two teachers. The group was taken aside to hear a tutorial on the basics of dealing with rotting bodies that was delivered with all the sensitivity of an explanation of the water cycle. The girls stood quietly absorbing the rules of self-preservation: wear a mask and gloves at all times, don't get the 'juice' on you, work in teams of two and always follow instructions.

I was part curious, part mortified. I repeatedly asked if they understood exactly what they were about to do. When they all nodded in the affirmative I suggested that maybe they had misunderstood the question. But each insisted that they hadn't, and that their involvement was voluntary.

'Yes. We do it to help,' said one.

'We are so sad for you,' said her friend.

With those assurances David and I picked up the camera and recording equipment, donned our own masks and gloves and followed the teen clean-team as they went about their macabre work. It was a steamy afternoon and the morgue was poorly ventilated. The odour of dead people hugged the ground, drifting up as we moved about, as if to snatch away the clean air. The schoolgirls were instructed to clean a corner where the first overflow of bodies had been piled. They put leftover limbs in one pile and unclaimed, unidentifiable strips of flesh and organs in another. By now most of the actual bodies had been relocated to more appropriate storage.

But not all.

He was lying flat on his back, arms placed neatly by his sides, as if enjoying a deep slumber. I guessed that he was in his twenties; tall with broad shoulders and a head of thick curly hair, and he had been physically fit. None of this apparent youth and vitality had helped to save his life, and so I was morbidly curious about the cause of death. At that point the veil of anonymity was ripped away. It dawned on me that many of the dead were just like me. Their faces were familiar, like people I had been passing on the street all my life. I knew a dozen people who could be him, and so for no other reason I concluded that he was Australian. My mind went the next irrational step further and judged that he must be from the eastern beaches of Sydney. He seemed too young and too uninjured to be dead. If he could speak, surely he'd agree. Although fire had singed his body the burn marks were superficial. It was as if he'd been rescued from a haze of smoke and had died afterwards from something completely unrelated to the explosions and fires. His death seemed somehow improbable. And yet there he was. Dead as dead can be.

Only when four schoolgirls were instructed to lift my mystery man by each limb into a black body bag did possible causes of death shockingly present themselves. His head lolled back, and a rich puddle of black blood oozed from a terrible wound in the back of his head. Then trickles from the eyes, nose and ears. Neither the schoolies nor I had noticed the likely fatal wound when he was facing upwards. Now it was on public display. More death without dignity. As they rolled his lifeless body into the bag there was the unforgettable sight of the contents of his stomach falling from yet another wound across his flat stomach. The charcoal colouring on his skin left by exposure to heavy smoke was merely death's disguise, a layer that had kept his secret for three or four days.

Throughout the two-hour exercise the Balinese schoolgirls were unflinching, maintaining fixed expressions the likes of which you'd expect from a world-class poker player. If they experienced any sense of revulsion, any urge to throw up or run and hide, they kept it to themselves. I found their neutrality unnerving. I searched each of their faces for reaction of any kind, maybe even a tear. But nothing came.

Later I reasoned that this was a display of Hindu indifference to the physical. To them the dead were merely empty vessels, abandoned by the soul that had transcended the mortal world for the next assignment. I have no such spiritual framework, and this ancient belief in the separation of flesh and soul could not persuade me from looking upon the same bodies and thinking it was still possible that they would rise up and continue their lives.

Crazy thoughts came to mind: how about an announcement over the loudspeaker? 'Okay, people. The exercise is over. Please return to your disco and resume dancing.' Or maybe the forensic team could go from bag to bag and gently tap each and every corpse on the shoulder or politely cough to interrupt their sleep. I was obsessing on this half-mad notion that if only we addressed the dead directly they'd stop being quite so dead.

By the end of the assignment in Bali I was consumed by collective outrage – on behalf of the dead who could no longer speak and the families who could. Everybody had questions for the murderers about what, where, when, etc., but for me it boiled down to *why* – and by extension the question that could never be satisfactorily answered: *How could you?*

This grief, which had been chasing me for days, finally came to dinner. Around the table was a team of workmates; James and Derek from Bangkok, and Kate and Michael from Sydney. In the small talk it emerged that a crusty former ABC journalist who I hadn't seen or spoken to in ten years had recently died. The brutal truth was that I'd never really liked him very much, but regardless, my reaction was instant and primal. The room went dark and people moved in slow motion. I could hear the voices around the table, but they now seemed to be at a great distance. There were tears, floods and floods of tears.

Not for a man I knew – but for two hundred people I didn't.

JONATHAN HOLMES has been working continuously in television current affairs and documentary for more than thirty years.

He was trained by and spent his early career with the BBC, where he spent twelve years, the last six as a producer for the weekly current affairs program *Panorama*.

In 1982, Jonathan came to Australia to take over as Executive Producer of *Four Corners*, where he spent four years. After a stint making documentaries in the USA, he returned to Australia in 1987 as Head of ABC TV Documentaries. In 1991 he was asked to become Executive Producer of a new program, *Foreign Correspondent*. He designed the format, recruited the Sydney team that was to supplement the ABC's overseas bureau reporters, and led the program for its first year.

Jonathan spent 1993 on a sabbatical in Sweden, from which he travelled twice to Moscow to produce stories with ABC Moscow Correspondent Deborah Snow – including the following report from Mongolia. Since then he has reported many *Foreign Correspondent* stories in his own right from all over the world. He spent two years in the ABC's Washington Bureau and is now reporting for *Four Corners*.

Last year Jonathan was awarded a special UN Association Silver Award in recognition of twenty-five years of journalistic achievement.

The Princess and the Camel: Mongolia

He wasn't on horseback, he didn't have a tufted spear and there was only one of him, not a horde. But the Mongolian official advancing towards me through a rainstorm in the Gobi Desert, decked out in spiked helmet and velvet ceremonial robe, *did* have an electric cattle-prod in his hand. To judge by the evil buzzing and the blue sparks it was emitting, he had every intention of using it. I had no problem at all in believing that this bloke was a direct descendant of the nomad warriors who back in twelve hundred and something had laid waste the civilised world.

'Really,' I thought, as I allowed myself to be herded back to our car like a runaway steer, 'does the job get any weirder than this?'

We wouldn't have been in the Gobi Desert at all if it hadn't been for Princess Anne. And until we arrived in Ulan Bator, we had no idea that we'd be sharing Mongolia with Her Royal Highness the Princess Royal.

Not that the coincidence was really bizarre. In the first week in July the Mongolians celebrate the feast of Naddam. In Ulan Bator, and in towns right across the country, herders from the open steppe gather to compete in the three traditional sports of the Mongol warrior: wrestling, archery and horse racing.

Even in the Soviet era, when Mongolia, though nominally an independent nation, was culturally, politically and economically a part of Moscow's empire, Naddam had been worth seeing. But now, in the northern summer of 1993, with the Soviet Union disintegrating, Mongolians were rediscovering their rich historical and religious identity, and Naddam promised to be spectacular.

So it was the obvious time to visit. Especially as behind the spectacle lay a counter-revolution in the making. Mongolia was throwing off the dead economics of Stalinism, which had tried to make steelworkers out of nomad herdsmen. It was looking for alternative economic opportunities, in tourism, in mining, in pastoralism – in fact in many of the ways that Australia has made a good living for 150 years. And, led by a Harvard-trained economist whose English was rather better than ours, the Ulan Bator Stock Exchange was due to open in a couple of weeks. It was potentially a wonderful *Foreign Correspondent* yarn – and a natural destination for a second-rank British Royal. Where opportunities for trade and financial services are opening up, the House of Windsor won't be far behind, touting the merits of British (but not, of course, Australian) commerce and industry.

A week or so earlier I'd flown into Moscow from my temporary home in Sweden, to join ABC Moscow correspondent Deb Snow, her cameraman Andy Taylor, and his wife Jo who, conveniently for the ABC, happened to be an experienced sound recordist. And all four of us had battled our way onto an Aeroflot flight from Shermetjevo Airport to Ulan Bator.

We had spent a most productive and exotic week. We'd filmed a hundred pairs of wrestlers knotting and grasping simultaneously in a dusty stadium – and the victors circling with slowly flapping arms, in imitation of the eagle of the steppe. We'd interviewed the Harvard economist and toured his new stock exchange. We'd been out on the endless grasslands, filming with a herding family and battling to look appreciative as we squatted in their yurt – the distinctive round Mongolian tent – swallowing curds and a fiery spirit distilled from mare's milk. We'd been to one of the ancient Buddhist monasteries, where aged monks, tolerated in tiny numbers by the atheist Soviet-era government, now found their rituals attended by thousands of curious and even devout Mongolians. And back at the Naddam, we had wondered as hundreds of Mongols, dressed neatly in velvet, belted gowns, knee-high riding boots, and bowler hats, swayed in their saddles as they sat their tough little mounts, so drunk that only a lifetime of horsemanship kept their knees grasping their horses' flanks.

The highlight of the week, without a doubt, had been the horse race. No mere matter of furlongs round some namby-pamby manicured racetrack, this. Two hundred small Mongolian horses careering at full gallop for twenty kilometres across the steppe, ridden bareback by jockeys who were kept light enough for the task not by dieting and sweat-baths, but by age. Not one of them was more than eight years old, and some were as young as five.

That night, in one of Ulan Bator's few restaurants, we bumped into a gloomy party of Fleet Street Royal Watchers. They told us that the Princess (an Olympic equestrienne, of course, and like all her family a fanatical follower of horseflesh) was furious because she and her entourage had been kept a full kilometre back from the racetrack. In fact, as far as we could gather, the tour had not been going well, either for HRH or for the Fleet Street hacks.

'Hardly got within twenty feet of her for a week,' complained the photographer from the tabloid *Sun* in a rich cockney. 'It's not her fault, mind. She's not a bad stick, knows the sort of thing we need. It's all them Mongolian minders. Got a way to go before they get the hang of this democracy lark, know what I mean?'

But Princess Anne was not our story; we followed our agenda, and she followed hers.

After a week's hard work, we had shot everything we needed for our main report. But the sparse airline connections between Ulan Bator and Moscow meant we still had two or three days before we could return. So our thoughts turned to the need for an extra 'postcard' for the program. The British Embassy, when I made an enquiring call, informed me that the Princess had a scheduled visit to the Gobi Desert the following day.

Could we come too? I asked.

'Well, strictly speaking there's only space for journalists specifically accredited to the Her Royal Highness's trip, old man. And you and your chaps aren't on the list, are you?'

No, we weren't. But I pointed out that there was no British TV crew with the Princess, so we'd hardly be threatening anyone's exclusive rights. And of course there was a good deal of interest in the royals in Australia.

'Well, of course there is, old man. Good point. I mean to say, she's your princess too in a way, isn't she? The problem won't be with us, anyway. Delighted to have you along. It's the Mongolians you'll have to convince. They can be a bit touchy about security. And there might be a bit of logistical difficulty finding transport for another four bods. Anyway, give it a go and if you have any problems let me know and I'll see what I can do.'

We got our Mongolian fixer to work. I no longer remember how we got onto the chartered press flight from Ulan Bator to a former Soviet air base in the middle of the Gobi. I do remember the fixer telling us that the real problem would be ground transport at the other end. He thought he'd arranged a car and driver to meet us, because he didn't think there'd be space on the press bus.

So at six the next morning we shuffled onto a Russian jet in the company of twenty or so bleary-eyed British journos.

'Cor blimey, it's the kangas!'

'Aren't you lot all republicans now? The Lizard thinks you should be anyhow. No caressing the Princess now, you disrespectful colonials.'

And so on, in a river of banter which hardly ever stopped. It was only a year since Prime Minister Paul Keating, whose republican leanings were a source of endless fascination for the British press, had appeared to put his arm around the Royal Person during a state visit by the Queen – and was instantly dubbed by *The Sun* 'the Lizard of Oz'.

On the flight, I learned from a helpful reporter from *The Daily Mail* that this was strictly the C-team of Royal watchers. The A-team was invariably camped outside whatever castle, palace, chalet, Caribbean island or luxury pub Princess Diana was inhabiting on any particular night, wherever in the world it might be. The Queen herself, when she was actually doing anything, merited the B-team these days. The C-team was called out to accompany minor royals on trips that seemed to promise the odd good colour story or splashy photo-op.

There had been precious few of either so far in Mongolia. So the Gobi Desert trip was going to be crucial. 'We do rather need to earn our airfares,' said the *Mail* bloke ruefully. 'I haven't had a single front-page story all week.'

'What we really need,' said the *Mirror* photographer, 'is the Princess on a Camel. That's the money shot.'

'Do you think you'll get it?' I asked, wishing desperately we had the camera running on this conversation.

'We live in hope, comrade. We live in hope.'

After a brief hour's flight, and with the morning sun still low enough to cast a golden light over the landscape, we landed in the Gobi Desert.

We could easily have been in the Australian outback. The Gobi is the great desert of central Asia, but it has much more in common with the Gibson than it does with the Sahara or Arabian Deserts. Or at least this patch of it did. A flat plain, covered in metre-high scrub that looked remarkably like saltbush, stretched to a red and ochre mountain range spread along the northern horizon.

To my eyes it was a stunningly beautiful place. But it was not what the Brits had been expecting – and more to the point, not what their editors or their readers would expect. And in the tabloid news business, expectations are there to be met.

'Call this a desert?' cried the *Sun* photographer in anguish as he came down the aircraft steps. 'This is not a sodding desert! Where's the sand dunes? Where's the camels? Where's the [adjectival] palm trees?'

The grumbling press pack, laden with cameras, tripods, and lenses the size of astronomical telescopes, was herded onto a bus. Its destination, we'd been informed on the plane by the smooth British equerry, was a gorge of reportedly spectacular beauty some two hours' drive from here.

It was not a big bus. It was quite clear that there was not going to be room for four Australian extras and a Mongolian fixer. And our promised car was nowhere to be seen.

'Well, see if you can rustle up some transport and catch up,' said the Brit helpfully. 'We'll probably have to stop and have tea with the local nabobs, so you should have plenty of time.' And with that, the bus disappeared towards the mountains in a cloud of dust.

But at least we would be able to get exclusive pictures of the Princess's plane landing in the Gobi Desert. It would make the perfect opening shot to the postcard. We could hear the drone of engines as the plane approached. Hastily Andy set up his tripod – and that's when we got the first hint of more serious problems ahead.

A reception committee was forming on the apron: a bevy of important-looking officials, all dressed in full ceremonial regalia – velvet knee-length belted robes, boots, and instead of the bowler hats of ordinary folk, wonderful spiked helmets with cheek flaps straight out of the Genghis Khan picture books.

One of these gentlemen now detached himself from the party and stalked in our direction. He spoke brusquely in Mongolian. Even before our fixer had translated, it was obvious what he was saying: 'No filming!'

'Tell him we have the permission of the British Embassy to cover the Princess's visit to the Gobi,' I said.

Exchange of views in Mongolian. 'He says the People's Republic of Mongolia decides what happens here, not the British Embassy.'

That 'People's Republic' was a dead giveaway. We were in the presence of an unreconstructed Soviet-style official. The counter-revolution under way in Ulan Bator clearly hadn't penetrated the official fiefdoms down here in the south.

'Tell him we have press passes issued by the People's Republic,' I said, proffering mine. Behind me, I knew without looking, Andy and Jo would be quietly continuing to set up; when the Princess's plane landed, they would get the best shot they could from where they were, then Andy would push his luck by going in for hand-held close-ups. Deb, the fixer and I had simply to keep the dialogue going and the official distracted. We'd all been in these scenarios so often before that none of us needed to spell out the procedure to the others.

Deb chimed in: 'Tell him the Queen of England is also the Queen of Australia. Tell him the Australian people will be very upset if we cannot document the visit of the Princess to Mongolia.' It seemed a reasonable hope that we could keep the guy distracted for an eternity while we explained the constitutional relationship between the Commonwealth of Australia and the House of Windsor.

A spurt of Mongolian, with much derisive gesturing at my press pass.

'He says he is under strict instructions from the Ministry of Information that only journalists with the appropriate accreditation may photograph the British visitor,' translated the fixer. 'You do not have the appropriate accreditation.'

I'd already noticed that the Fleet Street royal-watchers had press passes identical to ours, except that they had a red diagonal stripe across them. It looked as though the absence of a red diagonal was going to be a serious impediment.

But the royal plane was landing, and Andy was crouched over the camera, nursing his focus as he followed it on his longest lens.

Genghis, as I was beginning to dub him in my mind, was no fool. With three strides he had planted himself, arms folded and helmet glittering, in front of Andy's lens. Whatever else transpired, our opening shot was irretrievably ruined. And one glance at Genghis's implacable features was enough to convince all of us that we weren't going to win another round.

As we watched in helpless frustration, the royal party and its reception committee piled into a line of big black Zil limousines, and set off in the tracks of the press bus towards the mountains.

It is part of a producer's job to make sure 'the trains run on time'. Getting your crew stranded in the middle of the Gobi Desert while the story disappears over the horizon is not part of the job description. Deb Snow, a famously persistent and competitive journalist, was not a happy woman.

Still, our fixer kept assuring us that transport was coming. And sure enough, half an hour later, a small dust cloud approached and resolved itself into an ancient but serviceable limousine of indeterminate make and vintage. Within ten minutes we were off in pursuit of the Princess.

As we approached the mountains, we noticed a strange phenom-enon. Angry-looking clouds were boiling up over the crest of the range and spreading down towards us. As the road began to climb into a narrow valley, the sun went in. A few kilometres later, large individual rain drops began to spit down. By the time we caught sight of the line of Zil limousines parked outside an official-looking building by the roadside, the rain was coming down in sheets.

Obviously, HRH was having tea with the nabobs. We needed to go on up the gorge, to be ready when the rain stopped and the Princess arrived. But until Genghis's opposition was overcome, it was pointless to go further.

We decided the best tactic was for me to get inside the building and talk to the British Ambassador, whom we'd seen in the royal party. Perhaps he could persuade Genghis that we were all on the same side.

I had no waterproof gear – well, you don't think of taking it to the Gobi, do you? Within a few paces, I was soaked to the skin. A few paces more, and my heart sank. Stalking down to meet me from the building was none other than Genghis himself.

And that's when the electric cattle-prod made its appearance. It zipped and sparked through the rain. Genghis was clearly in no mood for conversation. As I walked, humiliated, back to the car I could see Andy trying to shoot proceedings out of the window.

Deb Snow was having none of it. Out of the car she came, arguing and remonstrating. To our shock, Genghis placed his hand on her chest, and shoved with brutal force. She reeled back against the car door. Then Genghis wrenched open the driver's door, leaned in and pulled the bonnet hatch.

The fixer was nearly frantic. 'We must go, sir and madam. Right now! Or it will be too late!' Genghis was stalking round to the open bonnet. He was clearly intent on grabbing our distributor cap and immobilising us right then and there.

'Go! Go!' I shouted. The driver slammed the car into reverse and backed off into the mud, and away we charged, slithering down the mountain road.

Despondently, we turned towards the airport. Andy had perhaps got some of the action on tape, but not enough to make a sequence, let alone a postcard. It seemed to me that we should call it a day. But Deb was made of tougher fibre. 'The Brit said that after the gorge they were going to visit a camel-breeder. That's where we're going.'

We stopped while the fixer and the driver conferred. They thought they knew where the camel-breeder would be. With much rather noisy sighing, Andy, Jo and I climbed back into the car.

We found him two hours later: a couple of yurts planted in the middle of nowhere, and a dozen or so shaggy, two-humped Bactrian camels, hobbled and grazing on the tough thorny vegetation.

The breeder was amicable enough. He confirmed he was expecting an important visitor that afternoon, though he had no idea who. But there seemed no pointing adding to our already massive stock of tapes by shooting a camel-breeder apropos of nothing.

So we mooched about and waited. Eventually the normal cloud of dust announced the imminent arrival of the C-team – and not far behind, the Zil limousines could be seen bouncing down the track.

The Fleet Street boys piled out of their bus.

'Oy, oy, it's the kangas again! Thought we'd lost you, Bruces and Sheilas. Thought you'd taken a shortcut back down-under!'

But there was no time for explanations. The Princess was coming. The *Sun* photographer swiftly drew a semi-circular line in the dust with the point of his one-legged camera stand. 'Here's the rules, Aussies. No one over the line, or you'll bugger up everyone else's shot. Got it?'

It made sense. If one of us broke ranks for a close-up, everyone else would have to do so too and we'd end up with an undignified scrum and no decent shots at all.

The Princess's motorcade drew to a halt. Deb and I were braced for the appearance of Genghis, but to our surprise and relief he seemed to have dropped out of the party. As the Princess emerged from her car, a cacophony of flashes and shutters broke out – and yelled instructions: 'Over here, Princess! Come on, Anne love, give us a smile! Oy, Your Royal 'Ighness, 'ave a chat wiv a camel for us, will yer?'

But the Princess wasn't playing ball – at least, not yet. With a smirk and a wave in our general direction, she dived into the main yurt for tea.

For forty minutes, we waited in the blazing heat. We prevailed on the Brits to allow Andy into the yurt with his camera, but the result, said Andy, was far from spectacular. The C-team spent the time in a frenzy of speculation, imprecations to the Almighty and pleas to the British equerry.

'Now come on, Hugh, yer've gotta make 'Er 'Ighness see reason. It's our last chance.'

'It really isn't up to me whether Her Royal Highness is invited to ride a camel, let alone whether she consents to do so.'

The Mail opined to *The Telegraph* that she wouldn't be able to resist the challenge of riding a Bactrian camel.

'Oh yes, she will,' said *The Telegraph*. 'She knows perfectly well what a twit you'll all make her look. Anyway she's already ridden a camel in Saudi back in 1985, and that was a real racing dromedary, not a lumbering pack-animal like these.'

'Fiver on it?' asked *The Mail*.

'You're on,' agreed *The Telegraph*.

The Sun was busy organising the photo-op, drawing lines in the sand, and trying to impress on the man from Mongolian TV not to cross them.

'Bloody Khan 'ere wanders into everyone's shot every bleeding time,' complained *The Sun*. 'Drives us all potty, 'e does, and honestly it's like talking to the Inscrutable Orient in person trying to get 'im to stop.'

And then to the inexpressible glee of the C-team, Hugh the

equerry approached us to announce: 'The Princess has been invited by Mr Yurgis to take a brief ride on one of his camels. The Princess has consented.'

Ten magical minutes followed. The emergence of the Princess; her introduction to the camel; her mounting the beast; the inevitable trespass by the Mongolian TV cameraman, who like most of his kind from the less-developed world had never apparently been introduced to the benefits of a tripod, and so used a hand-held camera with a wide-angle lens and needed to get within one metre of his subject for a decent close-up; the near-apoplexy of the Brits in response – Andy captured it all. Best of all, when I looked at the tapes that night there was a perfect shot: for five seconds it held a travelling close-up of the camel's haughty, contemptuous profile, then tilted up until the Princess's haughty, contemptuous profile came smoothly into view.

In truth, it was only shyness that made her look that way. As *The Sun* had assured us, she wasn't a bad stick in the end. She undoubtedly knew the gift she was giving her travelling press corps, and gave it willingly. And the ABC was the only Western TV station to secure its own footage of the Princess Royal on a Bactrian camel.

As far as I know, that footage has never seen the light of day. Thanks to Genghis's earlier efforts, we didn't have enough material for a self-contained postcard, and though we tried to work the sequence into our main story, it was never really going to fit.

Perhaps, in thirty years or so, when they compile the obituary of the King's sister, they'll find a way of using the Bactrian camel sequence. But somehow, I doubt it. Somewhere in the *Foreign Correspondent* archives, I'm afraid, the tape of the Princess riding the Camel is gradually fading away.

Originally a scientist at the Australian National University, **GORDON TAYLOR** soon became interested in film-making, and spent three years studying at the Australian Film, Television and Radio School, specialising in documentary film-making. Recruited by ABC Radio as a science broadcaster, he then moved on to other reporting roles at the ABC, in both radio and television.

On-air roles have included reporting on the radio current affairs programs *AM* and *PM*, science broadcasting on Radio National, as well as working as ABC TV's Science and Medicine Reporter.

In 1993, Gordon was posted to New Delhi to be the ABC's South Asia Correspondent, a post he filled for three years. While there, Gordon reported for *Foreign Correspondent*, including the plague in Surat.

Gordon has received many awards for his work, including a New York Television Festival Award for his *Foreign Correspondent* story on plague. Gordon is currently Program Manager at the ABC's specialist radio network, Radio National.

Plague in Surat

The Black Death. The words are immediately evocative: a metaphor for pestilence, terror and human suffering on a scale almost unimaginable. The nursery rhyme 'Ring-a-Ring-a-Rosie ...' quietly alludes to this most terrible of terrors, a pestilence that swept away perhaps a third of the civilised world in the fourteenth century '... a-tishoo, a-tishoo ...' continues the rhyme, '... we all fall down'.

The worst of all possible plagues, the Black Death evokes images of silent streets piled with corpses; of a time over 650 years ago, before science had a rational explanation for disease, or a cure. The 'Black Death' has come to be regarded almost as fable.

Who would have thought, then, that at the end of the twentieth century, 'the plague' would once again stalk victims? So it was that in September 1994 I found myself entering the all-but-deserted western Indian city of Surat. I travelled by train the two hundred and fifty kilometres north from Mumbai, the carriages almost completely empty, while the nervous train drivers and guard wore facemasks for protection. I found just one other passenger on the train. Rajeesh had already fled with his family, and was now returning to see if the city was safe. He travels against the wishes of his family '... Yes, definitely, they are telling me not to go back ...' because there have already been over forty deaths from 'the plague' in Surat. Rajeesh describes a city of scared people, and an exodus motivated by fear and confusion. 'There are lots of rumours spreading all over Surat city. When the first news came, [it was] that there is poison in the water, and nearly 60,000 people had died within six or seven hours.'

And what of the antibiotic tetracycline that can provide some protection? '... Even the Government authority can't give any of the antibiotics to people ... I searched from nearly twenty chemists in Surat, but I can't find it.'

Surat is normally a city of one and a half million people, so this stop on the line north from Mumbai is usually busy – and lengthy. Today it would be neither. The train slows for the station, and I can see the platform crowded with people, almost all wearing facemasks, and all wanting to escape the city. In just a few days, 200,000 residents fled Surat; in all, over 400,000 people ended up leaving. Even before the train has fully stopped, people are desperately clambering into the empty carriages. The halt lasts little more than a minute before the train pulls away with a full load of passengers.

I travel by car through the deserted streets to one of the many housing colonies. To a Western eye it looks poor, with dirt streets, few facilities and small unremarkable houses. But these colonies are a measure of the success and prosperity of Surat. Many of these people are migrants, drawn by the chance to make fast money in the city's burgeoning industries. They represent the new India. They are the infant middle class, upwardly mobile, educated and ambitious. And it's these 'colonies' that have been worst affected by 'the plague'.

Of the three hundred families in this suburb, only fifty remain. The rest have left, fearing for their lives. And with good reason. I come across a family group squatting outside the entrance to their home, quietly grieving. The matriarch of the family died only hours after becoming ill. 'We got to the hospital in five minutes,' says her husband. 'They did some tests and told us she had died. Still, we waited for an hour, and asked the doctor how this had happened, and they said 'What can we do? ...' Most of the family had never heard of 'the plague' until now, although the man's father remembers hearing stories as a child. 'This disease happened a hundred years ago, and our elders would talk about it. We've never even heard of it happening [in our lifetime].'

'The plague' is caused by a bacterium, *Yersinia pestis*, that infects rats. Fleas living on the rodents spread the disease, and by biting humans pass the virulent disease on to our species. The most common form, bubonic plague, begins innocently enough as a fever. After an incubation period of about six days, victims suddenly experience pains in the chest, difficulty breathing, vomiting of blood and high fever. But the most characteristic signs of this gruesome disease are the painful swellings or 'buboes' that occur in the glands in the groin and armpits, and the dark blotches which erupt under the skin from bleeding, giving the disease its name, the 'Black Death'. Mental confusion, hallucinations, and finally coma and death follow rapidly.

But the *Yersinia pestis* bacterium can also attack the lungs, resulting in the more virulent 'pneumonic plague'. It is this even more potent form of the disease that erupted in Surat. Fits of coughing release hordes of bacteria from plague abscesses in the lungs. Unlike bubonic plague, this more virulent form can be passed from human to human by a simple cough or sneeze. And pneumonic plague kills even more quickly. Violent, bloody coughing, and the characteristic dark purple blotches follow an incubation period of a couple of days. The bacteria quickly engulf the body and can affect the brain. Coughing and choking, the patient finally suffocates and dies.

A truly gruesome death. Little wonder, then, that when it first appeared in Surat, unannounced and undiagnosed, terror struck the city. But why recount this story when, as a foreign correspondent living in India, I daily came face to face with people in the most desperate of situations? This is a country where life is cheap, and a few hundred deaths amongst a population of one billion seem insignificant.

What was different here was that the fear touched me, and connected me in a way few other events would. As a correspondent I had 'parachuted' into war zones like Kashmir, and seen the incomprehensible violence of the guerrilla war by the Tamil Tigers in Sri Lanka. The difference with this story was that I also was a potential victim of a threat you can never see. I was feeling the same vulnerability as the people I observed.

On a rational level I was reassured by medical advice that a fit and healthy person is less likely to succumb to the disease. And it was thought that large doses of the antibiotic tetracycline would act as prophylaxis against the disease. Still, that unreasonable fear remained.

It was a fear I was to see in the faces of almost all those I met in Surat.

Just like medieval cities such as Florence and Genoa, the government and health authorities are unprepared. In the first days of the outbreak hundreds of doctors leave the city, fleeing alongside hundreds of thousands of their fellow citizens. For those who fall prey to the illness, there is only one hope for survival – the Civil Hospital in Surat. Ordinary patients are moved out, and the centre of the medical response becomes the hospital's antenatal ward, which has been cleared and turned over to the treatment of plague victims.

Dressed in blue camouflage fatigues, and with their rifles held tensely, paramilitary police guard every exit. Their presence is a measure of the all-pervading fear. After a hundred suspected plague carriers deserted the hospital, the government was forced to post these paramilitaries to prevent further escapes. But they too are fearful of the invisible threat of disease. They stand uneasily, fidgeting and suspicious.

Inside, the fear is palpable. An Indian government hospital is always a spartan and austere place. That seems to add to the sombre mood. Patients sit or lie in beds, with sadness and anxiety showing on their faces. One patient strains forward in bed as she is attended to by two nurses. But the effort is too great, and she slumps back onto the bed, crying.

Doctor Divya Thyagorajan is in charge here. Young and nervous, he tells me that the patient is a nurse from the hospital. She, along with another nurse and two doctors, have succumbed to the disease after working in the hospital. 'On the first two or three days you could say that it was total fear,' he explains. 'In fact, even we didn't know what we were dealing with … we were quite surprised. I mean, one has read about plague and things like that, but this is the first time that most of the doctors, and especially my age group, have come across it.'

Plague thrives on poverty, of which there's plenty here. Surat may well have been 'India's filthiest city', although countless others could compete for this unwanted title. But herein lies the paradox of Surat, for it is one of the most energetic, modern and industrialised cities in India. High-rise buildings dot the cityscape, along with modern textile mills, while fax machines, computers and leading-edge industrial technology are commonplace inside them. Satellite dishes sit awkwardly atop houses and blocks of flats, testament to the consumer electronics to be found within. This is a boom town: a frontier town of the twentieth century. Poor migrant workers are drawn here from across India, enticed by the prospect of fast money, and an escape from the stifling caste and class shackles of rural India. They come to work in the textile mills, churning out millions of metres daily of the bright cotton-silk used to make that quintessential of Indian cloths, the sari. Or they work on lathes in small gem shops in quarters of the city like the Zaveri Bazaar, where half the diamonds sold in the world are cut and polished.

But this unbridled enterprise and rapid industrialisation tests the limits of the city to house and service its ever-burgeoning workforce. More than half the people live in slums like that around Ved Road. The city's drainage and sewerage system doesn't reach here; so torpid black creeks become the slum's toilet. Sick and scabby-looking children play amongst the piles of refuse that are dumped in any vacant space. A bloated dead cow floats in a stagnant pool of water, left after the flooding of the Tapi River that flows through the city.

Thus the paradox that a medieval scourge was visited upon a city that epitomises modern India – with all its hopes of becoming another Asian Tiger, an economic powerhouse and regional superpower. The plague shows that, try as it might, India's destiny is linked, as it always has been, to its traditional agrarian society. It's also a clue to how the 'Black Death' came to infect the city.

Using the armoury of modern science, epidemiologists have now pieced together a scenario for the eruption of the disease. And it's the same as for every plague epidemic – a series of national disasters cause change in the germ and social circumstances. The migrant workers are a clue, as are events hundreds of kilometres to the south, a year earlier. The Beed District, near the town of Latur, lies in a remote part of the central Indian state of Maharashtra. In the early hours of the morning of 30 September 1993 a severe earthquake struck, causing immense damage. The houses in this area are made out of the local stone, and are built without cement, a simple mud mixture holding the rocks together. When the quake struck with massive force, the houses simply fell down on their sleeping residents. Rain then followed, washing the mud into the rubble and entombing the victims beneath. As many as 30,000 people were buried in the rubble. In the town of Killari I watched as a man dug the bodies of seven members of his family from what had been his home. All that remained was a large muddy mound.

As well as a massive death toll, the quake unleashed hordes of wild rats from the forests. Known to be carrying fleas with the *Yersinia pestis* bacteria, the rats quickly overran fifty or more villages in the weeks after the quake. Then the rats began to die. With their rodent hosts dead from the plague, the fleas then attacked the villagers, passing the disease on to humans. In the month before the outbreak in Surat, bubonic plague was diagnosed in villagers in the Beed District. Doctors believe that it was here that the disease transformed into the more potent variant, pneumonic plague. Unlike the bubonic form, which needs rats and fleas to transmit the bacteria, in pneumonic plague human beings themselves become the vectors. It's most likely that it was one of Surat's migrant workers, returning from his village in the Beed District, who carried the plague more than seven hundred kilometres north to Surat.

That humans are carriers of pneumonic plague was sobering. In Surat more than forty people died within a few days of the first diagnosis on 20 September. But the medical response was rapid once the doctors knew what they were dealing with. Not so the response of government, which was slow and ineffective. Garbage continued to mount up; antibiotics were scarce or nonexistent; nothing was done to stop the exodus from the city. And many of those leaving were carrying the bacteria, creating the opportunity for the disease to spread across India.

Many of Surat's doctors, angry at the government's inadequate response, come together to try and remedy the shortcomings. A sort of council of war is held each evening in one of the doctors' clinics. Gynaecologists, psychiatrists, anaesthetists, and even a neuro-surgeon, form a type of parallel administration in the beleaguered city. They try to convey their concern to those in charge – but nobody is listening.

'Well, it's not advisable to leave the city, because then it's dangerous for the nation,' says Dr Smarhar Amin. 'Of course this was our belief earlier also, and we conveyed it to the government officials … please don't let the people in the city get out of the city – that means quarantine. Quarantine the city …' The government never tried.

Quarantine was ironically invented in Genoa in the fourteenth century as the city was confronted by the arrival of plague from the east – *quaranta* was the forty days of isolation before plague ships could berth. 'Those travellers who have arrived from Gujarat, and especially those from Surat …' blurts a loudspeaker at Mumbai's Central Railway Station '… the Naval Hospital has opened a Plague Screening Centre. Before you leave the station please go there for a medical examination.' The train from Surat has just arrived, carrying hundreds more escapees from the city. It's a week after the first diagnosis and still the government's efforts at contain-ment are ineffectual. Passengers emerge from the carriages, most wearing face masks. Whole families hasten down the platform. Heads down and eyes averted, they hurry past the officials hovering at a makeshift stall on the platform. Almost every passenger avoids being tested. Any plague carriers can just walk out on to the streets of Mumbai and pass on the disease.

The *Yersinia pestis* bacteria did spread, carried by the 400,000 refugees who fled the city. Soon plague cases were reported in the capital, New Delhi, and in Calcutta on the other side of the country. Only now did the authorities do something about the threat. They aggressively tracked down carriers of the bacteria, called in epidemiologists from New Delhi to trace the human vectors of the disease, and enlisted the help of the World Health

Organisation. And at last they encouraged the scared residents of Surat to stay in their diseased city.

Quick treatment with the antibiotics streptomycin, chloramphenicol or tetracycline reduces the mortality rate of either form of the plague to less than 5 per cent. In the end, only fifty-four people died in the Surat outbreak, although unofficial estimates put the figure closer to three hundred. Many families immediately cremated their loved ones, as is the Hindu tradition, but didn't report the death. And belated action by the government prevented the plague taking hold across the country.

But the question 'what if …?' lingers. What if the plague had taken hold in the shanty towns and slums of Mumbai, with twelve and a half million people, India's largest city? What if the disease had spread across India, and into neighbouring Pakistan and Bangladesh, exposing more than one and a half billion people to the threat of the plague? What if the 'connectedness' of the modern world meant air travellers had spread the *Yersinia pestis* bacteria around the globe?

Certainly Surat proved that the 'Black Death' is not just a fable from medieval times, and that it must be taken seriously. But the Surat outbreak also suggests how we should react to any of the plagues of modern times. Surat showed that fear is the greatest enemy of effective control. It was fear that led to the mass exodus of 400,000 people, and to the consequent spreading of the plague as those fleeing acted as human vectors for the disease. Governments must be able to communicate effectively to the populace, allaying their fears, and educating them quickly in what they can do as individuals to prevent disease spreading.

But perhaps there is another lesson from Surat: that – confronted by plague, whether it be the 'Black Death', human influenza or more recently Sudden Acute Respiratory Syndrome (SARS) – sometimes governments *have* to act in a draconian way, limiting citizens' rights, forcibly isolating disease carriers, and even quarantining whole cities. They are choices that are unpleasant, but perhaps essential.

TIM LESTER has been a broadcast journalist for twenty-one years, including ten with ABC Television, reporting from a number of state capitals as well as overseas bureaux in Jerusalem, Bangkok and Washington.

Tim spent time in the Middle East in 1997 and 1998, was South-East Asia Correspondent in 1998 and 1999, the *7.30 Report*'s Political Editor in 2000, and North America Correspondent in 2001 and 2002. Among the many stories he has covered are: the Palestinian–Israeli conflict, including suicide attacks in Israel; a *Foreign Correspondent* feature with Hezbollah inside the Southern Lebanon Security Zone; the conflict between UN Weapons Inspectors and the Iraqi Regime in Baghdad; the sacking and imprisonment of Anwar Ibrahim in Mahathir's Malaysia; the repression of Aung San Suu Kyi and her democracy supporters in Burma; the historic general elections in Cambodia and Indonesia; the rise of militia violence in East Timor and the country's historic independence ballot (he was ABC TV's correspondent with the military on the first day of the landing of the Australian-led military mission to restore order); the anti-globalisation protests at the Summit of the Americas in Quebec; the economic collapse of Argentina; the September 11 attacks on New York and Washington; and the rise and election of Luis Inacio Lula da Silva to the Brazilian presidency.

He is currently the *7.30 Report*'s Business and Economics Editor, based in Melbourne.

Brazil: God's Slum

Through tinted windows, the 'City of God' looks calm and businesslike. Ramshackle shops and beer joints glow in the mid-evening darkness as they drift by our van. People work, drink or simply stand and take in the activity, but no-one seems to speak. The notorious Rio slum, or *favela*, appears frozen in silence. It's as though the people here have just been ordered to close ranks against the unfamiliar van that's driven into their dusty street.

Fear can distort people's sense of their role in the events around them. The apparent silence probably says more about my perception of danger than about the street itself. We have been told not to wind down our windows. So I can't hear this place – or smell it. It snakes by me, surreal and dangerous, not in anything much that we see, but dangerous by reputation. These people don't know we have crossed into the drug-gang fortress they call home, and most wouldn't care if they did. But at least a few would care. 'Cidade de Deus' or the 'City of God' is a stronghold of the Red Command. Its leaders see no benefit in advertising their cocaine and marijuana business to the world, nor the fact that the Red Command and Rio de Janeiro's two other brutal drug gangs employ many thousands of Brazilian boys as child soldiers to terrorise and kill those who might threaten their business. The drug gang would not want us here. And the drug gang would definitely not want one of its youngsters breaking ranks and speaking with us. But we're trying to meet someone who we're told is ready do just that. What we need is simple enough: to get in, stay hidden while we record his point of view, then get out again.

Cidade de Deus lent its name to a recently released movie, *The City of God*, about life among Brazil's urban poor. The acclaimed drama has given the slum notoriety. But Cidade de Deus is little different from Rio's seven hundred or so other *favelas*: it rises above the others only by virtue of the incongruity of its name.

Some 1.2 million Rio residents live in these government-service vacuums, abandoned by the state to cope as best they can. Their vista is a hotchpotch of tin, brick and concrete, with masses of rough tenements, badly-built houses and dirty alleys. Here, Brazil's law is no more enforced than its building regulations are. The toughest thug – with the biggest gun – rules. That said, these places are not without order. Authority is inseparable from terror and drugs, but in its own sad way, it works. As we're about to learn, the view from Cidade de Deus is that the *favela* must fight – and often kill – to protect its own delicate 'order' from the anarchy of the outside world.

We leave the dusty commercial strip and make our way down a dark, narrow side street. Our driver turns the van into a private yard and closes a huge swinging gate, sealing a two-metre-high perimeter wall. We are now hidden from scrutiny, and he encourages us from the van.

We go to work. Dave Martin takes his bag of camera lights from the back of the van, and begins unpacking. Dave is a bald, bike-riding cat lover with a lively temper when he's crossed, but on another level he's utterly unflappable. Like many camera operators, his tools absorb him. He can stand in the middle of a melee and watch it with the detachment of an observer in a lounge chair with a cuppa. A shrink – if he ever went to one – would tell him he responds inappropriately to stressful situations. That is to say, he stands in the middle of them. In clouds of tear gas as anti-globalisation protestors attacked the Summit of the Americas in Quebec city, or in the screaming crush as Malaysian troops stormed Anwar Ibrahim's Kuala Lumpur home to arrest Prime Minister Mahathir's long-time deputy, Dave just stuck his eye in the viewfinder, let his soul follow and recorded with perfect calm the madness around him.

In Cidade de Deus, a melee is the last thing we want. This interview is meant to redefine the 'low' in low profile – we're trying to prevent the rest of the drug network finding out about the colleague who is breaking ranks. So why exactly is Dave setting up lights? He's about to place the equivalent of a neon sign saying 'foreign media crew' above our heads. Oblivious, Dave's mind is deep in his viewfinder again. He's worrying instead about lighting angles, and whether Cidade de Deus suffers the kinds of power surges that turn television lights into fireworks.

Producer Vivien Altman and I shake our heads. 'Dave, if you turn on *one* light, let alone three, it's going to look like the sun's rising out of this guy's yard.'

'If we don't use lights, nobody sees anything – ABC viewers included.'

Dave wins. We try to convince ourselves that the light could be dismissed as some sort of party, or maybe preparations for one of the evangelistic meetings often held in poor homes around Rio. Maybe. It just makes us that bit more edgy.

I begin pacing and mumbling possible questions to myself, and after a while turn to see Vivien drawing on a cigarette as though she's taking gas in the second stage of labour. Vivien doesn't need me to say 'What are you doing?' She reads it from my look. 'I don't smoke,' she protests. There's a brief pause as the gathered few glance at Vivien's cigarette, then back at her, and chuckle. In the City of God, if smoking gets you through, then you smoke.

In Rio, the Red Command and its two rival gangs are both feared and revered. Even wealthier 'Cariocas' (as Rio residents know themselves) have traces of respect for the drug lords who terrorise their city. Part of the mythology that's grown up with the cocaine and marijuana trade is that the gangs enforce a kind of order that low-paid, poorly equipped and subsequently corrupt police can't hope to match.

'I live in a country where I can't leave my own house without feeling afraid,' Vitor Nacimento tells me. He's a twenty-year-old student who lives '… in fear, not only of the criminals but also of the police, as they are involved in this kind of violence …'

'Sometimes you feel much better with the people that are the drug dealers – that they don't want to rob [you],' Karla Ribeiro, a young biologist, told us. 'You feel safer than with the police.'

This sense that the drug gangs are the custodians of justice in their areas is keenly felt in the gangs themselves. Several months before we visited Rio, one drug boss ordered the arrest of Brazilian journalist Tim Lopes as he worked under cover at a drug party in a Rio *favela*. Apparently, they set up a court and tried Lopes, before torturing and beheading him. The fact that they bothered with a process at all says something about their sense of separation from Brazilian society. Tim Lopes, declared a criminal for revealing drug use and sexual exploitation, was never likely to be acquitted, but his killers no doubt insist his execution was just.

The city in which Tim Lopes lived and died is as gorgeous as it is brutal. Seven million people live in Rio de Janeiro, many of them jammed along its stunning Atlantic beaches. Others, including many of the desperately poor, live around the edges of its mountains. Few countries on earth have a greater gulf between rich and poor than Brazil, and increasingly crime has bled from the poor side to the well-to-do neighbourhoods.

The day after we arrived, Vivien returned to her room in our central city hotel to find her notebook computer and other equipment and papers gone. There had been no break in. The lock on her door was intact. Surely staff in the hotel hadn't turned to stealing? We later learned that Vivien was the victim of a thief with nerve. The man had apparently entered a succession of tourist hotels, wearing a suit and behaving like a guest. He searched for rooms where hotel staff were cleaning, entered and greeted the cleaners as though he were the guest staying in the room. He then took anything of value that he might reasonably be expected to leave with – and strode from the hotel.

The person we are about to meet is no suit-and-tie crook. He's a self-confessed killer with a tribal belief that what he does is critical for his community's survival. Like those who executed Tim Lopes, he has a fierce sense of violence as an instrument of fairness. He's a rake-thin eighteen-year-old veteran of Rio's drug business, who appears out of a van and walks through the darkness and across the yard towards us, tugging a balaclava over his chin with one hand. The other hand fidgets with two pistol grips sticking out above his belt. He looks hyperactive and nervous.

We are nervous, too. Nothing stirs my instincts for danger as much as teenagers with guns. It struck me most strongly when I worked in East Timor in the months leading up to its historic independence ballot. I was frightened by the rogue chance that things could go pear-shaped just because the person with the means to kill lacked the experience to keep events under control. With age comes predictability. It might be duller, but it's safer. And the danger is all the more random when drugs are in play. Might this person lack even what steadiness a teenager can mostly muster because that calm is lost in a cloud of cocaine? There's also my own doubts about whether I'll be able to 'connect' with a person under half my age whose life experience is so utterly different from my own.

Apart from sneaking into the City of God, there are other ways to meet and speak with some of Rio's young killers. We made a thirty-minute journey into the suburbs, introduced ourselves to Superintendent Carlos Miranda, and asked to meet some of the one hundred and twenty boys in his prison. They are teenagers, twelve years old and above. They sleep on concrete bunks behind bars. Their cells are small and dark. Some walls are decorated with bible passages and impressions of Jesus. Others are covered with naked centrefolds. One has pictures of Osama bin Laden and press coverage of September 11. I ask, but don't get an answer, whether the display is inspired by respect for the terror leader or just fascination with the event. Through the bars on some windows there's a distant view of Rio – striking even from jail.

Carlos tells us we can speak with the boys, but not identify them by name or show their faces.

I meet a seventeen-year-old who is introduced as 'J'. I ask where he is from. 'Jorge Turco,' he tells me. Our translator explains: 'It loosely means George the Turk.' It turns out George was the first trafficker to bring drugs to the *favela* where 'J' lives. The people there so respected George's contribution, they named the place after him. 'J' tells me he is *munto* (sad). Why? He's not with his boys. He's the father of twin two-year-olds. I tell him that in the weeks before I left for Brazil, my partner Diane and I had found out we were expecting twins. It serves as a small link, though it's hardly something I can chat with him about. Not like the Boston academic and father of twin girls I'd interviewed shortly before leaving. When I told him I was soon to join him as a father of twins he looked at me in horror for a second or two, then said simply, 'My house is a zoo.' 'J' barely knows the babies he conceived at fifteen, and he may never see them grow up. He's a drug soldier. Prison is not such a bad outcome for now. In his home *favela*, his life expectancy is dreadfully low.

I get a sense of the danger from another inmate, who also uses the first letter of his first name to protect his identity. 'L' was twelve when he began work as a cocaine courier. He is now sixteen and has been shot twice. He shows us the scars. Not that it's unusual for those in the *favelas* to have bullet wounds. 'L' tells me his father – also a drug trafficker – has four wounds. One of them pierced the back of his skull and he can no longer talk properly.

'L' then calmly explains how he's been involved in numerous killings. In four cases he acted alone. Why? 'In order to not disturb the business of the *favela*, I had to kill, set fire and bury the bodies, so the police wouldn't come and stop our business.' He's bordering on matter-of-fact in his tone, and there's a hint of 'What is it about this you don't get?'

Any fleeting sense that I understand him disappears when I ask what he will do when he leaves prison. 'I'll go back to working with drugs,' he says, 'because it is good, I make good money very fast. You get everything that you want.' I'd expected him to at least suggest he wanted to get away from his past. I'd underestimated just how much the conflict he's a part of has become his life.

Some of the boys crowd around us as we prepare to leave. One of them insists, through our translator, that he has an important question. 'Did you come to Brazil on a plane?' he asks. His question has enough gravity for the others to stop talking and listen.

'Yes,' I tell him, 'and we'll be leaving on another plane soon.' The answer impresses him enough to pause for a second, and then he grins and comes to the point. 'You better hope it doesn't fall out of the sky.'

Risk depends on your point of view. These teenagers are the shock troops on battlefields more deadly than almost any contemporary war zone. A Sao Paulo man in his early twenties told me about his fifteen closest teenage friends. Four are alive now. Violence and drugs killed all the others. To me, that's risk – and yet if you're born to it, perhaps it's just life. Viewed from Cidade de Deus, risk is engine failure on an Airbus.

As our interview subject moves to meet us in the walled yard, a sense of risk wells inside me. He is carrying guns. We're in a place we don't know; a violent place. As he reaches us, it becomes clear that here too the danger is wrapped up in perceptions. He sees risks as well – us.

I shake his hand. He introduces himself in Portuguese, as 'JN'. I try to break the edgy feel of our meeting by explaining a little about the ABC and *Foreign Correspondent*, and then when I know Dave is recording, I ask him about his guns. Clearly, he wants us to see he's got them. He pulls one of the pistols from the front of his pants and waves it around. 'I carry heavier things – rifles. This is the minimum for the *favela*,' he says. But why two? 'If this one fails – it jams sometimes – this one doesn't. With this one, all I have to do is to pull the trigger and shoot at them.'

'JN' is eighteen. He tells us he joined the Red Command, to deal in drugs and protect the *favela*, as a ten-year-old. Mixed with bravado, there are nerves. He fiddles with the safety catch on one of his pistols. There's also that conviction that the drug-supported hierarchy, of which he is a part, is vital to his people. And he has worked himself into a place of respect. 'There are no crooks in here, no rapists,' he tells me. 'We kill them.'

On his role as a Red Command soldier, 'It's a good job,' he insists. 'Easy money [and] power.' But doesn't he face dangers in

247

here? Outside there is also betrayal, he explains. And anyway, he couldn't leave now if he wanted to, because outside the protection the Red Command offers he's a marked man. 'The day I leave the *favela*, I go straight to the coffin.'

After less than an hour with us, 'JN' is more comfortable. He smiles a couple of times. I sense we trust one another. He spills the bullets from one of his pistols. We're not *quite* relaxed enough to laugh about it, but enough at least to help him pick them up. We wish him well. He disappears back into Cidade de Deus and Dave flicks the power switches on his lights.

In a few minutes we'll drive out of here, along the *favela*'s tracks, past the stores and beer joints and back to a place where the criminals wear ties and steal computers. For many thousands of Cariocas, the *favelas* are to be feared. For many thousands more, they're home: places with dangers, yes, but the greatest fear is saved for threats from outside.

DOMINIQUE SCHWARTZ has travelled extensively during her two decades as a journalist, filing news and current affairs reports for radio and television from more than fifty countries around the world.

After a cadetship with the ABC, Dominique went on to work for numerous Australian and international news organisations, rejoining the ABC in 1992.

She has covered conflicts in Africa, Central Asia, the Balkans and the Middle East, and has reported on a broad range of issues including the AIDS epidemic, the international drug and ivory trades, and the transition to majority rule in South Africa.

In October 1997, after six years globe-trotting for *Foreign Correspondent*, Dominique was appointed the ABC's Middle East Correspondent. During her three-year posting, she covered such events as the expulsion of United Nations weapons inspectors from

Baghdad, the Israeli withdrawal from Lebanon, and the outbreak of the current Palestinian *intifada* or uprising.

Her reporting on the *intifada* won her a high commendation in Australian journalism's Walkley Awards and saw her as a finalist in the Logies for Most Outstanding Television Reporter.

In 1996, Dominique won the New York Festival/Unesco Gold Award for a *Foreign Correspondent* story on a West African campaign to stop female genital mutilation, and more recently, was awarded South Australia's Barbara Polkinghorne Award for her contribution to media, writing and artistic expression.

Dominique presents the ABC's television news in South Australia.

The Insecurity Zone

In the early hours of Wednesday 24 May 2000, Israel withdrew the last of its troops and tanks from southern Lebanon, ending two decades of occupation and one of the region's most protracted conflicts.

Israel had first invaded its northern neighbour in 1978 to root out members of the Palestine Liberation Organisation who were using southern Lebanon as a base to mount attacks against the Jewish state. In 1982, Israeli troops again stormed north, reaching the Lebanese capital, Beirut, before pulling back to an 850-square-kilometre strip of Lebanese land along the border. Israel called this area the Security Zone as it was meant to protect Israel's northern residents from cross-border attacks.

The United Nations condemned the occupation, and over time, as more Israeli soldiers were killed, there was also growing disquiet within the Jewish state over the conflict which some called Israel's Vietnam. In March 2000, the Israeli Cabinet, led by Labor Prime Minister Ehud Barak, announced it would bring the boys home by July. Emboldened and sensing victory, fighters with the Lebanese Islamic movement Hezbollah stepped up their attacks. Israel's Lebanese allies in the Security Zone – the South Lebanon Army or SLA – crumbled, and in the end the Israeli withdrawal came sooner rather than later.

As the ABC's Middle East Correspondent, I worked on both sides of the border covering the events leading to this historic occasion. In the tense, dying days of Israel's occupation, ABC Middle East cameraman Andrew Sadow, *Foreign Correspondent* producer Vivien Altman and I spent a week in Lebanon and the Security Zone, filming with Hezbollah guerrillas and gaining rare access to the bases of the South Lebanon Army.

* * *

'Please!'

Morning tea was not what I was expecting, but Yasser was politely insistent. He had the air of an old-fashioned pie seller working his way through the grandstand at the footy as he pushed past the bushes carrying a low-sided cardboard box.

It was the perfect setting for an alfresco snack: a lush valley in southern Lebanon, resplendent in the spring sunshine. Nevertheless, it seemed incongruous that we should be stopping for a picnic in a war zone. Arabs, however, are nothing if not hospitable. Who was I to refuse? It's bad manners to decline food or drink and not particularly smart, either, if the invitation comes from a man wearing a machine-gun and a necklace of ammunition.

Not that I was feeling threatened. My day with Yasser and his fellow fighters had been sanctioned by the media-relations officer with Hezbollah – a man no doubt as keen as his Israeli army counterpart to put a human face on his side of the struggle. As we sat down at the edge of a small clearing, I wondered what nourished this Islamic army. Like most things in the Middle East, what appeared from Yasser's cardboard box was not what I'd imagined: canned pineapple juice and Mars bars.

'It's no wonder Hezbollah gets better foreign media coverage than we do,' quipped a young Israeli soldier when I later recounted my experience with his enemy. 'The bastards have better caterers!'

As it turned out, on that particular day in southern Lebanon, Yasser and I didn't have time to savour our chocolate bars. The roar of an Israeli fighter jet overhead sent us scattering into the scrub. As we lay on the ground, our faces in the dirt, Yasser asked me where I was from.

'Australia.'

His face brightened and he angled his head towards me. 'Do you know Melbourne?'

'Yes. I used to live there. My parents still do.'

'Oh,' he said with a smile, 'perhaps you know my sister then?'

I've not met many soldiers I couldn't get along with. Being on their side of the firing line helps, of course. It's not difficult to build an appreciation for people if your life may depend upon them. One of the privileges of being a journalist is that you get the opportunity to see both sides of a conflict, and all combatants as human.

Abed Taqqush never had that chance.

Abed was our driver in Beirut. He yearned for the day southern Lebanon would be free of Israeli forces. A passionate man, he hated the occupiers with the same intensity he loved his family – and fast cars. Although fifty-three years old, Abed took a childlike delight in terrifying correspondents with his driving impersonations of Michael Schumacher. Except that a Formula One driver doesn't take to the track with a cigarette in one hand and a mobile phone permanently pressed to his ear in the other.

'I'm talking to Germany!' Abed would bark out proudly, turning his back to the highway and a rush of on-coming traffic to grin at us in the back seat.

His phone would ring again.

'That was Switzerland! Everyone wants to work with me. I'm not just a driver, you know, I'm a producer. The best.'

And he was.

For three decades, Abed had been driving the crème de la crème of international correspondents around Lebanon, dodging bombs, bullets and kidnappers throughout the country's long civil war. He'd never left anyone in the lurch. He might not have known all the important people around town personally, but he knew their bodyguards and drivers, and that was often better. With a good word, you could find yourself slipped into a vacant slot on a VIP's schedule, or tipped off as to a convenient place to jump your quarry. And no official requests meant no official rejections. That meant anything was possible. It all boiled down to contacts and timing. Abed had both.

'*Habibi*, I'm going to kill you!' Abed always prefaced his death threats with a term of endearment.

'Get into the car!'

Vivien, Andrew and I finished loading the camera gear into the boot of his polished Mercedes and dutifully did as commanded.

'We are in very big trouble,' he said, his face like thunder. 'The Ministry of Information has lost your papers. I don't know how you'll ever get into the south now. The official is so angry, he stormed out of the office and I can't find him anywhere. I've been on the phone all the time you were filming. You didn't send your request from Israel, did you?'

'No, of course not,' I said, not sure what was going on. 'Vivien sent our details from Australia.'

'Aaaaaaah, I have such a headache,' Abed groaned, putting his hand to his forehead with a theatrical flourish. 'Do you have an aspirin?'

Getting the appropriate papers to visit occupied southern Lebanon – Israel's so-called Security Zone – was enough to challenge even the strongest constitution. First, we needed permission from the Lebanese government to clear its army checkpoints on the road south. Then, to drive through 'enemy territory', we required an escort from the Israeli-backed South Lebanon Army. Finally, to liaise with the peacekeepers there, we needed accreditation with the United Nations. After weeks of negotiating, we'd secured everything except permission to drive the sixty kilometres from Beirut to the frontline. Now, on what we had hoped would be the eve of our departure for the Zone, Abed was telling us our application had been lost. He wasn't the only person needing an aspirin.

Apparently our request had been the victim of another correspondent's unforgivable mistake. The first rule of journalism in the Arab world is that you don't admit to having visited Israel, and you certainly don't indicate you live or work there when asking favours of a country which is occupied by its forces. You can imagine, therefore, how impressed Lebanon's Ministry of Information was when it received a fax from an Israeli-based foreign correspondent requesting permission to travel to the

Security Zone. As Abed told it, the official in charge was so enraged he tipped the entire contents of his in-tray into the bin – our application included.

It took two days and who knows how many favours, but Abed did get our travel documents. He considered it a matter of honour.

'Habibi, promise me you will be careful. You must not let the driver stop anywhere on the road. It is too dangerous.'

Abed was dispensing some last-minute advice as we hurtled south. He swung from madman to mother as often as he changed lanes. Any moment now I was sure he was going to ask if I had a clean handkerchief in my pocket.

We stopped at the last Lebanese Army checkpoint. Our escort car was waiting on the other side. Abed eyed it suspiciously.

'I don't like this,' he said. 'I wish I could take you myself.'

It was time to switch vehicles and allegiances. From here on, the de facto ruling authority was Israel through its proxy militia, the South Lebanon Army. We hauled our gear out of the boot and agreed on a pick-up time later in the week.

'Remember, you cannot trust anyone. You are entering the land of the traitor,' Abed warned, his bug eyes shining with intensity only centimetres from mine. Before he could launch into another conspiracy theory, we hugged and said our goodbyes. He watched us as we crossed the line from Free Lebanon to the Occupied Zone, his dark face full of foreboding.

Abed is not the only one who drives fast in Lebanon. It must be in the genes. History has taught the Lebanese that in a land of roadside bombs and ambushes it's better to be a speeding target than a sitting duck. It seemed a shame, though, to be rocketing through a landscape so spectacular. Olive groves and orchards laced the terraced hillsides while minarets and church spires made a grab for heaven. Rustic villages straddled babbling brooks which cut through deep, green valleys alive with blossom, bees and wildflowers. But not all the groundcover was natural and not all of the activity agricultural. Camouflage netting climbed over SLA and Israeli military bases like a runaway creeper, tanks and armoured vehicles churned up the soil and bombed-out houses belied the bucolic idyll.

We stopped just a few times on our way to Qlaiaa – a Christian enclave amidst the Zone's largely Muslim population. Our only passport was our driver and the name of the man we were going to meet. A local SLA commander, Major Saed Ghattas.

I'd first met Saed in northern Israel. I had rung him in Lebanon to make arrangements for our visit, but he suggested we meet face to face.

'Perhaps you could drive up from Jerusalem one afternoon and I'll pop across the border to meet you,' he said.

I was sceptical. In all my time entering or exiting Israel, I'd never been able to just 'pop' anywhere. Security checks, luggage X-rays and a seemingly endless list of repetitive questions from humourless officials meant it always took me hours to clear immigration control. How much more difficult would it be for someone entering from Lebanon, I wondered, even if he was an ally? Ahead of Israel's planned withdrawal, the border was particularly tense, with Hezbollah regularly lobbing Katyusha rockets into Israeli villages.

But our rendezvous worked with the ease Saed had predicted. He walked through the border checkpoint, greeting Israeli officials in Hebrew with a comfortable familiarity. A handshake here. A backslap there. He was confident and charming, with a ready smile. Dressed in his civvies, with his wrap-around sunglasses, Saed could have almost passed as Israeli. That was hardly surprising. He shopped in Israel. He had friends in Israel. Many of his neighbours in Lebanon crossed the border every day to work in Israeli orchards or fruit canneries. There was little work in the Zone. Saed knew his way around Jerusalem better than his own capital. But his dream, he said, was to visit Beirut without a gun; without fear of capture or death. As a member of the South Lebanon Army, Saed had been branded a collaborator by the Lebanese government and sentenced, in absentia, to twenty-five years in jail.

'Your dream is to go to the moon or do something special,' he said. 'I dream of seeing my country. I don't know if this will ever happen.'

At thirty-five, Saed had become something of a career soldier. He'd taken three bullets. The first, he said, was at the age of fifteen while defending his home against Palestinian guerrillas. They had set up shop in southern Lebanon after being expelled from Jordan as troublemakers. The Fatah faction of the Palestine Liberation Organisation so colonised this part of southern Lebanon during the 1970s that it was known locally as Fatahland. From their bases there, Yasser Arafat loyalists mounted attacks on Israel, eventually prompting the 1982 invasion of Lebanon. It didn't endear the Palestinians to the Lebanese. Saed's second and third bullets, he said, came courtesy of Hezbollah – the Party of God – a Lebanese Shi'a movement backed by Iran and Syria, which first wanted to drive Israel out of Lebanon, and then out of existence.

In each of these conflicts, Saed had found himself, either directly or indirectly, on the side of Israel. It's just the way it worked, he said. 'It's not my fault I was born in southern Lebanon and I am friends with Israel,' Saed explained. 'Israel helps me. It provides for me. It's a geography thing.'

Geography is not an exact science. In the Middle East it can be particularly subjective. Everyone has a different map of what is, and what should be. For many of the Palestinians who left their homeland during the fighting which erupted after the creation of Israel, the clock stopped in 1948. In their refugee camps in Lebanon, generations of children are born into a time warp. There is no Israel on their maps, only Palestine as it existed under the British Mandate, with Jerusalem as its capital.

There are more than 365,000 Palestinian refugees in Lebanon. They have no rights as citizens. They're not allowed to work. They live in the past or the future, because the present is unbearable. At Ain el-Hilweh, south of Beirut, as many as five generations of one family live in houses built as temporary accommodation half a century ago. From hidden, locked boxes they pull out their most treasured possessions: the yellowed land titles and ornate iron keys to their properties in the West Bank and present-day Israel. But not only have the locks in Palestine long since changed, their country no longer exists.

Colonel Munir Maqdah, the militant camp commander at Ain el-Hilweh, says Palestinian refugees are the forgotten people – nothing more than a rallying cry for their Arab brothers; political pawns to be traded by their own Palestinian leadership. Dressed in fatigues, his AK-47 slung across his back, he swears he'll fight to return to his family's land. His teenage nephews – would-be Gucci kids dressed in black with their hair slicked back – tell me in one breath how they dream of living in Canada with fast cars and pretty wives, and in the other, how they're prepared to die for their homeland.

In Lebanon, everyone will tell you they're ready to die for their home and family. Many have. Far more have died for no good reason.

Uma Issam has only one picture of her son. It was taken when he was nine. It has the look of a 1950s *Women's Weekly* picture, all pastel-shaded and perfect. But beneath the pale pinks and faded yellows is a calm and beautiful face. Issam went out for bread and milk in Beirut one morning in 1982 and never came home. Uma Issam – literally, the Mother of Issam – still waits to hear his footsteps on the front path. Still stands on her balcony searching the street. She won't stay away from her house overnight. What if he should come home and she wasn't there?

Issam is one of 17,000 people who went missing when the civil war fractured the country along religious lines. Every Lebanese family would know of someone who'd met a similar fate. Uma Issam insists her Muslim son was kidnapped by Christian militiamen, who were backed by Israel during the war. She believes Issam is now in a jail in Israel and that one day soon he'll be released for a joyful reunion. She has to believe it. What else can she do? The Lebanese government offered her a death certificate so that she could get on with her life. But she refuses to sign it. Instead, every week she joins other campaigners at Martyrs' Square in Beirut to light a candle for the missing and call for more to be done to find them, or at least uncover their fate. They're keeping the hope alive, even if their loved ones are not.

Back in the Zone, however, faith was wearing thin.

'What hope is there when the Tigers finish twelfth on the ladder?' asks Hassib with a cheeky smile and a broad Australian accent.

Hassib, or Harry as he's known to his mates in Melbourne, ran the 7-Eleven store at Kew Junction for twenty years, before bringing his family back to his home village of Hesbaiyah. He's a die-hard Richmond supporter. His friends with the United Nations occasionally drop him some back copies of the Australian papers. It's pre-season, but he's hungry for any news he can get.

'What do I miss most about Australia?' he muses. 'Well, the footy of course … and democracy. During twenty years travelling the length and breadth of Australia I was never once asked for my passport. Now, if I travel to Beirut, no more than a couple of hundred kilometres, I get stopped five or six times. Every group has a checkpoint.'

Harry despairs about Lebanon's different communities ever living together in peace. He's not optimistic about the future here. He worries about his brothers and sisters and children. His grocery store barely turns a profit. No-one has money to spend. And security is getting worse. Just recently a car load of local soldiers was ambushed, most probably by Hezbollah guerrillas.

'Sure, those guys were members of the SLA,' Harry says, 'but many had no choice. They had families to feed, and Israel is the only boss around here with money.'

He sighs. 'Lebanon is like the pressed ham in the middle of a sandwich: Syria on one side and Israel on the other.'

It was the perfect allegory, with an endearing twist. Perhaps Harry had been in Australia too long – he seemed to have forgotten that neither Muslims nor Jews eat pork.

Harry may have been thinking about leaving southern Lebanon, but our contact with the SLA, Major Saed Ghattas, had no plans for going anywhere. Dressed in his Sunday best after a morning at church, he was now presiding over the barbecue. His two boys ran around the lawn with their cousins and friends, while the womenfolk dodged basketballs as they emerged from the house like an ant-train carrying plates of delicious food. Our trip through the Zone was beginning to feel like a culinary expedition: if it wasn't Mars bars with Hezbollah, it was pappadams and curry with the Indian peacekeepers, and now this feast. Not that we were complaining. After lunch, the tape recorder was turned up and we were invited to dance off our excesses. Saed excused himself and went to change. I made my excuses and joined the kids.

Rabiah was throwing hoops in front of the garage. He loves basketball. He wants to be a famous player like Michael Jordan. In the local league, he told me, all the Christians barrack for one team, Muslims another.

'So are all your friends Christian?' I ask.

'No, most of them are Muslim,' he says.

'Do you think there might be problems between Muslims and Christians when Israel withdraws?'

Mary answers from the lawn where she's sitting with some of the others. 'With us children, no. For our parents, maybe yes. They think differently – that's the problem here.'

Saed does worry about retribution by Hezbollah and its sympathisers. He fears a bloodbath may follow the Israeli withdrawal. He looks a different man in his military garb. More purposeful. His young recruits watch him intently as he explains tactical responses to an ambush. A few tanks rumble around, the odd soldier walks past, but his SLA base has the air of a holiday camp winding down at the end of summer. There's plenty of military hardware – much of it recycled from Israel's wars against its Arab neighbours – but I wonder how many of the estimated 2,500 SLA soldiers will hang around to use it.

If Saed is concerned about the Muslim and Druze members of his fighting force dropping out, he's not saying. 'It is a good thing for Lebanon if Israel leaves,' he says. 'I do not fight for Israel. I fight to protect my home and my family. I hope there will be peace when Israel leaves, but I am ready if there is not. I will fight if I have to. I will not leave.'

But we have to leave. We have an appointment to keep. Abed will be waiting. Four days after crunching up the gravel driveway, we're reversing out – our host family lined up to farewell us. It reminds me of my weekend visits to Grandma as a child. She'd always come outside and wave us off, passing last-minute packets of lollies or biscuits through the car window.

'Safe journey,' someone yells as we reach the road.

'Don't forget us,' they sing out in chorus, as we pull away.

'Any time you need anything in Lebanon, *Habibi*, just ring me. I will organise it. Okay? You promise?'

There was no such thing as closing a business deal with Abed. You just made periodic payments against an open tab. We were running late for our plane and Abed was clucking around us like a mother hen. He fought us for the luggage, then stacked it on several wayward airport trolleys before checking, for the umpteenth time, that we had our tickets and passports.

'What will you do without me?' he asked, flashing one of his electric smiles.

None of us wanted to say goodbye, so we hugged and spoke about next time.

'When you come back, the south will be liberated,' Abed said. 'Israel will be gone and we will all go to the south together. Insh'Allah.'

'Insh'Allah,' we replied. God willing.

I was in the ABC's Jerusalem office several weeks later, when reports came through that Hezbollah had driven a wedge through Israeli defences in the west of the Security Zone. If true, this was it. The dominos were falling. The withdrawal deadline was still six weeks away, but Israel would be out of Lebanon long before then. I called the international editor in Australia and began making plans to get to Beirut, as Andrew scrambled to pack the camera and edit gear. I was on the phone when I half-heard a radio report about a car coming under Israeli tank fire near the Lebanese border. Two people had apparently escaped, but one had died. As sad as it was, I didn't pay it much attention. Such attacks had become a regular event. A day before, two Lebanese children had been killed in a similar episode.

I was at home, rushing to pack a bag, when my mobile phone rang. It was Hilary Andersson, a friend and colleague from the BBC.

'Dom, I have terrible news,' she said, crying. 'Abed is dead. His car was blown up by the Israelis.'

I couldn't believe it. Not Abed. He said he wasn't going to the south until it was liberated. Surely it was a mistake.

It wasn't, of course. In the end, Abed couldn't help himself. He was a newshound like the rest of us. More importantly, he didn't want to let down his mates, BBC journalist Jeremy Bowen and cameraman Malik Kan'an. They wanted to go to the border to investigate the previous day's shelling and the death of the two girls. Abed agreed to take them. When they arrived, he parked his car not far from the previous day's burnt-out wreck. Jeremy and Malik got out to film. Abed stayed in the car to make a phone call. Vintage Abed. No doubt he was smoking as well. Across the border, in Israel, Jeremy could see an Israeli observation position. He stood in the middle of the road and waved his hands over his head to indicate they were civilians and had no weapons. Neither he nor Malik were wearing flak jackets or helmets. Several minutes later, a car zoomed past and there was a huge explosion. Abed's Mercedes was a fireball. Jeremy made a move towards the car, but found himself pinned down by machine-gun fire. All he could do was watch his friend burn.

The Israel Defence Forces investigated the incident and eventually apologised to the BBC, but defended the actions of its military. It was a war zone, after all, they said. Accident or premeditated strike, it didn't change the outcome. Abed was dead, just one day before the last Israeli troops pulled out of his beloved Lebanon. He would have loved the party. We covered the euphoric celebrations; the bumper-to-bumper traffic as Lebanese flooded south to be reunited with their land and loved ones; the dancing on abandoned tanks and storming of Israeli prisons. Then we drove back to Beirut and cried with Abed's widow Hana and their three children. Mohammad, Abed's eldest son, had been on the other end of the phone when the Israeli shell struck.

The next day we went looking for Major Saed Ghattas. The shutters were down on most of the businesses in Qlaiaa and smoke rose from the ransacked offices and bases of the SLA. We knocked on Saed's front door. There was no answer. Neighbours told us the family had gone. The next time we saw them, they were refugees in Israel, trying to get visas for the United States. Saed was further away from Beirut than ever.